THROUGH DIFFERENT EYES

THROUGH DIFFERENT EYES

Two Leading Americans—a Jew
and an Arab—Debate U.S. Policy
in the Middle East

HYMAN BOOKBINDER
and
JAMES G. ABOUREZK
Moderated by David K. Shipler

ADLER&ADLER

Published in the United States in 1987 by
Adler & Adler, Publishers, Inc.
4550 Montgomery Avenue
Bethesda, Maryland 20814

Library of Congress Cataloging-in-Publication Data
Abourezk, James.
Through different eyes.

1. Middle East—Foreign relations—United States.
2. United States—Foreign relations—Middle East.
3. Jewish-Arab relations—1973- . I. Bookbinder,
Hyman Harry, 1916- . II. Title.
DS63.2.U5A615 1987 327.56073 87-1357
ISBN 0-917561-39-2

Printed in the United States of America
First Edition

I disapprove of what you say,
but I will defend to the death
your right to say it.

Attributed to Voltaire

CONTENTS

PUBLISHER'S NOTE

*T*his book is a cooperative effort between two political opponents.

Hyman Bookbinder is special representative of the American Jewish Committee; for many years he presided over sessions of the Washington representatives of America's major Jewish organizations.

Former Senator James G. Abourezk is the founder and chairman of the American Arab Anti-Discrimination Committee, a nationwide organization of more than fifteen thousand members.

It would be hard to find two Americans who disagree more profoundly about U.S. policy toward Israel and the Middle East. In this book, they lay out their conflict as clearly as they can.

Here is how the book was created:

First, each author answered the question: Is U.S. policy in the Middle East in America's best interest? These statements comprise the opening section of the book.

Then each man wrote a rebuttal. These constitute the second section.

To carry the argument further, a live, face-to-face debate was held on February 18, 1987. Because of his knowledge of the issues and his reputation for fairness, David K. Shipler—former Jerusalem correspondent of the *New York Times* and Pulitzer Prize-winning author of *Arab and Jew: Wounded Spirits in a Promised Land*—was asked to moderate. An edited transcript of this debate appears as the third section of our book.

Finally, each author provided a brief closing statement.

The result is an extraordinary confrontation in print. It dramatically demonstrates the difficulty of settling the conflict between Jews and Arabs over Israel. While both men look at the same history, each sees something entirely different in it. To read these conflicting views together is to experience something akin to the Japanese film *Rashomon:* it makes us realize just how different the same facts look when viewed through different eyes.

Whatever the differences between them, however, the fact that two such bitterly opposed advocates have cooperated to create this book is, in itself, a tribute to the vitality of the American political process. We are pleased to have brought them together for this purpose.

James B. Adler
ADLER & ADLER, PUBLISHERS

OPENING
STATEMENTS

HYMAN BOOKBINDER

Introduction

*U*nited States policy toward Israel and the Middle East is clearly in America's best interest.

I readily accepted the challenge to uphold this side of the debate—as I have on earlier occasions with a number of outstanding Arab Americans, including Mr. Abourezk, on radio and television, and in public appearances before interested groups. This book now gives us the opportunity to propound on a more comprehensive basis how each of us, as an American, views the difficult Middle East scene, with special attention to the American role in helping resolve that tragic conflict. It gives me a special opportunity, by the very fact of this participation, to rebut the unfair charge that American Jews are unwilling to debate Middle East policy. Not only are we willing to do so, we are anxious to do so.

I am an enthusiastic supporter of American policy, and a confident admirer of Israel, even though—as will be noted from time to time in the pages that follow—I have expressed disagreement or disappointment with a particular American policy or a particular Israeli policy.

Looking at the entire picture over the years, despite differences that have surfaced even within any given administration and despite occasional tough battles waged between the White House and the Congress, I believe the underlying premises of American Middle East policy—a policy not only of the government, but of the American people—have been essentially correct and have well served America's best interest. Those premises include what has come to be known as the "special relationship" between Israel and the United States; the reaching out for friendship with any Arab nation sharing our goals of peace and stability in the area; and the protecting of our strategic interests and those of the free world in that area.

I write here as a Jewish American expressing *personal* views; no other individual and no Jewish organization, and surely neither the United States government nor that of Israel, is responsible for these views. But I do believe that I will be reflecting an overwhelming consensus among American Jews on the essence of the analysis I will be presenting, with the respectful anticipation that some of my words will not be endorsed by others who are equally committed to the "special relationship" but who make different judgments about particular events or policies. I am prepared for some criticism both from friends more "dovish" and from friends more "hawkish" than I am.

I write as an *American* and as a *Jew*. Above all, I want to believe that I write as a human being trying the best I can to live by universal principles of justice and freedom and fairness. I glory in the fact that over the years I have never felt that these three roles were in conflict. Of course my faith in America has shaped my reactions to world developments. Of course my Jewishness has never left my consciousness as I observe and react to such developments. But I cannot hide my pride in feeling that—with the inevitable exceptions that occur in any long, complicated history—my country, my people, and Israel have been on the right side of the struggle for world peace and justice. My hope is that these pages will adequately support this admittedly self-serving declaration.

I must say a bit more about my Jewishness. I do not pretend total objectivity in this review of American Middle East policy. I have indeed been emotionally affected by the history of my people, by the vulnerability of Jewish life that continues to this day. I write these words in late 1986—after seeing television pictures of the brutal attack on the Istanbul synagogue by Arab terrorists, crazed fanatics not content to kill twenty-one mostly elderly worshippers but insistent also on soaking their innocent victims with gasoline and burning them in their prayer shawls. I identify with these Turkish Jews, as I have throughout my lifetime with other Jews I have seen rejected, humiliated, tortured—and killed by the millions—only because they were Jews.

How can I possibly not be affected by my own personal situation? Both my parents came to America at the turn of the century to escape pogroms in Europe. They left two large families there. As a young boy I frequently wrote Yiddish letters to grandparents I'd never seen. And never did get to see. By 1945 they were among more than eighty blood relatives consumed by the Holocaust. Only two survived. One is now an American; the other is an Israeli. A special relationship between United States and Israel? How could I personally fail to see one?

I know, however, that horrors experienced by the Jewish people do not and cannot alone provide the basis for American Middle East policy. But neither can the condition of the Jewish people before, during, and after the Holocaust be ignored by a nation like ours committed to basic human rights. In the final analysis, I have always understood, it is the American interest itself which must be served. We shall be returning to that theme throughout this debate.

And I know, furthermore, that my opponent does not and cannot come to this debate with total objectivity either; he, too, is emotionally involved. He, too, has been affected by what he considers unfair treatment of *his* people. I can and do understand, for example, his disappointment over our rejection of or indifference to proposals over the years for what he considers fair solutions to the Palestinian problem. The Arab-Israeli conflict, unfortunately, has caused much pain to many people. That conflict, I will be arguing, need not have been as deadly and as prolonged as it has been. Many mistakes have been made, many opportunities have been missed. It is important that they be noted and discussed.

As in interpersonal relations, conflicts between peoples or nations are not always clear cases of right versus wrong. They can be painful disputes over one group's rights, real or perceived, as against another's. Too often in history, power has been the sole determinant of victory in such disputes. This need not, and should not, be the ultimate story of the Arab-Israeli dispute. Camp David is an eloquent reminder that compromise and accommodation are possible even after decades of hate and war and pain.

Final resolution of the entire Arab-Israel conflict does not require a debate on who has suffered most but rather on what kind of accommodations can yet be reached in order to reduce the pain and the fear of all who suffer. This debate should examine America's role in facilitating such accommodations. Knowing something about past debates on the subject, however, I express the hope that this debate will not deteriorate into an exchange of accusations about some specific atrocities, real or alleged. War itself is the basic atrocity. The war that started nearly seventy years ago, when Arabs chose to say no to a Jewish presence in the Middle East, still goes on. The American policy throughout these forty years has been to help end it. The Israeli policy, I am persuaded, has always been based on the search for peace, subject only to the condition that its very existence and security be assured.

These years of war between Arabs and Jews—with the significant exception of the Egyptian-Israeli agreement—have been costly in many ways. Above all, they have served not to reduce the suspicions and the hatreds and the prejudices of centuries but rather to intensify such attitudes. Much work will be necessary, even if peace should be achieved, in excising the bitterness that these years have caused. Even as the Abourezks and the Bookbinders continue to identify with their respective peoples in the Middle East, hope must be expressed that both in the Middle East and here in America, Arabs and Jews can work together to resist the pressures to hate, that they will instead remember that they are all God's children and bear common responsibility to seek a way to live as brothers and sisters. And as Americans, both of us have the obligation to serve the American interest even as we serve our peoples' needs.

It is in this context that I intend to deal with the following themes in my initial presentation:

■ Israel's legitimacy as a state is justified by its history, its achievements, and its sacrifices as it was compelled to fight and win military victories over those who have sought to deny its legitimacy and to destroy it. It has been in America's own interest to affirm its solidarity with and support of such a state, the only state in the Middle East that truly shares and observes the kind of democracy and pluralism for which America stands.

■ The "special relationship" between the u.s. and Israel has not prevented the United States from working with Arab nations that show moderation and flexibility. Neither Israel nor its American supporters object to this important American objective of seeking and strengthening Arab friendship. On the contrary, I believe that only in such a framework can America play the critical role of bringing Arabs and Israelis together in the search for accommodation and peace. Camp David is the impressive model for such a role, and we shall pay much attention to this achievement. It is a tragedy for all concerned that, except for Egypt, the Arab world generally has not abandoned its early determination to eliminate Israel; it has missed one opportunity after another to negotiate an honorable peace.

■ America's own *self-interest* has been well served by our Middle East policies. The close relationship between Israel and the United States has been of increasingly impressive strategic value to the United States. In the United Nations and in international affairs generally, no nation has shown greater consistency than Israel in supporting the United States. In contributing to Israel's independence and security, America serves its own best interests in a world threatened by totalitarianism, aggression, and terrorism.

■ The overwhelming majority of the American people support our Middle East commitments. It is a support reflected in the statements and actions of every president and every Congress since the Balfour Declaration in 1917 and especially since the state of Israel was formally established in 1948. It is a support that is encouraged, understandably, by the American Jewish community, but a support that extends into almost every part of American society. Both supporters and opponents of present Middle East policy have used traditional American methods for promoting their respective points of view—public relations, lobbying, political action.

America's interest in the Middle East extends beyond the Arab-Israeli conflict. Even if there were no Israel, we would be concerned about the implications of the rise in militant fundamentalism, the protracted Iran-Iraq war, the explosion of terrorism, and the ominous threat posed by Soviet intrusion in the area. In the debate, however, attention will be directed to the specific history and issues directly involved in the Israel-Arab dispute.

Israel—Its Origins and Its Appeal

On August 9, 1979, I was given an unusual opportunity to state what Israel has come to mean for me and for the world's Jews, if not for all the people of the world. The setting could not have been more poignant, more challenging, or more revealing.

There have been other notable days in my personal involvement in the Middle East story, some of which will be touched upon before we are through, but this day had special meaning.

Some months earlier, Jimmy Carter had appointed me to the President's Commission on the Holocaust. Chaired by Nobel Laureate Elie Wiesel, a Holocaust survivor, the commission was charged by President Carter with the responsibility of recommending appropriate ways to commemorate the Holocaust and teach others about that tragic event. To help in that task, we decided to spend ten days on a mission that would take us to Europe, to the Soviet Union—and to Israel, primarily to see several death camps and to study memorials and archives.

This is not the time to describe the gruesome details of what we saw and experienced in our travels through Auschwitz and Treblinka and Babi Yar. For me personally the days I spent in Poland brought back memories of those Yiddish letters I wrote as a teenager to my grandparents in Poland, letters that usually ended with the hope that someday soon I might be able finally to visit them and hug them. But, fifty years later, in August of 1979, as I went from one camp to another, I could only wonder in which of those camps their ashes had been strewn.

We then left for the Soviet Union, primarily to negotiate the release of valuable records and exhibition material. In Kiev, we saw firsthand what we had known from reports, that the great Babi Yar memorial did not reveal to visitors that the thousands of Babi Yar victims buried there had been Jews. The commission members decided to go to Denmark to seek the courageous Christians who had risked their lives to save some of the Jews.

And, finally, on August 9, we were in Jerusalem. The president of Israel, Yitzhak Navon, had asked to see the delegation. I was asked to present the commission members to the president and to say a few words. I had not prepared anything in advance and I did not keep a transcript, but I know that I said essentially the following:

> Mr. President, I have been to Israel quite a number of times. Each time I have been impressed, I have been proud, I have been overwhelmed with what my co-religionists have been able to build, despite all kinds of hardships and obstacles. You surely have so much reason for pride in what you have achieved even while you

have been at war with your neighbors from the day of your rebirth. But, Mr. President, today's visit is not like any of the others. Last week, we were in Auschwitz. We saw the ovens and the gas chambers. We were in Treblinka and saw the hundreds of rough slabs of stones, each one representing not an individual Jew but a Jewish village that once thrived with Jewish life and Jewish culture. We were in Kiev and saw that the Soviet rulers had killed our Jewish brothers and sisters a second time by denying them their Jewish identity. So today when we stepped on Israeli soil, I felt the meaning of Israel in many ways I had never quite experienced before. I just dare not wonder how many of those six million Jews might have been saved if there had been in those years a state of Israel with the rights and the power of a state. I see an Israel that has kept its promise to welcome any Jews anywhere who seek refuge or who choose to be part of the only Jewish state in the world. I know that Israel's legitimacy neither begins with nor derives from the Holocaust, but that terrible event and its aftermath is the most telling commentary on what Israel means for the Jewish people and should mean for all people.

I can hear critics like Mr. Abourezk protest at this point, "There he goes again! Invoking the Holocaust in an effort to shame us into silence or acquiescence. Of course Hitler was a criminal, of course the Holocaust was wrong. But are the Arabs responsible for that? Why does the Jewish problem have to be resolved at the expense of another people?" That's a fair question, one that makes it necessary to provide the background, albeit abbreviated and generalized, to place the rebirth and development of Israel in a historical context.

Scholars and historians have spoken and written millions of words debating the respective claims of Arabs and Jews to the "land of Palestine." The full history is so long, the claims so ambiguous, that almost any case can be made—and has been made—on the basis of one's selection of a starting point and one's interpretation of applicable criteria. I do not find it useful or wise to add to the jumble of centuries-old or even millennia-old statistics and presumed history to justify relatively recent events or policies. As generations of peoples replace earlier generations, historic realities simply must be accepted as the basis for resolving current problems. It surely would not be argued by Mr. Abourezk—or would it?—that American Indian claims and grievances against the original settlers for their conduct in the New World can serve today as appropriate grounds for undoing what has come to be the American nation. What *is* appropriate, of course, is concern for the welfare of descendents who may still suffer the consequences of historic developments—whether they be American Indians or, as we shall see, Palestinian Arabs.

I do not mean to dismiss an examination of early history, and surely do not mean to dismiss the historic Jewish claim to at least part of the land of Palestine. But even more useful is a realistic examination of what prompted the Zionist movement of the last century or so. We must try to understand what the various parties and nations involved did, and did not do, to make the inevitable as constructive and painless as possible.

In reviewing this relatively recent history, we find a constantly recurring central point of contention: do the Jews really have a right to create a Jewish state in Palestine? Even after its creation and recognition by the world's official body of nations, including the major powers, the question remains. The phrase "Israel's right to exist" defines the essence of the dispute that has continued for decades.

How ominous, and painful, that definition was to the Jews is perhaps best illustrated in the reaction of Abba Eban several years ago. For thirty-five years, this eloquent leader and spokesman had been a key figure in the building of the only Jewish state in the world. Generally considered a moderate in words and in policy, Abba Eban angrily rejected the very idea of having to justify, let alone ask others to acknowledge, Israel's "right to exist." "Nobody does Israel any service by proclaiming its 'right to exist,'" he said. "Israel's right to exist, like that of the United States, Saudi Arabia and 152 other states, is axiomatic and unreserved. Israel's legitimacy is not suspended in mid-air awaiting acknowledgment. . . . There is certainly no other state, big or small, young or old, that would consider mere recognition of its 'right to exist' a favor, or a negotiable concession. . . ."

Abba Eban, of course, is right. And yet it is necessary to discuss the issue because it is *the* issue that remains the most serious stumbling block to resumption of a peace process among Israel, the Arab states, and moderate Palestinians. It is an issue raised ominously and unambiguously, for example, in the Palestine Liberation Organization (P.L.O.) covenant. It is the issue inherent in the arguments still being made by critics like Mr. Abourezk about the founding of the present state of Israel. They occasionally acknowledge in muted tones that "Israel is a fact," but they lay the greatest emphasis on the illegitimacy, as they see it, of the Jewish, or Zionist, claim for recognized presence in the area. Their current failure to endorse the eminently reasonable American policy since 1975—that the P.L.O. must explicitly recognize Israel's right to exist before the United States will deal with it—is an example of how they give encouragement to the rejectionists and make so much more difficult a breakthrough for comprehensive peace.

So it is useful to recall the basic facts leading to the present state of Israel.

For as long as I can remember—and that's for almost all of my seventy years—I have heard the words "Next Year in Jerusalem." Jews everywhere have heard this expression for close to two thousand years. These words reflect the never-suspended link between the Jewish people and Israel, the land of Palestine. Ever since the destruction of the Second Temple in A.D. 70, the Jewish people's passion for a return to Zion has been a dominant theme in their dreams, their prayers, their expectations. Throughout that time, Jewish immigrants established new communities in Palestine, the nature and extent of those settlements were shaped in part by the nature of the political rule over Palestine at any given time, as well as the condition of Diaspora Jews around the world. Not until the nineteenth century, however, was the prospect of Jewish sovereignty seriously raised. In the latter half of that century, rabid anti-Semitism and pogroms in Europe resulted in significant increases in immigration to Palestine. During this period there was also a flow of Jewish emigrants from Yemen, Morocco, Iraq, and Turkey. Unrelated to the growing Zionist movement in Europe, these Jews from Muslim lands were motivated by their ancient dreams of "return to Zion" and fears of Arab intolerance and persecution.

Earlier centuries had seen many changes and fluctuations in the Palestinian population mix. Jews were always part of that mix, though with varying proportions of the general population. Toward the end of the nineteenth century, during the Ottoman rule, there were a substantial number of Arabs, though no independent Arab

Palestinian political entity had ever been established. These Arabs did not approve of Jewish immigration. An Arab-Jewish confrontation over the issue seemed inevitable.

The British became actively interested in this conflict during World War I; some of their principal policymakers talked frequently with Arab and Jewish leaders about the future of Palestine. On November 2, 1917, Britain's foreign secretary, Arthur Balfour, issued the historic declaration that bears his name. Jewish circles were enthusiastic when they learned the British government would now "view with favor" the establishment of a Jewish home in Palestine.

Here, then, was the first major pronouncement, by an authority in a strong position to affect the future of that area, that the time had come to resolve a difficult and complicated problem by recognizing the appropriateness and the need for both a Jewish and an Arab presence in a place to which both sides lay claim. The Balfour Declaration was clear and momentous:

> His Majesty's government view with favour, the establishment in Palestine of a national home for the Jewish people, and will use their best endeavours to facilitate the achievement of this object. It being clearly understood that nothing shall be done which may prejudice the civil and religious rights of existing non-Jewish communities in Palestine, or the rights and political status enjoyed by Jews in any other country.

No less clear was the swift American approval of the declaration. "I am persuaded," said President Woodrow Wilson, "that the allied nations, with fullest concurrence of our own government and people, are agreed that in Palestine shall be laid the foundations of a Jewish commonwealth." There it was—seventy years ago—the unambiguous commitment by our nation to a Jewish homeland in Palestine. Whatever conflicts and hesitations later arose about specific obligations and the implementation of this American commitment, that judgment has been the bedrock of American Middle East policy ever since. Remaining true to that judgment and that commitment over the years has been one of the best examples of American trustworthiness and fidelity.

The Balfour Declaration provides the occasion for asking the question that was destined to be asked over and over again: *What*

might have been the history of these last seventy years if in 1917 the
Palestinian Arabs, and the neighboring Arab states, had recognized
the wisdom and the reasonableness of the Balfour proposal, with the
built-in protection of Arab rights, and implemented that proposal?
How many Jewish and Arab lives might have been spared? How
prosperous and developed an area might the Middle East be today
if the many wars that ensued had been avoided?

Even though the United States and other nations endorsed the
Balfour Declaration, the Palestinian Arabs and the Arab world generally continued to protest. It was clear that the battle for a Jewish
home would be protracted and it would be difficult. When the
British acquired the League of Nations mandate over Palestine in
1920, the Arabs continued to wage not only nationalist-motivated
riots against the Jews but also an increasingly religious war against
"Jewish infidels." The massacre of sixty-seven Jews in Hebron in
1929 and the destruction of their synagogues ended the existence of
that city's Jewish community, which had been in existence for 2,000
years. Between 1936 and 1939 alone, 517 Jews were murdered by
Arab extremists, according to Julian Landau in *Israel and the Arabs.*
Arab moderates too were frequent victims of these terrorists.

Yielding to Arab pressures against Jewish immigration and Jewish sovereignty, the British turned away from the Balfour commitment in the period between the two world wars. In 1937, the British
government established a *Royal Commission on Palestine,* headed
by Lord Peel. The Peel Commission's proposal for a small Jewish
state comprising only 7 percent of the British mandate was reluctantly approved by most of the Jewish inhabitants, but even this
proposal was totally rejected by the Arabs. Again, I must ask, "What
if . . . ?". In a further attempt to appease the Arabs, the British issued
in May of 1939 the notorious White Paper prohibiting Jews from
purchasing any land in most of Palestine and limiting Jewish immigration to 75,000 for the years 1939–44. These were, of course, the
years of the Hitler terror, years of the most compelling need for
refuge in Palestine.

These were the years too when the Jews of Palestine found it
necessary to take up arms—on the one hand, they formed Jewish
brigades to fight alongside the Allies to defeat the Axis armies, and
on the other they defended Jewish inhabitants of Palestine. The
Jewish attitude during the war was best expressed by David Ben-

Gurion, that "Jews should go on fighting the White Paper as if Hitler did not exist, and to help [Britain] fight Hitler as if the White Paper did not exist." And so some Jews found themselves fighting Arabs at home while other Jews were fighting Arabs—such as the Mufti of Jerusalem—who had joined Hitler's side in the war.

Despite the war, despite the British resistance, despite the hostility of the Arabs, the Jewish population in Palestine continued to increase. Between 1939 and 1947, it grew from 400,000 to 630,000.

By 1942 the Zionist movement had decided there could be no further delay in demanding and securing a clear political status for the Jews in Palestine. At a historic conference in New York's Biltmore Hotel in May, a call was issued by the American Zionist movement for the establishment of a "Jewish political community" in Palestine after the war. In November that call was approved by the worldwide Zionist Action Council and became the official guideline for political action by the World Zionist Organization. The United States and Britain were designated as the prime targets for official government support of the Zionist goal.

The years immediately after World War II were characterized not only by fierce clashes between Jews and Arabs in Palestine, with tragic incidents prompting charges of unjustified terrorism by both sides, but also by violent clashes between British authorities and Jewish activists, again resulting in mutual charges and countercharges of cruel, unprovoked attacks. Perhaps the most dramatic, unforgettable, and unforgivable outrage of this period was the British refusal in 1947 to let *Exodus 1947*, a boatload of 4,500 Jewish refugees, discharge its passengers at Haifa.

But these years, too, had a positive influence on many people and governments around the world, undoubtedly affected by the now documented story of the Holocaust. Once the world had accepted the reality of six million Jews—one-third of the world's Jewish population—having been so cruelly exterminated, remaining doubts about the basic Zionist cause started to fade. The Arabs were not asked to accept the blame for the Holocaust, or to pay the price for it, but they were asked to try to understand why the Holocaust added an extraordinary sense of urgency to the need for a Jewish homeland. History, from ancient to current, had made the Zionist goal a reasonable and necessary one. The challenge was to reach this goal with maximum consideration for the welfare of all who might be affected by the inevitable next stage.

In the United States, support for a Jewish state had developed rapidly. A sense of responsibility for the remnants of European Jewry who had managed to survive Hitler's war against the Jews, and for the Jews who had sacrificed so much to start building their own state in Palestine, persuaded our nation's leaders to support the Zionist effort. But American support had been clear and firm even before the Holocaust. Wilson's endorsement of the Balfour Declaration had been followed by President Warren Harding's "approval and hearty sympathy for . . . the restoration of Palestine as a homeland for the Jewish people" and by President Calvin Coolidge's statement that "the proposed plan furnished the Jewish people an opportunity to devote their great qualities to the upbuilding and preservation of their own homeland and in their own sphere," and his confidence that "the people of the United States will not fail to give that earnest and substantial aid which will be necessary if it is to meet with a full measure of success." President Herbert Hoover continued this national commitment when he added his own "expression to the sentiment among our people in favor of the realization of the age-old aspirations of the Jewish people for the restoration of their national homeland."

The special urgency for a Jewish homeland during the Hitler period prompted President Franklin Roosevelt to "favor the opening of Palestine to unrestricted Jewish immigration and colonization, and such a policy as to result in the establishment there of a free and democratic Jewish commonwealth. . . . I know how long and ardently the Jewish people have worked and prayed for the establishment of Palestine as a free and democratic Jewish commonwealth. I am convinced the American people give their support to this aim."

With the end of the war, it fell to President Harry Truman to give leadership to implementing the goal stated by his five predecessors in the White House. Noting that American support had been expressed since World War I, [that the period after that war had freed from colonial control had a large area of the Near East, including Palestine, and established a number of independent Arab states, which were now members of the United Nations,] Truman declared the time had come for establishing a home for the Jewish people in Palestine. "Most of the liberated peoples are now citizens of inde-

pendent countries," he stated. "The Jewish national home, however,
has not been fully developed. . . .It is only natural, therefore, that
this government should favor at this time the entry into Palestine
of considerable numbers of displaced Jews in Europe, not only that
they may find shelter there, but also that they may contribute their
talents and energies to the upbuilding of the Jewish national home."

I have cited these expressions of support from every president
since the time of the Balfour Declaration because it is absolutely
essential to understand what has recently come to be known as the
"special relationship" between the u.s. and Israel is grounded in
what may be the most long-standing American foreign policy consensus. And as we shall see, on the central question of Israel's
legitimacy and American support thereof, that consensus has continued through seven presidencies, from Eisenhower to Reagan. It
is an American consensus that long predates the emergence of the
much discussed organized "Jewish lobby"—about which more will
be written later.

During the Truman administration, American support for the
principle of a Jewish state had to be translated into explicit action.
With Truman publicly committed, with similar expressions of support from other nations, and with a stubborn, arrogant Arab League
insisting upon total British rejection of Jewish hopes, the British
decided they could no longer handle the situation by themselves.
They turned the matter over to the United Nations.

A u.n. Special Committee on Palestine took only three months
to report, on August 31, 1947, that a majority of seven of its eleven
members approved the partition of Palestine. The boundaries of the
proposed Jewish state were to correspond to Jewish population centers and encompass about 13 percent of the original area allotted by
the British for the Jewish national home. On November 19, 1947,
the General Assembly of the United Nations overwhelmingly approved the partition plan—with both the United States and the
Soviet Union, the two major postwar powers, voting for it. Britain
abstained. Despite misgivings about the proposed size and other
limitations, the Jews were nevertheless enthusiastic in their reaction.
A new, hopeful chapter had finally begun. A Jewish homeland was
to be.

In my judgment, this is the point at which the issue of Israel's
legitimacy, its "right to exist," should have become a moot issue.

This was the historic moment when the world authority, enjoying the confidence of the world community, had assessed all the arguments, all the history, all the anguish surrounding a difficult conflict, one that unresolved could again threaten the peace of the world, and it had made a decision designed to meet the basic needs of both Arab and Jewish claimants to the land of Palestine. For hundreds of years the residents of Palestine, Arabs and Jews, had been governed by others. Now, at long last, justice would be done, and done in the only realistic way possible, by a fair partition. How would the parties respond? How would the area's neighbors respond? What if . . . ?

The Arabs could have seized the opportunity afforded by the u.n. partition plan to create a Palestinian Arab state, while limiting the Jewish state to the very small area stipulated in the plan. Instead, Arab diplomats proclaimed the "three nos," which tragically became the model for subsequent decades of conflict. No partition, no further Jewish immigration, no Jewish state. The seriousness of this rejection was made unmistakeably clear in the course of the u.n. debate when Jamil Husseini, spokesman for the Palestine Arab Higher Committee, declared, *"The partition line proposed shall be nothing but a line of fire and blood."* [Emphasis added.]

Husseini's words were soon translated into bloody terror. Relatively passive from 1939 to November 1947, the Palestinian Arabs responded to the provocations of the Jamil Husseinis with a campaign of terrorism, plundering, and killing throughout Palestine. Roads were mined, convoys were ambushed, apartments in Jerusalem were blown up, Jewish university students were massacred, the Jewish Agency was bombed, the Hadassah Hospital was attacked. The Jews were counting their dead by the hundreds.

Within a few months, the riots and the Jewish responses had deteriorated into a full-scale civil war. Both Arabs and Jews sought territorial gains in the course of the fighting. In January of 1948, the first detachments of an "Arab Liberation Army" entered Palestine from Syria and Jordan.

Palestine's Jews had to accept the reality that Jewish presence and a future Jewish state would have to be defended by their own arms and their own blood. They fought back, primarily under the direction and discipline of the Haganah and the Jewish Agency, rejecting terrorism as a policy and resisting it in practice, but determined to disrupt British military installations and Arab military targets.

Several splinter groups of Jewish forces, such as the Irgun and the Lehi gang, acted independently of the regular forces. Israel's critics frequently cite the Deir Yassin tragedy in an effort to discredit Israel's struggle for independence—to make it seem like a typical Jewish operation rather than the exceptional event of the period. In this one case, some two hundred Arab civilians were among those killed by Irgun forces as they fought off Arab soldiers engaged in a blockade of Jerusalem. But, unlike the proud claims of responsibility made by Arab terrorists (a practice to be repeated over and over again by the P.L.O. in later years), Jewish leaders in Palestine roundly condemned the targeting and killing of civilians. (It must be noted that the Irgun insisted it had appealed to residents to surrender.)

For almost forty years, partisans on both sides of this tragic conflict have argued over which side committed the most heinous crimes. Such an argument will never be resolved, and need not be. The more important purpose of study and analysis must be understanding the causes of the tragic fighting and the opportunities for peaceful resolution that were not grasped by all parties involved.

Despite the overwhelming support in the United Nations for the partition plan, no police action was taken by the U.N., which might have ended the fierce fighting, so that the plan itself might have been implemented. On February 16, 1948, the U.N. Palestine Commission reported to the U.N. Security Council, "Powerful Arab interests, both inside and outside Palestine, are defying the resolution of the General Assembly and are engaged in a deliberate effort to alter by force the settlement envisaged therein."

The Arabs proudly acknowledged their role in forcing war upon the adversaries. On April 16, 1948, Amin al Husseini, Mufti of Jerusalem, told the Security Council, "The representatives of the Jewish Agency told us yesterday that they were not the attackers, that the Arabs had begun the fighting. We did not deny this. We told the whole world that we were going to fight."

Notwithstanding this very clear indictment of the Arab role in forcing the war, the U.N. was prevented from taking effective action by the Arab opposition and by the British refusal to cooperate. An American proposal for a temporary trusteeship over Palestine was rejected. Faced with the U.N.'s paralysis, but acting in the spirit of its partition plan, the Jews of Palestine decided they need not and could not wait any longer.

On May 14, 1948, as the British finally left the area, David Ben-Gurion officially proclaimed the establishment of the State of Israel. Within minutes, President Harry Truman granted the new state American diplomatic recognition. Three days later, the Soviet Union did the same.

Once again, the Arabs had a choice. They could opt for peace and reconciliation, or they could go on fighting. It did not take them long to announce their choice. On May 15, Azzam Pasha, secretary general of the Arab League, declared in Cairo, "This will be a war of extermination and a momentous massacre which will be spoken of like the Mongolian massacres and the Crusades."

Backing up those words, the armies of Egypt, Transjordan, Iraq, Syria, Lebanon, and Saudi Arabia immediately invaded Israel with the declared objective of preventing, by force, the birth of the Jewish state. It may be arguable whether any major Arab spokesman at the time actually used the words "sweep the Israelis into the sea," but surely those words reflected the reality of the early years of Israeli statehood—the reality of Arab hopes and the reality of Jewish fears. More than five years after statehood, the king of Saudi Arabia, Saud ibn Abdul Aziz, still found it possible to declare, "The Arab nations should sacrifice up to 10 million of their 50 million people, if necessary, to wipe out Israel. . . . Israel to the Arab world is like a cancer to the human body, and the only way of remedy is to uproot it, just like a cancer . . ."

The hostilities "ended" after eight months with a series of armistice agreements between the new Jewish state and Egypt, Lebanon, Transjordan, and Syria. The war had been a costly one, for both Jews and Arabs. Israel had at that time somewhat more than 600,000 inhabitants and had lost 6,000 of its people. In order to understand the staggering nature of that loss, it would be as if the United States today lost *more than two million people* in a war or other calamity. But the costs of that war for independence went beyond the immediate casualties. The war and its consequences were a sobering warning that Arab determination to keep the Jews from building their state, by killing them or driving them out, would not end with Arab signatures on armistice agreements.

The 1948 war created some new and critical realties that were to affect the years—and, tragically, the wars—to come. As the fighting ended, Israeli resistance to Arab invasions and terrorism resulted in enlarged areas of Israeli dominance. Surely not unknown in the history of wars among nations, the victor lay claim to some of the lands it had been compelled to occupy in self-defense. The fact of consolidated Arab aggression, and the costs involved in defending against it, persuaded the Israelis that they needed control over some of the captured lands for their security. They held on to the coastal plain, upper Galilee, and the Negev, while surrendering other areas. They had been unable to prevent the Transjordanian conquest of the Old City of Jerusalem, including the Jewish quarter. Arab desecration of Jewish shrines, cemeteries, and homes in the quarter, and the subsequent barring of Jews from important Jewish holy sites, including the Western (Wailing) Wall, would be painful challenges and provocations for the Jews for the next nineteen years.

But most problematic of all, the 1948 war had caused population shifts that cried out for creative, compassionate, and constructive solution. The early plans for a Jewish state sought to minimize the number of people who would feel compelled to, or would choose to, leave their birthplace in order to live with their own ethnic, religious, or national group. The U.N. partition plan was limited in its allocation for the Jewish state for precisely this reason; the Jews had agreed to it in order to minimize the problem, even while they declared all along—both before and after the establishment of the state—that Palestinian Arabs who wished to live in a Jewish state, with full citizenship rights, were welcome to and urged to stay.

Despite such assurances, it is understandable that some Arabs, perhaps most, would accept the inevitability of the changed situation and would choose relocation. How many would have done so if the U.N. partition plan had been accepted peacefully by all the parties will never be known. What we do know is a terrible war took place; Arab leaders urged and in some cases even ordered Palestinian Arabs to leave their homes, help destroy the Jewish enemy, and then return after the Jews had been driven out; there were tragic instances of terrorism on both sides, which frightened many Arabs; and while the Israeli authorities were officially and sincerely urging the Arabs to stay, some Jews did urge and threaten Arabs to leave.

Pro-Arab propaganda over the years has sought to place the

principal, if not the entire, blame for the Arab exodus on Jewish threats and violence. But the record is too complete to permit any conclusion other than that the principal cause for the exodus was the exhortation by Arab leaders for the Palestinian Arabs to leave. Thus, a British eyewitness quoted in *The Economist* reported that of the 62,000 Arabs living in Haifa, only about 5,000 remained. "There is but little doubt," the observer noted, "that the most potent of these factors were the announcements made over the air by the Arab Higher Executive, urging all Arabs in Haifa to quit. . . . It was clearly intimated that those Arabs who remained in Haifa and accepted Jewish protection would be regarded as renegades." *Falastin*, a Jordanian newspaper reported, "The Arab states which had encouraged the Palestine Arabs to leave their homes temporarily in order to be out of the way of the Arab invasion armies, have failed to keep their promise to help these refugees."

Fifteen years after the war, *Akhbar et Yom*, an Egyptian journal commented, "The 15th May 1948 arrived. . . . On that very day the Mufti of Jerusalem appealed to the Arabs of Palestine to leave the country, because the Arab armies were about to enter and fight in their stead."

It is a historic fact, of course, that more Arabs heeded these Arab appeals to leave than the Jewish appeals to stay. As a result, between 500,000 and 600,000 Arabs abandoned their homes and their lands. They became the "refugee problem" for a while and then the "Palestinian problem" that was to make an Israeli-Arab accommodation so difficult. But it is not sufficiently recognized that hundreds of thousands of Arabs remained or returned to their homes in what had become Israel. Their acceptance and integration was not without problems but soon most observers accepted it as remarkably successful under the circumstances.

That shift of more than a half-million Arabs leaving Palestine was one population change. Meanwhile another was taking place. An equal number of Jews, some 580,000 of them, who had lived for centuries in Arab lands were finding it necessary or desirable to flee from their angry and resentful Arab rulers and seek refuge in the new state of Israel. They could not, for example, ignore an Egyptian threat during the 1947 U.N. debate, "The lives of a million Jews in Moslem countries will be jeopardized by the establishment of the Jewish state." Thus, in the few years during and immediately following the war of independence, a major exchange of Jews and Arabs was taking place.

Such changes are never happy ones. Leaving the land of one's forebears with its memories, attachments, and personal friendships, and going to some unknown environment, can be a searing experience—even when one knows there may be people with common interests and loyalties waiting to receive you. But history provides many precedents for major population shifts, and some provide evidence that they can occur without much pain and, in fact, with positive gains for those involved. In roughly the same time frame as the Arab-Israeli dispute, the world witnessed such massive population shifts as those between India and Pakistan, between the two Germanys, and between the two Koreas. It is estimated that after World War II, there were forty million refugees. For most of them, resettlement—not repatriation—was the practical answer.

It is instructive to compare the disposition of the two parts of the historic population swap in the aftermath of the 1948 Arab-Israeli conflict. Israel, a tiny state struggling for its very life, succeeded in absorbing from Arab lands and integrating a group of Jews almost as numerous as its own indigenous population, despite major cultural differences between the Ashkenazi Jews from Europe and the Sephardic Jews from Arab lands. The Palestinian refugees were dispersed among Arab lands with total populations many times that of the refugees. But with the possible exception of Jordan, very few of them were permitted to be fully integrated among their fellow Arabs. The reason was as cruel as it was obvious: to keep the refugee issue alive and useful as a political weapon to fight Israel. Added to Arab failures to endorse partition plans that could have created a new political entity for these Palestinian Arabs, is the record of refusing to welcome and rehabilitate Jews for productive and peaceful coexistence in Arab lands. That failure explains much of the tragic story of the next few decades.

The 1948 war was brought to a halt with *armistice* arrangements, not with *peace* treaties. Before agreeing to negotiate an actual end to the war, the Arabs demanded that Israel accept the borders that had been proposed in the partition plan—borders they could have had if they had not chosen to wage war against that plan. Consequently they created a pattern they would repeat regularly in later wars, a doctrine of limited-liability wars, i.e., refuse a proffered compromise, wage war to win total demands, and if defeated, fall back to the original compromise position. They were to follow this pattern while persisting in their refusal to acknowledge Israel's "right to exist."

Acknowledged by the Arab states or not, Israel by 1949 clearly had established itself as a nation. On May 14, 1949, exactly one year after its own proclamation, Israel was admitted to the United Nations.

The next thirty-eight years would see the development of a proud, free, democratic, pro-Western Israel. A country facing not only the challenges of any new nation but also the burden of preparing for and fighting wars with Arab neighbors—and also the "burden," happily assumed, of absorbing survivors of the Holocaust, immigrants from hostile Arab lands, Soviet Jews permitted to emigrate, fleeing Ethiopian Jews, and any Jews choosing citizenship in the only Jewish state on earth.

American identification with this Israel became more explicit and firm over the years as the benefits to the United States became clearer and clearer. A special relationship was inevitable. In the next section I will explain how and why.

Building and Defending the Jewish State

Over the years I heard Golda Meir speak these moving words a number of times. Each time they evoked both pain and pride. But especially that first time. She had the ability to reduce profound thoughts to simple eloquence when she said, "Someday we may be able to forgive the Arabs for killing our children. But we will never forgive them for making us kill theirs."

She spoke those words soon after the Six Day War in 1967. Even while she and her countrymen were still grieving over their sons who died in battle, she could embody in those words the basic humanity that had motivated the Zionist founders of Israel. They had dreamed and planned to create a nation free of the persecution and violence and hatred that had been the Jewish experience for so many generations. *Shalom*—peace—was to be their frequent greeting, their constant dream, but they were not permitted to enjoy it.

After the Yom Kippur War in 1973, I heard Golda Meir repeat those poignant words, this time adding, "When we determined to work for our own Jewish state, we knew there would be difficulty, that some of us would even have to give our lives. It was difficult having to bury comrades who had been killed. Later, when we fought our war for independence, it was even more difficult having to bury some of our sons. But, never, never, did we think that it would be necessary ever to bury grandsons of ours in defense of the state. But that is what thousands of Israeli families have been doing these last few weeks."

Burying any sons or grandsons killed in war—Jewish, Christian, Muslim, Arab, or Israeli—is painful beyond description. No mother's or father's anguish should be compared to another's. And yet it must be noted that there is a special pain involved in the deaths of those thousands of Israeli youths. Many of them were the sons or grandsons of Holocaust victims with hearts still broken over the gruesome deaths of their parents and grandparents. And now, in defense of the land which gave them refuge, their children were again the victims of a war against Jews.

The 1967 and 1973 wars, tragically, were not the only occasions for burying fathers and sons, grandfathers and grandsons, soldiers and civilians, men and women and children, Jews and Arabs—the victims of war and terrorism. For the first thirty years after Israel's formal status as a state, every Arab nation persisted in its rejection of Israel and engaged, directly or indirectly, in a war against it.

In 1978, Egypt became the first Arab state to say *yes* to the existence of Israel; I will examine that historic development in the next section. But even with this important exception, it is a tragic fact that Israel has been at war with its Arab neighbors every day of its existence.

Over the years Golda Meir's voice was heard not only to honor the memory of those who died in defense of Israel, but also to affirm her country's readiness to take steps with her neighbors to prevent future wars and additional deaths. On October 9, 1962, for example, after fourteen years of increasing hostility and escalating arms build-up on both sides, then Foreign Minister Meir addressed the U. N. General Assembly, "My government rejects war as a means of settling disputes," she declared. "From the day that the State of Israel was established, my government has called for settling all outstanding differences by direct negotiations." Then she delivered a challenge:

> We do not rest content with calling upon the Great Powers to find a way to disarmament, and to settle outstanding problems by negotiation and conciliation between them. We are prepared to put this into practice in the dispute in which we are involved with our neighbors. As we have done in the past, *we call again upon the Arab states to agree to complete disarmament with mutual inspection, covering all types of weapons, and to accept that method of direct negotiations as the only means of solving all differences between them and Israel.* [Emphasis added.]

That challenge was never met, as we were to be reminded time and again.

Concurrently with its search for peace and its resistance to Arab violence, Israel set about to do what it had always wanted to do— build a democratic Jewish state. Despite endless war forced upon it, a thriving society was organized under the most difficult circumstances, one with which the United States found it easy to identify— and one with which Jewish people everywhere could and did proudly identify.

Defining a Nation

What kind of state did the founders of Israel dedicate themselves to building? These words from the Declaration of Independence of the state of Israel are clear, the commitment firm:

> The State of Israel . . . will devote itself to developing the land for the good of all its inhabitants. It will rest upon foundations of liberty, justice, and peace as envisioned by the Prophets of Israel. It will maintain complete equality of social and political rights for all its citizens, without distinction of creed, color, race, or sex. It will guarantee freedom of religion and conscience, of language, education and culture. . . . We call upon the sons of the Arab people

living in Israel to keep the peace and play their part in building the State on the basis of full and equal citizenship and due representation in all its institutions.

This declaration of May 14, 1948, has served, in effect, as the constitution for the state of Israel and is its primary legislative source. It is more than mere rhetoric; a body of laws enacted by the Knesset flows directly from this source. Implicit or explicit in all of these laws, is the guarantee of equality before the law of *all* Israeli citizens—Jews, Muslims, Christians, Druze, and others. No other Middle East nation comes close to such a guarantee.

A system based on fundamental guarantees of equal treatment for all its citizens and blended with the concept of a "Jewish State" has resulted in some difficulties and in occasional violations in practice. Before it could actually be tested, this idea of a Jewish state in a pluralist frame was hotly debated both in Jewish and non-Jewish circles. Would it really be Jewish? Would it really be pluralist? Given the inherent difficulties involved in implementing this unique combination of societal goals, and given the tragic history of conflict, the record is most impressive. Until recent years, when the P.L.O. and other Arab forces set out to instigate turmoil within Israel itself, the history of Arab-Jewish relations inside the new state provided heartening evidence that tolerance and cooperation could be achieved between these two groups. But only in the context of peace and mutual acceptance.

In the spirit of the Declaration of Independence, citizenship was granted to members of every religious or ethnic group, with special naturalization preferences for Jews; political rights were protected for every Israeli citizen, resulting in every Knesset since independence having a number of Arab members; religious freedom was guaranteed for every faith; educational opportunities were provided for all, with consideration given to respective cultures and heritages; freedom of the press, including the Arab press, was protected, with restrictions limited only to national security considerations; social equality, aimed at reduction of inherited cultural gaps, was sought.

Despite these official policies and the nation's commitment to full rights and opportunities for all citizens, the wide cultural and social gap that predates the state of Israel has not been eliminated entirely. As in the United States and other democracies, results in Israel do not always match expectations. Laws are sometimes ignored or poorly administered. The system itself provides for the correction of neglect or evasion. Civil rights organizations are permitted, even encouraged, to help improve the system.

This is not the place to detail what the Israeli system has in fact produced since 1948. Suffice it to say that despite the overriding preoccupation of the state with warding off and defeating military threats, despite the terrorism that always threatens to strike, the Israelis did, both literally and figuratively, "make the desert bloom." Their achievements in agriculture, industry, science, education, the arts—a story so often told and extolled, there is no need to repeat it here.

More impressive than these visible, tangible achievements is the strength of the political system itself. That the constant threats and pressures from hostile forces did not provide the justification or rationale for a less democratic society, for an authoritarian system with few if any freedoms enjoyed by the people, is a tribute to the underlying democratic ideology firmly held by Israel's founders and retained tenaciously by their sons and daughters. The democracy of the Israeli system makes it possible for a demagogue like Meir Kahane, the American-born extremist who seeks the ouster of all Arabs from Israel, to function politically and even to win a seat in the Knesset, but there is no expectation that he can ever be a real force in Israeli politics.

It is impressive that a new, burdened, developing nation readily shared its experiences, knowledge, and discoveries with other developing nations. Between 1957 and 1973, for example, Israel sent some of its best people to black African nations where they trained thousands of Africans in agriculture and economics, industrial development, and health services.

Between 1967 and 1973, under intense pressure from the Arab world, most of the African nations severed relations with Israel, with the unfortunate consequence that most of these very successful technical assistance operations came to an end. It is now known that even after 1973, informal arrangements with some of those black nations permitted the continuation of some vital assistance programs. In recent years, several black nations have resumed diplomatic relations and technical assistance activities with Israel. There is general expectation that soon relations will be restored with most of the other black nations.

It is nothing short of mind-boggling to contemplate what the present economic and social conditions would be today, not only in Israel but in the neighboring Arab countries, if these last thirty or forty years had seen peaceful cooperation among all the nations in the area, including a common market, cooperative water and shipping arrangements, and technical assistance. Instead we have a history of anti-Israel Arab boycott, oil embargoes, and diversion of billions of dollars to the build-up of military capacity rather than economic growth and productivity.

Meeting the Arab Threat

We must take a closer look at what prevented such cooperation from occurring.

The armistice agreements of 1949 declared clearly that neither party "shall commit any warlike or hostile act against the military or paramilitary forces of the other party, or against civilians in territory under the control of that party." Israel and the United Nations considered the armistice agreements a step toward total and permanent peace, but the Arabs considered them an intermission in hostilities; the state of belligerency for them had not ended.

As early as August 9, 1949, a U.N. commission found Egypt was illegally blocking the Suez Canal. After several more years of intolerable Egyptian hostility, Israel's U.N. Ambassador Abba Eban, on October 30, 1956, found it necessary to set forth the record of Egyptian provocations:

> During the six years during which this belligerency has operated in violation of the Armistice Agreement, there have occurred 1,339 cases of armed clashes with Egyptian armed forces, 435 cases of incursion from Egyptian territory, 172 cases of sabotage perpetrated by Egyptian military units and fedayeen in Israel. As a result . . . 364 Israelis were wounded and 101 killed. In 1956 alone . . . 28 Israelis were killed and 127 wounded. . . .

It is important to keep in mind, whenever reference is made to Israeli casualties that Israel has always been a very small country—in size and in population. Every Israeli victim is known to many and is thought of as a family loss.

In the 1950s, the cumulative effect of six years of Egyptian harassment of Israel could not be ignored by Israeli leaders, and was not. After Egypt began importing large quantities of arms from the Soviet Union, after it nationalized the Suez Canal, after it entered into an alliance with Jordan and stepped up attacks on Israel by fedayeen "suicide fighters," and after the United Nations demonstrated its inability or unwillingness to enforce its decisions against Egypt, the Israelis felt compelled to take action. In 1956, they moved against Egypt, soon capturing Gaza and the Sinai. France and Britain approved the initiative and joined Israel at the Suez Canal.

u.s. President Dwight Eisenhower, while sympathizing with Israel's plight, disagreed with the actions Israel thought essential for its security. When both the United States and the Soviet Union demanded a halt to the action, Israel withdrew from the Sinai, the second time since 1949. Arrangements were made for a u.n. peace-keeping force, but once again the Arab side did not agree to renounce its war aims or to engage in peace negotiations. Israel's withdrawal from the Sinai was interpreted throughout the Arab world as a supreme victory for Egypt's Gamel Abdel Nasser—and Nasserism was to become the underlying ideology of the period.

While the Sinai effort of 1956 gave the Israelis confidence in their military capability, its political outcome gave them ominous warnings—Nasser and Nasserism were committed to continuing the struggle against Israel and there would be obstacles to gain international approval and support for its countermeasures.

The period between 1956 and the Six Day War of 1967 saw a number of simultaneous developments. An Arab world that was constantly beset with internecine intrigue and betrayal, with ad hoc alliances forged and soon ignored, could unite and agree on only one objective—the destruction of Israel. The Palestinian refugee problem became a Palestinian liberation cause, with the p.l.o. coming to the fore. The Soviet Union increased its presence and influence in the Middle East, providing huge quantities of sophisticated arms to Egypt and Syria along with critically important political support. Terrorism, directed not only against Israel itself but against Israeli or Jewish targets anywhere in the world, became a major element in the Arabs' war against Israel.

The Six Day War

A series of major Arab provocations finally compelled Israel to strike back.

Fatah—which means "conquest in the service of Islam"—was the Syrian-backed Palestinian group led by Yasir Arafat; it had its own military wing that conducted terrorist attacks on Israel beginning January 1, 1965. Some seven months earlier, it had joined with other Palestinian groups to form the p.l.o. Before long the p.l.o. created its own Palestine Liberation Army. Syria launched attacks from the Golan Heights against Israeli villages below, and escalated such attacks in late 1966 after it signed, with Soviet endorsement, a mutual defense pact with Egypt. After suffering thirty-nine attacks from Syria in the period from February 1966 to April 1967, Israel struck back on April 7, downing six Syrian MIG fighters. On May 15, 1967, the u.n. complied with an Egyptian demand that the u.n.'s peace-keeping force be evacuated from its position along the border, and soon thereafter Nasser announced a blockade against Israeli shipping to Eilat. Muslim leaders called publicly for a jihad ("holy war") against Israel. On May 30, King Hussein of Jordan jumped on the bandwagon by agreeing to allow Egyptian and Iraqi forces into Jordan and recognizing the p.l.o. as the sole representative of the Palestinians.

Despite the clear evidence of Israel's waging a legitimate war of self-defense, there are some who continue to allege that Israel was the aggressor. But the words of Arab leaders at the time leave no doubt. Some examples:

Egypt's President Nasser: "Our basic objective will be the destruction of Israel. The Arab people want to fight." (May 27) "The armies of Egypt, Jordan, Syria, and Lebanon are poised on the borders of Israel . . . this act will astound the world. Today they will know that the Arabs are arranged for battle, the critical hour has arrived. We have reached the stage of serious action and not declaration." (May 30)

Iraq's President Aref: "The existence of Israel is an error which must be rectified. This is our opportunity to wipe out the ignominy which has been with us since 1948. Our goal is clear—to wipe Israel off the map." (May 31)

On June 5, 1967, with a government of national unity in place and convinced beyond any reasonable doubt that a major Arab offensive was close to execution, the Israelis waged a preventive attack. Within hours, the Israelis had inflicted critical losses on the Egyptian Air Force. Within two days, after Jordan refused to respect an Israeli appeal not to enter the war, Israeli forces had conquered East Jerusalem and the West Bank. On the fourth day, Israel reacted to Syrian provocation by taking the Golan Heights. And within six days Israeli forces had reached the Suez Canal in the south, the Jordan River in the east, and were sixty miles from Damascus in the north.

Once again, Israel had won a military victory. The Israelis were euphoric and so were their friends and supporters. But, again, there was concern that despite the sacrifice and the victory, the final outcome would not bring peace, or that Israel's legitimacy, its "right to exist," would finally be acknowledged by its Arab neighbors. Israel was determined this time not to make unilateral concessions without appropriate assurances from the Arabs.

American reaction to the Six Day War was most positive. That reaction was a reflection of what had been developing in American-Israeli relations and laid the basis for that special relationship which was to become so explicit in the years ahead.

President Eisenhower's action in 1956 in compelling Israel's withdrawal from the Sinai had been a serious blow to u.s.-Israel understanding and friendship. But even that could not alter an affinity that had been developing between the two nations since 1948. Americans empathized with a small nation taking on a hostile Arab world, which, supported and encouraged by the Soviet Union, was determined to wipe it out. Americans identified with a nation keeping its promise to absorb every Jew who survived Hitler's terror and every Jew choosing to live in a state that could assure them protection from anti-Semitism and persecution. Americans admired a nation, especially in that part of the world that believed in and was building a viable society based on the democratic, humanistic, and pluralist principles on which America was founded.

American Jews identified easily with the fears and then the pride engendered by the 1967 war. But there can be no doubt that the overwhelming majority of Americans experienced similar feelings. The loss of this democratic nation, whose independence the United States had helped to win, would have been considered a major defeat for America.

American identification with Israel's welfare and security, albeit not incorporated in any explicit agreements, had been recognized by every president. I have already cited declarations of support *before* the establishment of the state—from Wilson to Truman. That uninterrupted pledge of support continued.

Despite President Eisenhower's opposition to the Sinai operation in 1956, his attitude about basic u.s.-Israeli friendship could not have been stated more strongly or more explicitly:

> The State of Israel is democracy's outpost in the Middle East, and every American who loves liberty must join the effort to make secure forever the future of the newest member in the family of nations. We pray that a strong Israel and her Arab neighbors will join in the creation of a just and lasting peace which will bring to all an era of prosperity and enlightenment.

President John Kennedy spoke of this basic American policy with particular eloquence:

> The United Nations may have conferred on Israel the credentials of nationhood, but its own idealism and courage, its own sacrifice and generosity, had earned the credentials of immortality. . . . It carries the shield of democracy and it honors the sword of freedom. . . . Israel is a cause that stands beyond the ordinary changes and chances of American public life. . . . Friendship for Israel is not a partisan matter; it is a national commitment.

Lyndon Johnson, president during the 1967 war, clearly stated his basic view of Israel:

> Israel is a vital, progressive land, a symbol of courage and the strength of her people. . . . We share many common objectives . . . chief of which is the building of a better world, a world in which every nation can develop its resources and develop them in freedom and peace.

When Israel successfully met what was generally regarded as a threat to its existence in 1967, and did it so impressively, there could be little doubt about American reaction. Public opinion polls showed that Americans from every area and from every walk of life shared in the exhilaration of a clear Israeli victory. Because of the more than fifty years of American identification with the fate of a Jewish state in the Middle East, it was considered an American victory almost as much as an Israeli triumph. For the Soviets, on the other hand, it was a bitter defeat.

Generally supportive and sympathetic as American attitude had been through the years, the United States had not been an active participant in Middle East diplomacy or in *direct* support for Israel. In order not to jeopardize relations with the Arab world, it had even embargoed arms shipments to Israel in 1949. Its financial help was limited to modest technical assistance grants. But the Six Day War was to change that. American concern for Israel's victory in the war itself was unmistakable, for example, when the Sixth Fleet was ordered to the area after ominous warnings were issued by the Soviet Union.

More important, the Six Day War led to major and critical American participation in the United Nations diplomatic process after the fighting was over. That participation defined the essence of the vital role played by the United States for the next twenty years, the role that is really the subject of the present debate between Mr. Abourezk and me, a role I applaud because it has been conceptually sound and in the American interest, occasional misjudgments and confusion notwithstanding.

The u.s. role since 1967 has been to blend as effectively as possible three simultaneous, at times *seemingly* incompatible goals: (1) ending the isolation and assuring the security of Israel; (2) developing friendship and trust of moderate Arab states and Palestinians; and (3) protecting its own geopolitical and economic interests, especially with regard to Soviet ambition in the area.

It soon became clear how difficult it would be to meet these goals after the 1967 war. Despite the fact that the Arabs had come out of the war humiliated and divided, they did unite within two months in a defiant rejection of all talk of Arab-Israeli reconciliation. At the historic Khartoum Arab Summit they followed Egypt's Nasser in proclaiming again the three angry "nos"—no peace, no negotiations, no recognition of Israel. Lands taken by force, Nasser insisted, could be retaken only by force.

The Israelis, despite their astounding military success, understood that ultimate victory could be achieved only at the negotiating table, and they were prepared to make concessions to reach an agreement. They made it clear, however, that they would never return to unmodified 1967 borders, the borders that had invited terrorism and had been so costly to defend. And, after nineteen years of Arab perfidy in preventing Jews from visiting their most precious shrines, they would never yield effective control over East Jerusalem.

Despite Arab rejectionism, the u.s. ambassador to the u.n., Arthur Goldberg, did finally secure unanimous Security Council approval on November 22, 1967 for Resolution 242. The key operative sections of this historic resolution are the following:

1. *Affirms* that the fulfillment of Charter principles requires the establishment of a just and lasting peace in the Middle East which should include the application of both the following principles:
   (i) Withdrawal of Israeli armed forces from territories occupied in the recent conflict;
   (ii) Termination of all claims or states of belligerency and respect for and acknowledgement of the sovereignty, territorial integrity and political independence of every state in the area and their right to live in peace within secure and recognized boundaries free from threats or acts of force;
2. *Affirms further* the necessity
   (a) For guaranteeing freedom of navigation through international waterways in the area;
   (b) For achieving a just settlement of the refugee problem;
   (c) For guaranteeing the territorial inviolability and political independence of every state in the area, through measures including the establishment of demilitarized zones.

The Soviet Union did join the United States in urging approval, but insisted on its own interpretation of key sections that to this day has made full implementation so difficult. Similarly, Egypt and Jordan nominally "accepted" 242 but insisted that it required *immediate* and *total* withdrawal by Israel from all territories occupied in the war. Most of the other Arab nations rejected the resolution out of hand.

Arab rejection, either outright or by contrived interpretation, reflected the traditional, basic obstacle to Middle East peace. *Resolution 242's basic premise was recognition of Israel's "right to live in peace within secure and recognized boundaries."* The Arabs were not willing to go along.

Israel recognized it would have to return some, probably most, of the occupied lands in exchange for genuine recognition and peace. It accepted 242's principle of the "inadmissibility of acquisition of territory by war," but insisted the resolution called for negotiations to determine the final disposition of disputed lands. The Arab contention that the resolution itself required *total* and *prior* withdrawal before negotiation has been fully repudiated by the principal architect of the resolution, Ambassador Goldberg. The Soviet proposal for total withdrawal, he has pointed out, was rejected by the Security Council. Reference to "territories," rather than *"the* territories," was deliberate; final decisions were left for direct negotiation between the parties involved. And, Ambassador Goldberg insists, no withdrawal was required *before* such negotiation.

Failure to resolve the territories question soon after the Six Day War led to years of conflict and increasing bitterness in the Arab-Israeli dispute. It is time to raise the question I've asked before— and, tragically, it will have to be asked again and again.

What if the Arabs in 1967 had agreed, albeit reluctantly and even resentfully, to the reality if not the legitimacy of Israel, and had negotiated secure, recognized borders? How many thousands of lives, Jewish and Arab, might have been saved? How much more Arab land might have been recovered in the context of a conciliatory peace negotiation than is likely today? How much might have been done to provide for Palestinian welfare and self-governance?

Israel's standing as a military power and as a gutsy, determined people enhanced its reputation in the United States and in other democratic nations, but there were many negatives associated with the victory. For Israel there was the draining cost—in money and in personnel—of administering the occupied areas. The normal resentments of "occupied" people provided easy customers for the poison peddled by the P.L.O. and hostile Arab leaders. The Soviet bloc and many of its Third World allies broke relations with Israel. With military options less successful to the Arabs in the aftermath of the 1967 war, they chose the United Nations and world diplomacy to wage all-out political war against Israel. Oil-rich Arab nations were determined to use their economic clout to support this political war against Israel. Victorious in war, Israel was becoming the pariah nation in the world, more isolated than ever.

The threat to Israel during this period, however, was not just political. The military threat took on new forms. A "war of attrition" was proclaimed by Nasser and fighting took place also along the Jordanian and Syrian frontiers. In addition, Palestinian terrorist operations were expanded, both in Israel and around the world. The most horrendous and most publicized atrocity was the murder of eleven Israeli athletes at the Munich Olympics in 1972. While the true needs of the Palestinians had been largely ignored by the Arab states until 1967, the "Palestinian question" became for them a convenient weapon, an easy rationalization for refusal to negotiate peace with Israel.

Though no serious, direct military threat seemed imminent at the time, a major Arab remilitarization was occurring. Between 1970 and 1973, the Soviets sold about *three billion dollars* worth of arms to Egypt and Syria, financed principally by Arab oil-producing states. Almost 1,000 planes and 4,500 tanks were part of the build-up.

Egypt acquired a new president, Anwar al-Sadat, after the sudden death of Nasser in the summer of 1970. Sadat's early years were marked by erratic and contradictory policies toward other Arab nations and toward the Soviet Union. The one unchanging policy was insistence that Israel return every inch of Egyptian territory— but he was alternately in favor and opposed to negotiating directly for such return.

Israeli doubts about Sadat's reliability were prompted by his confusing behavior. Soon after a letter in early 1971 to U.N. special envoy Gunnar Jarring expressing his willingness "to enter into a peace agreement with Israel," Sadat told a Palestine National Council meeting in Cairo that he would support the P.L.O. "until victory" and said Egypt would never accept Resolution 242. Two days before that speech, Hassanain Haykal, Sadat's unofficial spokesman and editor of *Al Ahram*, had clearly spelled out the two-stage plan against Israel:

> Arab policy at this stage has but two objectives. The first, the elimination of the traces of the 1967 aggression through an Israeli withdrawal from all territories occupied that year. The second

objective is the elimination of the traces of the aggression, *by means of the elimination of the State of Israel itself.* [Emphasis added.]

The Yom Kippur War

On October 6, 1973—Yom Kippur, the holiest day in the Jewish calendar—Egypt and Syria staged a coordinated, surprise attack against Israel. With only 130 Israeli tanks facing 1,400 Syrian tanks on the Golan Heights, and fewer than 500 Israeli soldiers warding off 80,000 Egyptians, the first two days were disastrous for Israel. With its reserves rapidly mobilized, Israel finally threw back the invaders and pushed the fighting deep into Egypt and Syria. Only when a major Israeli victory seemed certain did the Soviet Union and the U.N. join the American efforts for a cease-fire.

Egypt and Syria had done the actual fighting, but eight other Arab nations had sent troops and/or equipment to the battlefronts: Morocco, Algeria, Tunisia, Sudan, Saudi Arabia, Kuwait, Jordan, and Iraq. Moreover, *economic* war had become an important complement to the actual fighting. Oil-producing states not only gave generous financial assistance to Egypt and Syria, but boldly used oil as a weapon, including embargoing oil for the United States. For a while it worked; numerous nations found it advisable to scold Israel regularly and to vote for hostile U.N. resolutions.

The Soviet Union had been a major, indispensable partner to the Yom Kippur attack, having supplied the Arabs with more than 200,000 tones of military equipment in 900 air flights and 100 ships. At one point, the Soviets put their own forces on alert and threatened to interfere. American conduct was somewhat uncertain and delayed, but before the fighting was over, Israel was assured of massive replacements of lost matériel and was encouraged by American readiness to alert its own forces, and subsequently by critical diplomatic support and generous economic and military assistance.

The United States and the Soviet Union both made it abundantly clear by their actions that they were indeed major adversaries in the Middle East conflict. The beginning of a more conscious, a more explicit "strategic relationship" between Israel and the United States was being forged. No discussion of the appropriateness of American Middle East policy today can ignore this fundamental reality.

American identification with Israel during this conflict did not mean unquestioning acceptance of the Israeli position. The United States interest was not only to protect Israel, but to retain its own ability to exercise a mediating role in establishing peace in the area. It was generally believed that in the war, Secretary of State Henry Kissinger did not welcome a total, crushing defeat of the Arabs, which might make reasonable accommodation more difficult. By taking on the role of "honest broker," the United States did not always enjoy the full confidence of the Israelis. There were to be occasional crises in the u.s.-Israel relationship even as basic strategic cooperation was being strengthened. And there were times when Israel's supporters in the United States—in the Jewish community and in general—would be critical of positions taken by the administration.

The Yom Kippur war ended, on October 22, when the Security Council adopted Resolution 338. It was brief and to the point:

The Security Council,

1. *Calls upon* all to the parties present fighting to cease all firing and terminate all military activity immediately, no later than 12 hours after the moment of the adoption of this decision, in the positions they now occupy;

2. *Calls upon* the parties concerned to start immediately after the cease-fire the implementation of Security Council Resolution 242 (1967) in all of its parts;

3. *Decides* that, immediately and concurrently with the cease-fire, negotiations start between the parties concerned under appropriate auspices aimed at establishing a just and durable peace in the Middle East.

Once again, there were hopes that a process had been agreed to that would assure a productive "peace process." It called for all parties to implement *immediately* after the cease-fire Resolution 242 *in all of its parts,* and that concurrently with the cease-fire, negotiations *under appropriate auspices* be started between the parties to establish a durable peace.

However, a u.n.-sponsored peace conference in Geneva in December of 1973 demonstrated that such a conference was *not* appropriate for a productive peace process. Inclusion of several Arab delegations meant that the most hostile, the most intransigent participant would determine the tone and substance of Arab participation; inclusion of the Soviet Union assured introduction of unhelpful, irrelevant elements of super-power rivalry.

In light of this telling experience, the United States chose to confine itself to the promotion of bilateral agreements between Israel and its immediate adversaries. In what was to be at times a controversial and troublesome role, Secretary Kissinger gave brilliant leadership to a series of disengagement negotiations. By January 18, 1974, Israel and Egypt had signed an agreement calling for Israel's withdrawal from both banks of the Suez Canal, permitting Egypt to control the canal and regain national pride and authority over a very important strategic and economic asset. Israel, in return, secured access to the canal for shipping to and from Israel.

On May 31, 1974, after weeks of exhausting shuttling between Jerusalem and Damascus, Secretary Kissinger could point to another disengagement agreement, this one between Israel and Syria. Under its terms, Israel returned territory it had reached in 1974, plus the town of Kuneitra, in exchange for a cease-fire, a separation of forces, and an exchange of prisoners. A second Sinai disengagement accord signed in September of 1975 was hailed as a major step in Israeli-Egyptian reconciliation and a new high in Israeli-u.s. cooperation.

These agreements represented a major achievement for the United States, one that served our national interest by demonstrating our ability to influence and promote peace to the benefit of both Israel and Arab states willing to negotiate with the u.s. America's trusting relationship with Israel, moderate Arab leaders were beginning to recognize, was an important asset, if there was to be any progress toward peace.

The next few years saw no progress in the peace process. It was a period during which the u.n. welcomed Yasir Arafat; its now automatic anti-Israel majority adopted one resolution after another excoriating Israel and demanding recognition of the p.l.o., and acceptance of a Palestinian state. The most notorious resolution, adopted on November 10, 1975, condemned Zionism as a form of "racism." This verbal violence was accompanied by a steady stream of terrorist activities. During 1974 and 1975 alone, there were 36 border crossings by Palestinian terrorists from Lebanon, and 110 shellings of Israeli settlements from Lebanon by Soviet-built Katyusha rockets. Israeli retaliation kept pace with this increased terrorism.

Both American presidents who served during these years carried on in the spirit of their predecessors, but articulated even more explicitly the stake that America had in the search for a Middle East peace that included security for Israel. Thus, Richard Nixon declared, "The United States stands by its friends. Israel is one of its friends. . . . It is prepared to supply the military equipment necessary to support the efforts of friendly governments, like Israel's, to defend the safety of their people."

His successor, Gerald Ford, declared that "America must and will pursue friendship with all nations . . . but never at the expense of America's commitment to Israel. . . . Our commitment to Israel will meet the test of American steadfastness and resolve. . . . My commitment to the security and future of Israel is based upon basic morality as well as enlightened self-interest. Our role in supporting Israel honors our own heritage."

Despite a shaky and ambiguous first year, the next president of the United States, Jimmy Carter, played a historic role in achieving the first major breakthrough in Middle East peace—Camp David.

The Long Road to Camp David

Before we examine the Camp David story, it might be useful to take stock of the American posture in the Middle East as it had developed up to that point.

As we have seen, in the period between the Balfour Declaration of 1917 and the end of World War II, the United States identified with the goal of Jewish resettlement in Palestine. One president after another, and one Congress after another, considered it morally right and diplomatically appropriate to express America's understanding of the conditions that had prompted the Zionist dream for a return to the ancient homeland of the Jews. A nation committed to "life, liberty, and the pursuit of happiness" could not be indifferent to a people yearning for those same goals. It served America's interests in the court of world opinion to be associated with such a cause. This first chapter in American Middle East policy development was, essentially, based on humanitarian and philosophic considerations.

Having led the Allies to victory against Hitler, the United States could not be indifferent to the group that had been singled out by Hitler for total annihilation. The plight of those Jews who managed to survive the Holocaust provided additional incentive for American identification with and support of a Jewish homeland. When President Truman, with overwhelming American support, recognized Israel minutes after the U.N. vote, a second and more direct chapter in the evolution of Middle East policy was initiated. American policy would not be confined to expressions of humanitarian concern; it would be forthright in its diplomatic operations. Israel's legitimacy, its "right to exist" as a sovereign state, would have American backing. So emphatic was this support that adherence to the commitment would soon be a measure of American steadfastness and reliability in world affairs, no less than any other commitment, such as NATO.

A third chapter in the developing involvement was evidenced in American reaction to the Six Day War and the Yom Kippur War. Even without any explicit or formal guarantees, it was clear that the United States could not and would not be indifferent to the outcome, or unresponsive to Israel's material needs when its existence was in jeopardy. But America's interests always went beyond Israel's own. While giving Israel moral, diplomatic, and even material support, the U.S. sought to obtain the trust of the Arab world too, so that peace could be negotiated.

When, at long last, a major Arab leader was ready to accept the fundamental premise of American policy—Israel's legitimacy—the United States was in a position to be that "honest broker."

The Promise of Camp David

Today a new dawn is emerging out of the darkness of the past. A new chapter is being opened in the history of co-existence among nations. . . . Men and women of good will have labored day and night to bring about this happy moment. Egyptians and Israelis alike pursued their sacred goal undeterred by difficulties and complications. . . . Let there be no more war or bloodshed between Arabs and Israelis . . . no more suffering . . . no more despair or loss of faith.

ANWAR AL-SADAT

It is a great day in the annals of two ancient nations, Egypt and Israel, whose sons met in our generation five times on the battlefield, fighting and falling. . . . Now we make peace, the cornerstone of cooperation and friendship. . . . Now is the time for all of us to show civil courage in order to proclaim to our peoples, and to others: no more war, no more bloodshed, no more bereavement—peace unto you, Shalom, Salaam—forever.

MENACHEM BEGIN

Today we celebrate a victory, not of a bloody military campaign, but of an inspiring peace campaign. . . . Mothers in Egypt and Israel are not weeping today for their children fallen in senseless battle. The dedication and determination of these two world statesmen have borne fruit. Peace has come to Israel and to Egypt.

JIMMY CARTER

That was March 26, 1979. The north lawn of the White House. The signing ceremony for the Egyptian-Israeli Peace Treaty. I was there among the hundreds of men and women privileged to hear those historic words. That picture—a picture since printed by the millions—of those three world leaders clasping hands and smiling broadly, that picture still gives me goosebumps whenever I recall that day of joy, of thanks, of hope, of promise, and, above all, of pride in what my own country had been so instrumental in creating.

How could I not feel that way? Sixty years after Balfour, thirty years after the aborted U.N. partition plan, a full-fledged *peace treaty*—not a cease-fire, not an armistice, not another disengagement agreement—was finally being signed by Israel and an Arab state. Not just any Arab state, but by far the largest and most important of the Arab states. No more Israeli sons dying in battle; no more Egyptian sons being killed in battle. Golda Meir must have been smiling.

Sixteen months earlier, in November 1977, Egypt's President Anwar al-Sadat had gone to Jerusalem and told the Knesset; "Israel has become an established fact recognized by the world. . . . We really and truly welcome you to live among us in peace and security." That was it. That was what had been missing all those years, a clear acknowledgment by an Arab leader that there was room in the Middle East for a Jewish state.

That Knesset speech, we soon learned, did not lead automatically to agreement and a peace treaty. The speech had indeed removed the principal obstacle to reconciliation, resistance to Israel's legitimacy. But Sadat had spoken boldly about the high price Israel would have to pay to get more than a positive speech. Nothing less than total withdrawal, Sadat demanded, and acceptance of a new Palestinian state.

The terms were harsh, but Israel's enthusiasm would not be dimmed. Sadat's courageous action in going to the Knesset had been actively encouraged by Menachem Begin, who had become prime minister only six months earlier. The trip and speech started a process that Sadat and Begin—and after a short period of hesitation and confusion, President Carter too—were determined to pursue. All three of them, in the course of those sixteen months between the Knesset speech and the signing ceremony, would earn plaudits for their courage, their imagination, their steadfastness.

But it was not to come easily. For Sadat and Begin the risks were obvious, and they were serious. While Sadat could be reasonably certain of carrying his Egyptian people with him, he had little hope of support from the Arab world. He knew he was risking Arab hostility, perhaps even violence. Begin risked his own political support at home, but more important, he could not ignore the terrible possibility that any compromise he offered or agreed to might risk the security, perhaps the life of Israel. Carter, sensitive to their respective concerns, understood the political risks to himself and the damage to America's standing in the world if his efforts should fail.

The period between Sadat's speech to the Knesset and the summer of 1978 failed to bring any hopeful developments in what had been expected to be an active peace process, despite numerous private meetings between Israeli and Egyptian diplomats and many American intercessions. The Carter administration, increasingly impatient with the public and private sparring between the parties, decided in early summer to use its influence to speed up the process.

I was given the opportunity for a close look at the difficulties of that period when I was invited to be a member of a citizen group accompanying Vice President Walter Mondale on his mission to Egypt and Israel during the first week in July. The meetings Mondale had with the two nations' highest officials were private, but we were briefed sufficiently to understand the delicacy of his mission. We were to learn later that Mondale obtained some important concessions from Sadat, including withdrawal of his earlier insistence upon self-determination for the Palestinians and, procedurally, approval for his foreign minister to meet later that week with Secretary of State Cyrus Vance and Foreign Minister Moshe Dayan in London.

That was "quiet diplomacy" being practiced by an American vice president on behalf of the administration. But the mission provided an illustration too of the kind of "public diplomacy" required to move both parties to compromise. The Begin government was taking the position that u.n. Resolution 242 did not require withdrawal on *all* fronts, in an apparent strategy to protect its options on the West Bank, which Begin insisted on calling by its biblical names—Judea and Samaria. The American position was that Resolution 242 did contemplate withdrawal on all fronts, the precise nature of such withdrawal to be negotiated by the parties directly involved. Foreclosing any such withdrawal in advance, in the American view, could well destroy any chance for progress. Mondale, knowing full well that his own reputation as a true friend of Israel would be threatened, agreed to make a clear statement on the subject in his speech to the Knesset. He knew of course that the Egyptians and other Arab leaders would be analyzing his speech carefully.

"In the Sinai," Mondale told the Knesset, "Israel has proposed a peace treaty in which there would be negotiated withdrawal, and security would be achieved while relinquishing claims to territory. *This approach can be applied in the West Bank and Gaza.*" (Emphasis added.) He received no complaints, as far as I could tell, from any of the Americans accompanying him, including those from the Jewish community. It is difficult to measure how much this Mondale mission contributed to what culminated two months later at Camp David. I cite it here, as a personal footnote, as an example of the unique role that the United States played in the search for peace in the Middle East.

The story of Camp David itself, the thirteen-day marathon negotiating session during September, has already been chronicled thoroughly elsewhere; it will continue to be a fascinating subject for historians and researchers for many years. How each of the participants revealed new strengths, new personalities, new abilities, will continue to intrigue us all. Debates will continue over the wisdom of specific provisions of the accords and then of the treaty itself; perhaps even over the ultimate wisdom of the process in light of the fact that only one of its stated goals—peace between Egypt and Israel—has been achieved, and even that one has had its complications and frustrations.

President Sadat was gunned down by Muslim fanatics who hated him for his turning to the Christian West for economic help as well as for making peace "with the Jews" at Camp David. Prime Minister Begin, exhausted and frustrated in the aftermath of the war in Lebanon—and saddened by the death of his beloved wife—stepped down. President Carter, despite the great political lift Camp David gave him and his administration, failed to win re-election. But the Camp David achievement endures, not only for what it has achieved but also for what it meant and can still mean.

■ Above all, for eight years now, it has meant peace between Israel and Egypt. The major battleground of past wars has been silent and without any real fear of that silence being broken. There have been problems between Egypt and Israel, the result primarily of failure of other Arab states to accept the challenge of the Camp David Framework for Peace to "proceed simultaneously to negotiate and conclude similar peace treaties with a view to achieving a comprehensive peace in the area."

■ Camp David—and the treaty that followed—proved with deeds that when an Arab leader made clear his acceptance of Israel's right to exist and live in peace, Israel was prepared—even when its reputably most "hawkish" prime minister was its leader—to be flexible and generous in its response. Israel's critics have failed to acknowledge that for peace Israel agreed to withdraw from an area three times its own pre-1967 size, abandon the only oil fields it had access to, along with three superior air bases, a strategically vital naval base, a modern road network, and even several urban and rural settlements over the violent objection of courageous pioneer residents. While such Israeli flexibility and generosity cannot serve as a precise model for any future Israeli-Arab peace negotiation, given the history of these last eight years, the basic meaning of the Camp

David Framework remains and has been articulated by most Israeli leaders: *for credible assurances of peace, Israel is prepared to take risks.*

■ Camp David sought to provide a basis for solving the difficult Palestinian question. It still can. Israel and Egypt agreed to work for the establishment of an elected self-governing authority on the West Bank and in Gaza, with a built-in timetable for ultimate resolution of the Palestinian problem in which Israel, Egypt, Jordan, and elected representatives of the inhabitants of the West Bank and Gaza would be involved. Here again, Israel demonstrated flexibility and moderation. While resisting, as it still does today, any commitment to a new, independent Palestinian state, Israel agreed to the Camp David accords language that stated that "final negotiations must recognize the legitimate rights of the Palestinian people and their just requirements." A far cry indeed from the position of an earlier prime minister, Golda Meir, who was reputed to have declared, "There is no such thing as a Palestinian." (Mrs. Meir denied ever having said this, insisting that she had referred only to the nonexistence of a Palestinian *state,* but for years her alleged quotation was accepted widely as portraying the Israeli position.)

The plan for full autonomy for West Bank and Gaza residents was without precedent. No other country or authority had ever offered such self-governance to the Palestinian Arabs. It stood in sharp contrast to the failure of Jordan throughout its nineteen years (1948–1967) of occupation to offer independence or autonomy or any form of self-governance when it could have done so unilaterally.

■ Camp David demonstrated that the United States could play a significant role as the "honest broker." It was dramatic evidence that American commitment to Israel's security did not make it unsympathetic to reasonable Arab demands or goals. Camp David was a triumph for American diplomacy and thus enhanced its standing in a very critical area of the world. The most important Arab leader of that period had placed his confidence in the United States, and it had paid off.

■ Camp David strengthened and also clarified the "special relationship" between the United States and Israel. Israel recognized that, despite its insistence upon direct negotiations with the Arabs and its determination always to have the defense capability to defeat by itself any combination of Arab adversaries, it had to look to the

United States both for diplomatic support and for material assistance. The United States recognized the need to demonstrate, beyond question, to the Israeli people that it was a reliable and generous partner, that the Israelis could therefore take some additional risks for peace.

In a dramatic, final action to assure acceptance of the pending peace treaty, Jimmy Carter had left for Cairo and Jerusalem on March 6, 1979—twenty days before the treaty was to be signed. To the Israeli Knesset, some of whose members still needed reassurance, Jimmy Carter went beyond any of his predecessors in defining the special relationship and in promising to back it up with deeds:

> Seven Presidents have believed and demonstrated that America's relationship with Israel is more than just a special relationship. It has been, and it is, a unique relationship . . . a relationship which is indestructible because it is rooted in the consciousness and the morals and the religion and the beliefs of the American people themselves. . . .We recognize the advantages to the United States of this partnership. . . .The risks of peace between you and your Egyptian neighbors are real. But America is ready to reduce any risks and to balance them within the bounds of our strength and our influence. . . .We have been centrally involved in this region, and we will stay involved politically, economically, and militarily. We will stand by our friends. We are ready to place our strength at Israel's side when you want it to ensure Israel's security and well-being. . . . In the context of peace, we are prepared to see Israel's economic and military relationship with the United States take on new and strong and more meaningful dimensions even than already exist.

America could not and would not be an automatic supporter of any and every Israeli position. Differences with Israel had surfaced during and following Camp David—as they were to develop in the post-treaty years. Israel had to appreciate the very difficult role the United States was determined to play: to combine an outspoken special commitment to Israel's security and welfare (as articulated in Carter's speech to the Knesset) and a readiness to serve as "honest broker" between adversaries. Israeli flexibility and moderation, consistent with its perceived minimum requirements for security, would be necessary to permit the United States to be accepted as that

honest broker. Israel would be expected to give American suggestions serious and sympathetic consideration.

Reactions to Camp David

The euphoria at that White House ceremony did not last long. Each
of the three principals had expressed the hope that the Israel-Egypt
peace treaty would be the model for others to follow—that piece by
piece a Middle East comprehensive peace would eventuate, and that
the Palestinian issue would be on its way to resolution. But once
again, we were to witness Arab unwillingness or inability to see the
opportunity for peace and accommodation. Five days after the signatures were affixed to the Egypt-Israel treaty, an Arab League Summit
communiqué excoriated Egypt for having "chosen, in collusion with
the United States, to stand by the side of the Zionist enemy . . ."
The league then suspended Egypt from its ranks, called for the
immediate withdrawal of all Arab ambassadors from Egypt, and
recommended severance of political and diplomatic relations with
Egypt. Syrian and P.L.O. reactions were particularly violent. The
Soviets joined with the Arab rejectionist front and much of the
Third World in assuring U.N. hostility and refusal to implement
treaty undertakings.

Particularly distressing to me was the reaction of the Arab
American community. Except for the American Lebanese League,
the community's organizations and spokesmen were highly critical
of the treaty and of America's role in the entire Camp David process.
It echoed the demands of the Arab rejectionist states and the P.L.O.
One umbrella group, the National Committee on the Middle East,
condemned the treaty as a "war pact based on capitulation and
injustice." In a *Washington Post* article, Mr. Abourezk belittled
President Carter's interest in the Sinai, criticized the promised
financial help to Israel and Egypt, and warned that unless Israel
yields to the demand for a new Palestinian state, "there will be no
peace."

Reaction in the American Jewish community was, as noted,
altogether different. Understanding this difference goes to the heart
of this debate between Mr. Abourezk and me. After all, what did
Israel get out of Camp David except the *promise* of recognition and
peace with at least one of its neighbors? For that promise, it surrendered land and facilities that had provided physical defense against

another threat to its existence. Egypt, the leading Arab nation, obtained not only the promise of peace with a neighbor who had repeatedly defeated it in war, but recovered all its land, its oil fields, its airports. The Palestinian Arabs, moreover, were being offered for the first time an opportunity for self-governance.

How, then, should Americans with emotional ties to the Middle East have reacted? Was it too much to expect that Arab Americans would cheer the fact that the major Arab nation had achieved not only land and restored territory, but also a close, trusting relationship with the United States? Was there not cause for appreciation that the United States was prepared to provide financial assistance to Egypt in addition to political and diplomatic support? Should they not have recognized an enhanced American role in the Middle East as being in our national interest?

American Jews were not enthusiastic about every aspect of the accords or the treaty; they shared some of the apprehension of the Israelis. Their joy on March 26 was based on pride that their government had played such a critical role in laying the groundwork for acknowledgment by the major Arab nation of Israel's right to exist, and following from that, the prospect of a more comprehensive peace—a peace to be enjoyed by Jew and Arab alike.

For American Jews, moreover, there was pride in the broader process that had been involved. In the days immediately preceding the actual signing, I wrote an essay that appeared in the *Jerusalem Post* and in some American Jewish newspapers. In "Breakthrough for the Democratic Process as Well as Peace," I expressed appreciation for the fact that "American Jews played a constructive role in helping to bring about the present situation—both in their relation to the American government and in their relation to Israel." I noted that there had been times when we invoked our rights as American Jews to offer criticism and advice to our own government when we thought it was wrong, when it was unduly critical or demanding of Israel. And there were times when, as friends of Israel, we had found ways—at times, public ways—to offer criticism and advice to our Israeli friends.

"No government, American or Israeli," I wrote, "is infallible or always fully sensitive to every possible consideration. It can benefit from the advice and prodding it gets from its citizens or its friends. . . . Jewish dissent from official Israeli policy may have contributed

to Arab intransigence . . . but may also have contributed to that
Israeli flexibility that made the breakthrough possible. . . . Democ-
racy has proved itself in Israel. It has proved itself in the United
States. . . ."

Sadly, the years since that treaty signing have not produced the
comprehensive peace envisioned by Camp David. Major problems
remain unresolved. Tensions and violence have increased. Arms
build-ups continue. But none of this is the consequence of Camp
David. It is the consequence of resistance to Camp David.

The question I raised earlier now cries out more urgently than
ever before. It is now more than eight years since the Camp David
accords for peace were agreed to—three years *after* the five-year
autonomy period decreed for the Palestinians in the West Bank and
Gaza. Is it unreasonable to speculate that if the Arab response to
Camp David had not been angry rejection, if Palestinians had been
permitted to explore the possibilities of autonomy, if Jordan had felt
free to negotiate without fear of dire consequences from the P.L.O.
and pro-P.L.O. elements in the Arab world, if indeed the "spirit of
Camp David" had guided Arab attitudes following the signing of the
Egyptian-Israeli peace treaty—is it unreasonable to speculate that
much of the violence and bloodshed of these eight years might have
been avoided, that billions of dollars spent on arms might have been
used instead for economic growth and improvement of living standards?

Above all, it must be asked, if the first five years, as anticipated,
had been used for good-faith implementation of the autonomy provi-
sion, might not the Palestinian issue be much closer to solution
today? This *could* be the ninth year of Arab-Jewish cooperation in
the development of the West Bank and Gaza, with substantial
Palestinian self-governance, perhaps in federation with Jordan, and
perhaps with territorial compromise which assured Israel's security.

Instead, these years have been years of violence, of diplomatic
stalemate, of increased polarization between and within the major
parties to the conflict, of new political realities in the administered
territories, which makes accommodation increasingly problematic.
The root of so much of our current problem was the immediate
rejection of the Camp David accords by the Arab world. It was that
rejection that affected both the Egyptian and the Israeli approaches
to the autonomy negotiations. Stunned by its expulsion from the

Arab bloc, Egypt felt compelled to demonstrate its loyalty to the Arab, and particularly the Palestinian, cause, by taking a tough stand in the negotiations on the details of autonomy arrangements. Stunned by the strident, threatening rejection of the accords and the peace treaty by the Arab bloc, the Begin government felt compelled to insist upon minimal authority for the Palestinians under autonomy lest it lead to a P.L.O.-dominated, hostile, independent state, committed to the destruction of the Jewish state.

American hopes that Camp David would usher in a new period of trust and accommodation were soon dashed. But there had been too much invested in the peace process for the United States to abandon the effort—and there was substantial, bipartisan support for the effort. For the remainder of his administration, President Carter, and then President Reagan through his administration, were determined not to permit the "peace process" to be abandoned. American efforts have continued, at times vigorously and prominently, at times hardly visible, but eight years after Camp David there was no real progress to point to, one dashed hope following another.

Jimmy Carter and Ronald Reagan differ greatly in style and in general political philosophy, but their administrations were not in any basic disagreement on Middle East policy, demonstrating again the national consensus that has developed over the years. Camp David was a reflection of that consensus and also the basis for continuing bipartisanship on the Arab-Israeli dispute. In a major statement outlining his "Reagan Plan" on September 1, 1982, the president declared, "The Camp David agreement remains the foundation of our policy. Its language provides all parties with the leeway they need for successful negotiations." Four years later, at the dedication ceremony for the Carter Presidential Center in Atlanta, President Reagan singled out Camp David as a major achievement. Six years into the Reagan administration, Camp David was still the context for America's search for solutions to the seemingly intractable problems of accommodation with the other Arab nations and a just solution to the Palestinian problem.

President Reagan had begun his administration with commitments to the historic special relationship that were at least as strong as those of earlier administrations—and that were to lead to unprecedented forms of strategic cooperation, which I will examine more closely in the next section. In 1979, before he was elected president, Ronald Reagan had made it unmistakably clear how he felt about Israel. "Our own position would be weaker without the political and military assets Israel provides," he wrote. "Israel has the democratic will, national cohesion, technological capacity and military fiber to stand forth as America's trusted ally."

But even such strong feelings did not prevent some serious strains and conflicts in u.s.-Israel relations after Reagan's election, as these two allies—*allies,* as they were increasingly to refer to one another, not just friends—had differing views on how best to pursue the road to peace. In his first year as president, a difficult situation was created when the Reagan administration prevailed in the battle over the sale of AWACS planes to Saudi Arabia. The inherent strength of the relationship, however, was demonstrated over the next six years when it survived two major threats: the war in Lebanon and the Reagan Plan.

The War in Lebanon

A major strain in u.s.-Israel relations developed in the course of Israel's most difficult, most controversial, most divisive period in its history. For about a decade, Israel had been contending with the ominous presence and increasing challenges of the p.l.o. in Lebanon, where it had moved after its expulsion from Jordan. Between the civil war in Lebanon that this p.l.o. move had exacerbated and the massive intervention by Syria, Lebanon had virtually ceased to be a viable state. The p.l.o. felt free to wage war against Israel from its positions in southern Lebanon. Despite the introduction of a u.n. Interim Force in Lebanon (UNIFIL) and a u.s.-negotiated cease-fire between Israel and the p.l.o. in July of 1981, the p.l.o. threat to Israel grew more and more menacing as it amassed huge stockpiles of arms in southern Lebanon, attacked Jewish and Israeli targets abroad, and attempted occasional raids into Israel. A series of provocative incidents and retaliations throughout the first months of 1982 reached a climax in June when Shlomo Argov, Israel's ambassador to Great Britain and one of its most respected diplomats, was shot down in London by Palestinian terrorists as he left an evening meeting for his home.

Despite President Reagan's urgent request that the "abominable" attack on Argov not lead to military action, Israeli troops pushed into Lebanon on June 6, 1982. Determined to destroy the P.L.O.'s ability to inflict heavy damage on Israel from major installations within Lebanon, Israel declared its intention to attack and destroy such P.L.O. strongholds, but only up to forty kilometers north of the Israeli border. It took only a few days to accomplish this, and in the course of this action, Israel also inflicted heavy losses on the Syrian Air Force.

Despite apprehensions in the United States and elsewhere about this initial thrust, there was general understanding and even public statements of approval of Israel's determination to wipe out the base of P.L.O. terrorism that had made life unbearable for those living in the northern part of Israel. Israel, it was widely believed, was invoking its right, under international law, to pursue those who threaten the security of its citizens. "Peace for Galilee," as the operation was called, was a legitimate goal.

The initial Israeli incursion was welcomed by many Lebanese. I observed this myself firsthand, even as late as March of 1983, when I went into Lebanon, as far as Sidon. With an interpreter to help, I talked with scores of ordinary Lebanese, including some in refugee camps. Many poured out their anger at the harsh treatment they had been subjected to by the P.L.O. They seemed genuinely hopeful that the Israeli presence would lead to Lebanese stability and, with that, their own greater freedom and security. Even after allowing for the fact that they were talking to an American Jew, I had the clear impression they were genuinely grateful to both Israel and its American ally for the better future that they felt was now possible. I recall, too, the many expressions of appreciation for the Israeli action— some public, some private—from American Lebanese Christian groups and individuals.

The Lebanese incursion became unacceptable and controversial—inside Israel itself, among American administration officials, and within the American Jewish community—when the Israelis failed to stop, as originally announced, at the forty kilometer line. Determined to complete the goal of totally demolishing the P.L.O.'s military capacity to strike again, the Israelis pushed further north in the direction of Beirut. They soon found themselves the target of sharp criticism—both for the inappropriateness of the action itself, and for what seemed like duplicitous action.

This negative reaction came on top of the failure of Israel, at the time, to successfully rebut Arab claims of tremendous casualties inflicted upon the Lebanese. The Palestinian Red Crescent, headed by Yasir Arafat's brother, had gotten the world's media to broadcast his fabricated figures of "10,000 civilian deaths and 600,000 homeless" in southern Lebanon during the first few weeks of the incursion. The utter ridiculousness of such charges was soon revealed when it became known that there were only 510,000 residents in southern Lebanon. Even columnists Evans and Novak, surely among the most critical observers of the Israel scene, accepted the Israeli estimate that the right numbers were 460 dead and 20,000 displaced.

The combination of Israeli actions beyond Peace for Galilee and exaggerated casualty figures resulted in some of the sharpest criticism Israel had ever faced. Its spokesmen insisted that the action around Beirut had been necessary to complete the rout of the P.L.O.; to rid Lebanon of all foreign forces; and to help create a central, stable, pro-democratic Lebanese government. The first of these objectives was achieved; the P.L.O.'s base in Lebanon was indeed destroyed. But the other objectives turned out to be unachievable. Syria, at the end, was even more extensively and solidly entrenched. Lebanon did not develop stability; it suffered assassination at the hands of Syrian agents of its first post-incursion president, Bashir Gemayal, and it has continued to be the scene of endless strife and wars within and between Christian and Muslim groups.

By its active participation in cease-fire negotiations and then in peace-keeping operations in Lebanon, the United States demonstrated not only its support for peace in the area but also its determination to play an important role in that geopolitically vital area of the world, and that it was not about to abandon that area to anti-American elements, Arab or Soviet. But American involvement was not without cost or political controversy at home. Almost three hundred Americans lost their lives in two tragic Arab terrorist attacks, one against the Marine barracks in Beirut in October of 1983, and the other against the U.S. embassy three months later.

Except possibly for the 1956 Sinai action by President Eisenhower, the Lebanon war was the greatest challenge ever to the U.S.-Israeli special relationship. Not only government-to-government relations were disturbed for a while, but people-to-people relations as well, as reflected in American public opinion polls. Anguish in the

American Jewish community was widespread; Israel, we feared, might not be living up to its own high moral standards.

I remember my own deep personal anguish during those early months. But it did not take long for that anguish to be eased and then overtaken, by admiration for the way Israel conducted itself at a moment of crisis, and by calmer reflection about what had caused it to take drastic, if ill-advised, action to defend its people. On June 10, 1983, one year after the initial Israeli incursion into Lebanon, I expressed my feelings in a *New York Times* article. I had looked back over that difficult year and felt that while the wisdom of Peace for Galilee was still subject to debate, "Israel has successfully met two critical challenges which were provoked by the Lebanese action—the challenge to the 'special relationship' between Israel and the United States, and the threat of a significant breach between Israel and world Jewry."

Early in that year, American displeasure had been so intense, I wrote, that there was talk of reduced aid, continued suspension of promised plane deliveries, and refusal to implement "strategic cooperation" agreements. But by year's end, the administration was supporting record levels of military and economic assistance, and was joining with Israel in sharing important military intelligence. The mutual benefits in u.s.-Israeli cooperation were simply so overwhelming that even disagreement over Lebanon was easily overcome.

Any anguish that Jews felt over possible excesses in the Lebanon war was outweighed by pride in how Israel and the Israeli people met the most painful episode during that war—the massacre in the Sabra and Shatila refugee camps. Very few observers believed that official Israeli policy either called for or approved of the brutal killing of hundreds of Palestinians in the two camps, but there were concerns about the failure of Israeli forces to prevent the Christian Phalangists from perpetrating the massacre. Demands for a full investigation and full disclosure were voiced everywhere. When 400,000 Israeli citizens demonstrated in Tel Aviv demanding such an investigation, Jews everywhere were proud of this eloquent testimony to the vitality of Israeli democracy. And when the government appointed a special commission, with full powers to investigate, there was pride in seeing the Jewish state doing what no other state in the Middle East had ever done or was capable of doing. They were heartened by the words of Israel's President Navon: "The very fact that a moral issue has raised a storm in Israel attests to the character of the state of Israel and constitutes a mark of honor."

"The basic case for Israel," I concluded in that article, "remained so strong and persuasive that even a controversial Lebanese action could not destroy it. . . . Israel's enemies should learn from this year's events that its ties to America and to world Jewry can sustain occasional differences, can tolerate occasional dissents."

The Reagan Plan

The war in Lebanon provided further encouragement to the Reagan administration to launch a major initiative to produce peace negotiations. Important differences between Egypt and Israel over the Palestinian autonomy issue endangered progress on that key part of the Camp David accords. A forthcoming meeting of the Arab League in Fez, Morocco, offered some hope, however slight, of reversing its earlier action in Rabat, which had affirmed the P.L.O. as sole representative of the Palestinians and endorsed its goal of an independent state. The administration's plan to get King Hussein to direct negotiations with Israel had been thwarted as a result of congressional refusal to approve American arms sales to Jordan, sales that the administration had offered to induce Jordanian moderation. And now there was the problem of American diplomats throughout the Middle East reporting Arab impressions—unjustified, but nevertheless strongly held—that the United States had been in collusion with Israel in the Lebanese war. All of these considerations seemed to argue for an American initiative— one that would both move the peace process and also restore American credibility.

On September 1, 1982, that initiative came in the form of a nationally televised speech by President Reagan. His statement, since known as the Reagan Plan, was the most comprehensive and detailed policy pronounced by the administration in recent years on how to resolve the Arab-Israeli conflict. Asserting that his administration had "embraced the Camp David framework as the only way to proceed," Reagan spelled out what he thought should be the essentials of a final settlement. In exchange for satisfactory security arrangements, Israel would be expected to withdraw from the West Bank and Gaza, the actual borders to be negotiated. Self-government for the Palestinians would be best served through association with Jordan, not by creation of an independent Palestinian state in the territories. Jerusalem "must remain undivided" but "its final status must be determined through negotiations." Further settlements in the West Bank were "not necessary for the security of Israel" and the ultimate status of existing settlements was to be determined in "final status negotiations." Full autonomy for the Palestinians was to mean "real authority over themselves, the land, and its resources, subject to fair safeguards on water."

Israeli official reaction to the Reagan plan was swift and absolute. Within twenty-four hours the Begin cabinet protested that the plan went beyond Camp David or "contradicted it entirely." The rejection was based not only on the substance of its principal elements, which troubled the Israelis, but also by bitter resentment over the process. The essence of the plan had been discussed with Hussein and other Arab leaders but not with America's closest ally, Israel. Israel's resentment was easy to understand.

Reactions in the American Jewish community were mixed, but generally moderate. Tom Dine, director of the American-Israel Public Affairs Committee (AIPAC), declared there was "a lot of value" in the plan, although he later stressed the negatives in it. I helped draft the position of the American Jewish Committee, whose president, Maynard Wishner, in a speech on September 12, declared that the plan "deserves thoughtful and thorough consideration" and represents "a reasonable approach to be dealt with on its merits." If King Hussein were willing to join Israel in discussions of the Reagan Plan, Wishner added, he would call upon Israel for "pause and restraint in its settlements policy." On two earlier occasions, the American Jewish Committee had felt that the prevailing situation had called for Israeli willingness to halt settlement activity in order to encourage progress on the negotiating front.

Arab reaction to the Reagan Plan was also mixed, but generally negative. Egypt and Jordan were mildly positive, but Syria, Libya, and South Yemen denounced the initiative. The P.L.O. complained about Reagan's rejection of a Palestinian state. The Arab League at Fez reiterated its backing of the P.L.O. and an independent state, but, in the view of some observers, approved language that could be interpreted as implicit recognition of Israel.

Having recently reread the text of the Reagan Plan, and with the

benefit of more than four years of hindsight, I believe now that the
Reagan proposals should have elicited a more positive reaction both
from the state of Israel and from the American Jewish community—
despite the legitimate criticism that the plan went too far in specifically endorsing a number of critical provisions which would have
been best left to open-ended negotiations. But the Reagan plan
meant more than a set of specific suggestions; it was and should have
been considered primarily as advocacy for a more active peace process which had to take place if progress was ever to be achieved.
Those specific suggestions were all in the context of Reagan's acknowledged concern for Israel's security and his absolute commitment to use American strength if that security were threatened.
"The United States will oppose any proposal—from any party and
at any point in the negotiating process—that threatens the security
of Israel," he said at one point. "America's commitment to the
security of Israel is ironclad." He understood the strategic importance of the region to the United States and the need "to deter the
Soviets and their surrogates from further expansion." However, he
added, "Our policy is motivated by more than strategic interests.
We also have an irrevocable commitment to the survival and territorial integrity of friendly states."

If Israel should have been more positive, surely the Arabs should
have been, as well. That they were not was evidence once again that
for many of them the goal was not really fair and honorable accommodation and peace but rather continued isolation and ultimate
destruction of the Jewish state. Their rejection of a proposal that,
to the Israelis, seemed too forthcoming to the Arabs became yet
another reason for Israeli toughness.

It is my judgment now that Israel would have been well advised
to have said something like this soon after the Reagan speech: "We
welcome the Reagan initiative. While we regret his spelling out at
this point the details of a possible agreement and while we reserve
the right to oppose any recommendations that we deem threatening
to our security, we are prepared to go to the negotiating table at once
with King Hussein and any other legitimate Arab leaders to discuss
the Reagan Plan, or any other suggestions that might be put on the
table." In recent years, there have been occasions when Israeli leaders have come close to making this kind of statement. The fact is
that when the day comes that Israel does sit down with Arab leaders,

much of the Reagan Plan will of necessity be on the negotiating table. But the longer it takes for that day to come, the more difficult it may be to reach agreement.

Ten Years after Camp David

It is almost ten years since Anwar Sadat made his historic trip to Jerusalem. He paid with his life for this courageous act. But he did not die in vain. Camp David would not have been possible without him—as it would not have been possible without the courage of Menachem Begin and Jimmy Carter. It has meant peace between Egypt and Israel, albeit for half the decade a very cold peace. It has survived through difficult times as both an inspiration and as a vehicle for further progress. It provides, still, the most imaginative, the most realistic, the most forthcoming plan for at least the first phase of self-governance for the Palestinians.

By serving as the instrument for bringing about the Camp David breakthrough, and by remaining faithful to its purpose, the United States has served the cause of peace and of fairness in the Middle East—and by so doing it has served its own national interests as well. It has demonstrated all these years that it was and it remains the only great power in a position to serve such a historic role.

In testimony given to the Foreign Affairs Committee of the House of Representatives in 1986, Assistant Secretary of State Richard Murphy has summed up this American role:

> Since the 1940s, the u.s. has been the crucial external actor in the effort to establish and maintain peace and security in the Middle East. This fact reflects the depth of our political, economic, and strategic concerns in the region, which eight administrations, both Democratic and Republican, have consistently sought to protect. . . .
> A fundamental commitment to Israel's security and well-being has long been constant in our Middle East policy. At the same time . . . we have maintained close ties with pro-Western Arab states. We have worked hard to build these links in order to promote several important u.s. strategic objectives: to deny opportunities to the Soviet Union in this critical geographic region; protect free world access to the world's largest reserves of oil; check the growth of radical anti-Western movements; and promote the process of

building peace between Israel and its neighbors by relying on our relations with both sides to the conflict.

It is this American role that made possible Camp David and several other agreements between Israel and Arab states. The respect that the u.s. has earned in the community of nations for this role may be grudging in some places, it may be resented in others—but it is one that deserves the support of all its own people. *All its people— and that includes Arab Americans and Jewish Americans.*

Serving the American Interest

*I*n the preceding pages, I have recalled some of the history of relations between the United States and the state of Israel. I have cited the commitments voiced by every president of the United States since Woodrow Wilson. I have pointed out how these declarations have moved steadily from expressions of moral and humanitarian concern to assertions of mutuality of interest. In the pages that follow, I will deal more explicitly with the benefits to our own American national interest which derive from the close partnership that has developed between the most powerful nation on earth and one of the smallest.

It is, of course, axiomatic that proponents of any public policy assert, and usually truly believe, that the policy they advocate serves the national interest. There are no absolute, totally objective criteria for measuring, let alone defining, the "national interest." In the final analysis, that judgment, in a democratic society, is reflected in the policies supported by the people themselves or by those selected by them for leadership. The evidence is overwhelming that the American people and their elected representatives have indeed made the judgment that—with the inevitable differences and fluctuations that are part of any long history—America's basic policy in the Middle East over the years has been sound and that it has served the American interest.

When President Reagan declared, as cited earlier, that the United States has "an irrevocable commitment to the survival and territorial integrity of friendly states," he hit the core of the American attachment to Israel. *Israel is our friend.* Friendship is often easier to feel, to sense, than it is to define or explain. Israel is a friend because we feel it shares with us the underlying premises of a free, democratic, pluralist society. It is a friend because we know it resists the forces of totalitarianism and autocracy and terrorism—our common enemies. It is a friend because we have felt its pain as it was compelled to fight over and over again for the basic right to exist as a free people, when its athletes were murdered in Munich in 1972, when its children were slaughtered in Maalot or Kiryat Shemona in 1974, when a busload of civilians were killed along the coastal road in 1978.

Even if there were no explicit quid pro quo benefits accruing to the United States from this friendship, it clearly would be in our nation's interest to be seen by the community of nations and by freedom-loving people everywhere as a nation that does indeed stand by this kind of friend, that it is prepared to back its words with appropriate action.

America's policies in the Middle East are not limited to a single relationship, that with Israel. Our readiness to be supportive of Arab nations was impressively demonstrated in our dealings with Egypt at Camp David and our generous assistance to Egypt since then. That too has been in our national interest, and the American people have supported that relationship. We are prepared, and should be, to hold out our hand of friendship to Jordan or other Arab states, or to responsible Palestinian elements, whenever they act constructively.

Even if this were the whole story—moral and political identification with other "friendly" nations—it would constitute a good case for United States involvement. The case, however, is significantly enhanced when one takes into consideration the ways in which the relationship with Israel has become much more than a one-way assistance program. Given the tremendous difference in size and power and influence, it would be ridiculous to suggest that it is an evenly balanced relationship, that Israel does as much for the United States as the other way around. But it is fair and accurate to suggest that the United States is a significant beneficiary of the partnership with Israel.

No friendship, no partnership, no alliance is without complication or suspicion or disappointment. Shakespeare's sober observation that "the course of true love never did run smooth," applies also to relations between nations. Our ties with traditional allies and neighbors—France, Britain, Mexico, Canada, to name only a few—have been marred from time to time by differences over trade policies, immigration, defense levels, and other critical issues. We have not permitted such differences—or occasional misstatements or misconduct by an official of a friendly government—to wipe out the basic affinity we have for one another.

Israel and the United States have not always been in agreement on how best to pursue common goals. Israeli settlement policy, arms sales to Arab states considered moderate by the United States, timing and intensity of Israeli retaliatory raids, tactics on resuming the peace process—these and other substantive issues have at times seemed so serious that they resulted in impatience and public scolding and vituperative responses. Painful as some of these public disputes were at the time, it is clear that they never did really threaten the essential compatibility of views of these two allies. Every dispute has been overcome by basic trust.

Perhaps even more threatening to the *quality* of the trust between these nations have been occasional events or incidents that have caused suspicions, irritations, resentments. Some allegations of misconduct—such as the tragic sinking of the USS *Liberty* during the Six Day War—have never been clarified sufficiently to warrant firm conclusions. Other incidents—such as the Pollard spy case—have indeed revealed misconduct or gross negligence.

Critics of close U.S.-Israeli ties have every right, of course, to discuss such developments and interpret them as they wish. But the basic debate over the value and appropriateness of the special U.S.-Israel relationship is not well served by preoccupation with these occasional blunders or transgressions. These cannot and should not be ignored; wrongdoing should be faced honestly and dealt with firmly. But it should not blind us to the bigger picture.

Strategic Cooperation

That bigger picture, of course, has no more vital component than America's principal foreign policy challenge—how to deal with and triumph over our number one adversary, the Soviet Union. There are differences among Americans about how best to deal with that challenge. That debate should and will continue. But surely every American should want to have as many nations as possible in the world identifying with us and sharing responsibilities, consistent with their resources and national goals, in the u.s.-Soviet rivalry and potential conflict. Israel's ability and willingness to be such an ally of the United States is beyond question.

Whatever hopes one may have for reducing u.s.-Soviet tensions, whatever progress can be made in eliminating the threat of nuclear catastrophe, one cannot be indifferent to the Soviet Union's interest in dominating the Middle East. If the Soviets or their radical allies succeed in acquiring a stranglehold on the area's resources, the economies of the major industrial nations will be jeopardized. The United States cannot be indifferent to the possible neutralization of Western Europe and Japan, to the encirclement of China, to the virtual isolation of the United States—the likely consequences of unchallenged communist domination of that critical area.

Israel is located midway between Europe and the Persian Gulf. It is at the crossroads of three continents. Its geographical values are obvious and vital.

Israelis, in addition to sharing the free world's general concern about communist domination, surely cannot be expected to be indifferent to Soviet alliance with its determined enemies. They are reminded too often, for example, that Syria's dream of wiping out Israel is backed by Soviet arms. Even as they seek regular diplomatic relations with the Soviet Union, they cannot ignore the immediate threat they face from the communist Goliath.

President Reagan recognized the strategic asset in Israel before he became president. In the 1979 article previously quoted, he referred to Israel's ". . . geopolitical importance as a stabilizing force, as a deterrent to radical hegemony and as a military offset to the Soviet Union." After he entered the White House, his public references were more guarded, but the essence of his assessment remained firm. He agreed to implement this assessment of Israel's value to the United States when on November 30, 1981, the United States and Israel signed a Memorandum of Understanding (mou) with far-reaching provisions, though short of the military pact preferred by Prime Minister Begin. Designed to meet threats posed by the Soviet Union or Soviet-controlled forces, the mou provided for joint naval and air exercises, a framework for cooperation in military research and development, American use of Israeli medical facilities, and limited American purchases of Israeli military goods and services each year.

This MOU, however, was never implemented. Before its provisions could take effect, Israel had a falling-out with the United States over its decision to extend Israeli law to the Golan Heights. Complaining that this action had undermined the spirit of the MOU, the United States acted precipitously and in anger when it suspended the agreement. Then the Israeli action in Lebanon further delayed progress on the MOU, though the validity and the urgency of closer strategic cooperation was made even clearer by experiences in that war.

Concern over the American suspension of the agreement led to an extraordinary endorsement of the principle of U.S.-Israeli strategic cooperation. For only the second time in American history, a large and distinguished group of military officers offered public advice to an American president. In March of 1983, more than 260 retired generals and admirals joined in a statement imploring the president that "transitory political strains . . . not be allowed to detract from the fundamental congruence of strategic interests cemented by a common heritage of Western values and democratic ideals." Stressing the importance of "the victory of Israeli-modified American weapons and tactics over those of the Soviet Union," this group of experts feared that the full value of that experience might be lost. "We therefore urge you," they concluded, "to revitalize the strategic cooperation between the United States and Israel, thereby enhancing the safety and well-being of the free peoples of the world."

Secretary of Defense Caspar Weinberger, never considered a particular friend of Israel, was similarly affected by the Lebanese experience. He told an American Jewish Committee audience on May 13, 1983, "Leaving all sentiments aside, looking only at our own national interests, it is clear that we in the United States have an important stake in Israel's security."

Before that year ended, the growing consensus around the need to have regular and intensive strategic cooperation resulted in the creation of the Joint Political Military Group (JPMG). Created in the immediate aftermath of the bombing of the Marine compound at Beirut, JPMG has served as a forum for consultation about common threats posed by Moscow or the countries within its sphere of influence. Meeting twice a year, the JPMG identifies possible areas of cooperation and monitors ongoing strategic dialogue between Israeli and American officials at all levels of responsibility. Contact is assured between working-level officials familiar with the nuts-and-bolts problems of defense operations.

As a rule, operations of JPMG are classified, but the nature of its operations was described by President Reagan after concluding the arrangement with then Prime Minister Yitzhak Shamir, "This group will give priority attention to the threat to our mutual interests posed by increased Soviet involvement in the Middle East. Among the specific areas to be considered are combined planning, joint exercises, and requirements for prepositioning of U.S. equipment in Israel."

Some of the operations resulting from JPMG cooperation and stimulation are public knowledge. They include:

■ joint U.S.-Israeli exercises with the Sixth Fleet designed to strengthen U.S. anti-submarine warfare capabilities in the eastern Mediterranean.

■ access to Israeli ports provided for regular visits by the Sixth Fleet.

■ Israeli facilities made available for storage and maintenance of U.S. materiél for American use in a conflict.

■ Israeli KFIR fighter aircraft made available to the U.S. Navy to help train American fighter pilots.

■ military training exchanges between Israeli forces and U.S. Marines.

■ formal arrangements for American access to sophisticated Israeli hospital facilities in case of conflict.

■ sharing of Israeli experience in the use of American equipment against Soviet weapons.

■ facilities for a Voice of America transmitter, at a location that makes Soviet jamming much more difficult.

Israel, compared to the United States or the Soviet Union, is a very small nation. Critics of our ties to Israel seek to downplay, even deride, how a small country like Israel could be of any real help to a major power. But military experts have testified about the value of steps like those cited above in that particular setting, and it can be assumed that the Soviets recognize that value too. They know that for many years now, Israel's knowledge and experience with Soviet equipment have helped the u.s. develop more effective weapons, countermeasures, and tactics. They know that Israel's demonstration of the vulnerability of sams and migs in Lebanon has made it necessary for the Soviets to concentrate on renovation and improvement rather than expansion of their equipment. They know that Soviet influence in the area has suffered from this discrediting of their weapons, thus discouraging provocative action by them or their clients in the area. They know that because of geography and the sophistication of Israel's naval and air operations, the entire Soviet fleet in the Mediterranean could be destroyed if the situation got out of hand.

Above all, Israel's enemies and potential adversaries know that, even without the present formal cooperation and obligations, Israel had in earlier years demonstrated a willingness to perform in the service of friends. King Hussein knows that in 1970 Israel, at the suggestion of the United States, mobilized to stave off a Syrian invasion of Jordan in support of a p.l.o. insurrection against the king. Egyptian leaders know that timely action and warnings by Israel prevented Egyptian President Nasser from trying to overthrow the Saudi government—and, later, their President Sadat was warned about a Quaddafi plot to assassinate him.

America does have other "friends" in the Middle East, but none provides for the United States the reliability and dependability that can be taken for granted as Israel. The key to this is political stability. There may be keen political conflict between Labor and Likud, but the basic political system of Israel is not threatened. Its deeply rooted democratic system provides absolute assurance that its pro-u.s., pro-Western commitment is solid, no matter which party is in charge. It will abide by commitments; it will protect American interests on its soil. In Israel there can be no catastrophe similar to the fall of the Shah of Iran and the consequent loss of vital equipment and intelligence-gathering facilities.

Israel, in a word, is the only friend in the Middle East today on whom the United States can count without qualms, without fears of betrayal or of uncontrollable turmoil.

Israel does not relish this picture of potential military counterbalance to the powerful Soviet Union. This is not the role it wishes to play in the international arena. Yet its entire history since 1948 has argued for maximum preparedness. Tragically, that preparedness must include defense against Soviet-supplied adversaries and even against the possibility of direct Soviet intervention. Its interests are compatible with American interests in the area. American resources have been generously shared with Israel. It is only right and natural, therefore, that Israel's resources be available, as required, to the United States. That's what strategic cooperation is all about.

Such cooperation does not always yield positive results. The Reagan administration's clumsy efforts in 1985 and 1986 to establish contact with Iran's "moderate" elements, involving direct and third-party sale of arms, was viewed as a cynical arms-for-hostage deal in clear conflict with official American policy. Israel's cooperation with White House officials in this gambit was embarrassing to Israel, but it illustrated Israel's willingness to help a trusted ally when such help was deemed important.

Flora Lewis, the distinguished *New York Times* columnist, writing on November 21, 1986, correctly observed, "The Israeli view . . . is that Jerusalem's 'strategic consensus' with the United States means it should not only receive help from America, but offer its services."

Over and above "strategic cooperation" as such, the u.s.-Israeli relationship has yielded our nation invaluable security intelligence for many years.

For more than two decades, Israel has had substantial firsthand experience in waging war against adversaries supplied with increasingly more sophisticated Soviet weapons. The several Arab-Israeli wars during this period have provided ideal opportunities for testing and evaluating both American and Soviet military technology. Israel's victorious defense against Soviet weapons has provided the United States with invaluable data on the performance capabilities and the technical specifications on a wide range of armaments. Israel has regularly given American intelligence both captured Soviet tanks and electronic elements from downed Soviet planes. An entire Soviet radar station captured by Israel and an intact MIG-22 delivered by a defecting Iraqi pilot were made available to American experts.

A study by the Heritage Foundation, "America's Security Stake in Israel" (July 1986) declared that "Israel has contributed significantly to the evolution of U.S. military tactics . . . [Israel] has affected the evolution of American military technology." The study detailed many improvements that Israel had made in American weapons resulting in increased combat capabilities, survivability, and endurance, which are provided to American authorities.

A good start has been made in using Israeli research and production facilities for participation in American weapons programs. In May of 1986, Israel became the third ally to cooperate in research programs for the Strategic Defense Initiative (SDI).

Israel's extraordinary intelligence capability is generally recognized. While much of the history must remain unknown to the general public, enough specifics have surfaced to support the high regard enjoyed by Israel's intelligence operations. Arab nations, European nations, and the United States have been the beneficiary of warnings about assassination plans, terrorist plots, or military movements.

In its impressive report, the Heritage Foundation concludes:

> Israeli-American strategic cooperation is not a panacea that will blunt all Soviet threats in the Middle East, but without it, the world will be a more dangerous place. Such cooperation deters the aggressive action of Moscow and its regional clients, encourages Arab states to opt for a negotiated settlement rather than military action in the Arab-Israeli conflict, and strengthens NATO's southern flank. Israel has much to offer the U.S. in terms of military intelligence, technical innovations, access to air bases and naval facilities, and a pre-positioning site for fuel, medicine, ammunition, and weapons. Washington should work closely yet discreetly with Israel in order to transcend the zero-sum nature of the Arab-Israeli conflict.

The Costs of Security

Protecting America's interests is an expensive undertaking. This is an obvious, tragic fact of life. For our direct defense establishment we now appropriate about $300 billion a year—almost $1 billion each day. This level is controversial—some, including the administration, think it is too low; others think it is too high—but nobody seriously suggests that it be reduced by more than $20 or $30 billion.

In addition to these hundreds of billions of dollars expended each year by the U.S. Department of Defense, we seek to protect our

interests in the world through a comprehensive diplomatic establishment funded through the State Department, by our participation in
the United Nations and other international bodies, and by a range
of bilateral economic and military assistance programs around the
world. Some of these programs are purely humanitarian, but even
these should be seen as part of a basic American design to enhance
our standing and influence in the world.

Our defense outlays are, of course, not limited to equipping an
army, navy, and air force to protect our own shores. They provide
for operations around the world, in cooperation with our allies,
because the threat to us and the free world *is* global. Our soldiers,
sailors, and pilots—tanks, ships, and planes—must be sustained
wherever our geopolitical strategy takes them.

The United States is far and away the principal, but not the
only, participant in the collective defense of the entire free world.
Proportionately, however, we spend substantially more than our
principal allies—about 7 percent of the gross national product,
compared with 5 percent in Britain, 3 percent in West Germany,
and 1 percent in Japan. Soviet expenditures are estimated at about
13 percent. Only one nation in the world spends substantially
more than any of these nations—Israel, with a recent average of
more than 20 percent.

From the first day of its existence, Israel has found it necessary
to devote a substantial part of its productivity to defense. A tiny
nation of a few million, facing adversaries with populations thirty or
forty times its own and bent on its destruction, Israel has had no
choice. It has had to develop a qualitative edge to compensate for
its numerical deficiency. It has had to keep a high proportion of its
people in uniform or ready reserve. It has had to impose on all its
people the highest per capita tax rates in the world.

When the burden became absolutely unbearable, Israel had to
turn to the United States for help. That help, in recent years, has
been generous and it has been supported by the overwhelming
majority of both houses of Congress. For several years now, the
level of military and economic assistance to Israel has averaged
about $3 billion, all in grants. Some additional emergency aid has
also been voted. This help serves several purposes: it pays for part
of Israel's current defense needs; it helps Israel repay u.s. loans;
and it makes up partially for the $2 billion oil bill Israel faces as a

result of having abandoned the Sinai oil fields under the Camp David agreement.

Israel is the largest beneficiary of "foreign aid." The second largest is Egypt, at a level of more than $2 billion. These grants to Egypt, American officials decided and the Congress agreed, were necessary to help Egypt develop a viable economy without having to submit to Soviet or Arab blackmail, but also as a gesture of American evenhandedness. There is no question that there would be no such level of aid to Egypt without a comparable level of aid to Israel.

Seen as *aid,* the sums appropriated by the Congress for Israel are indeed very substantial—in absolute numbers, in comparison with other countries, and on a per capita basis. But seen, as it should be, as a contribution to the defense of our American interests in that critical area, *the $3 billion paid annually represents the least expensive and most effective national security expenditures the United States makes.*

It is instructive to compare this outlay with American expenditures to provide for the defense of other critical areas. The *New York Times* military analyst estimated that no less than $129 billion in our combined defense budget of $300 billion is allocable to the defense of Europe, and $47 billion for defense of Japan and other countries of East Asia. Because these sums come from *defense* rather than *foreign aid* appropriations, little attention is paid to them. But it is a fact that each of the thirteen European members of NATO gets an average of almost $10 billion worth of defense assistance from the United States, and our six allies in East Asia average almost $8 billion each.

If these nations chose to provide more adequately for their own defense by increasing the share of their gross national product used for defense—not to the 20 to 25 percent level the Israelis have imposed on themselves, but to the 7 percent level of the United States—many billions of American dollars could be saved. But they have chosen not to do so, and because we consider defense of Europe and other critical areas to be in our own national interest, we have assumed that responsibility. Among other aspects of that responsibility is the maintenance of hundreds of thousands of American troops abroad.

Israel needs dollars from us because, as its leaders have repeatedly emphasized, *it does not ask for our troops.* Israel insists that it will defend itself solely with its own personnel. It chooses to impose an onerous tax burden on its people to provide the great bulk of its own defense, which, as we have stated earlier, is also in defense of American interests and that of the free world. Under our present legislation and budgetary systems, American assistance to Israel is labeled "foreign aid," but in the truest and fullest sense of the word, our assistance is an investment in the defense of our interests in the Middle East.

For some years now, suggestions have been made to transfer assistance to Israel from the foreign aid to the defense budget. It is no secret that both Democratic and Republican administrations have resisted these suggestions, primarily because aid to Israel has been far and away the least controversial part of the foreign aid package, that removing it would endanger approval of foreign aid generally because of widespread antipathy to such aid. No matter where "aid to Israel" is placed in the budget, however, Americans should appreciate the value of the investment.

Despite the general antipathy to foreign aid, and despite the great concerns about intolerable federal budget deficits, every recent Congress has approved, with overwhelming bipartisan support, at least the levels of assistance to Israel requested by the respective administrations. There is no other area of foreign policy that commands this kind of consensus.

What explains this? Why is our Congress so pro-Israel?

In the final analysis, it is because the *American people* believe it is right and it is in our American interest to be and act pro-Israel,—and not, as some would suggest, only because of a particularly powerful Jewish lobby that has somehow fooled or intimidated the Congress.

Shaping the National Policy

*T*hat American Middle East policy has remained, over the years, as supportive as it has of the special relationship is quite remarkable, given the problems associated with the Middle East. Allegations to the contrary notwithstanding, the Middle East has been one of the most discussed foreign policy issues of recent years—probably exceeded only by the basic U.S.-U.S.S.R. conflict. By almost any standard—articles in learned journals, newspaper editorials, and op-ed pieces, TV news and public affairs coverage, university and think tank studies, books and magazine articles, public opinion polls—Middle Eastern issues have been reported and debated more fully than most issues. Congressional hearings and floor discussions have been extensive.

Major events and related developments have made such review and debate inevitable. Wars, terrorism, American hostages, oil embargoes, U.N. resolutions and debates, Soviet-Arab collaboration, assassinations and upheavals in Arab nations, political turmoil in Israel, American peace-seeking efforts—all of these and more are constantly prompting discussions of Middle East policy. All of this goes on in the context of an ever present American fear, in the continuing aftermath of Vietnam, of excessive commitment and possible American entanglement.

Public officials—in the administration and in the Congress— have been affected by the substance of this public debate and by the course of events. But it is only realistic to note that their attitudes are affected also by their perceptions of what the public thinks about the issue. And they are affected too by the effectiveness of the direct representations made to them by concerned individuals and groups. *Public opinion* and *lobbying*—on Middle East no less than on any other political issues—are part of the American system of policy shaping.

There are many complicated, sophisticated nuances in Middle East policy about which most Americans cannot be expected to have expert opinion. But over the years they have developed some basic attitudes about the central issues involved. A Roper poll in June 1986 asked a cross-section of Americans the standard question, "At the present time do you find yourself more in sympathy with Israel, or more in sympathy with the Arab nations?" Of those making a clear choice, 87 percent selected Israel and 13 percent the Arab nations—about seven to one. Over the years, the ratio has been as high as ten to one, and during the very unpopular Lebanese war in 1982, as low as three to one.

In another question, Roper found that whereas Israel was deemed by a clear majority of Americans to be a "reliable ally,"

Egypt was so considered by only 31 percent, Jordan by 18 percent, and Syria by 4 percent.

The special relationship between Israel and the United States was implicitly endorsed by a wide margin in an interesting poll conducted in 1982 by Penn & Skein. Respondents were asked, "Is the United States too close to Israel, not close enough, or does it have the right kind of relationship with Israel?" Fifty percent replied it was "right." Thirty-four percent thought it was "not close enough," and only 16 percent felt it was "too close." Even in that difficult year of the Lebanese war, *five out of six* Americans endorsed either current or even stronger ties to Israel.

The essence of these findings is matched by other polls asking the same or similar questions. Public officials know that they can take actions deemed supportive of Israel, with the understanding that popular acceptance is likely.

Throughout this presentation, I have quoted presidents and other high government officials invoking both the moral and strategic case for the u.s.-Israeli relationship. If cynics wish to dismiss these as nothing more than "politics," they cannot dismiss similar declarations by the very broad spectrum of American leaders in every walk of American life. A few illustrations are in order.

Only weeks before he was so cruelly gunned down, the Reverend Martin Luther King, Jr., had declared:

> Peace for Israel means security, and we must stand with all our might to protect its right to exist, its territorial integrity. . . . Israel is one of the great outposts of democracy in the world, and a marvelous example of what can be done, how desert land can be transformed into an oasis of brotherhood and democracy. Peace for Israel means security, and that security must be a reality.

In the years since his untimely death, American black support for Israel has been voiced regularly through an organization formed by two of King's closest associates, the late A. Philip Randolph and Bayard Rustin—*Black Americans in Support of Israel* (basic). Black and Hispanic members of Congress have consistently supported aid to Israel and have rejected arms sales to Arab nations at war with Israel.

Leaders of American labor have spoken out forcefully through-

out the years in support of Israel. Even during the difficult days
of the war in Lebanon, AFL-CIO president Lane Kirkland declared
that American labor "will neither swerve from our support of
Israel, nor yield ground to those who would push our democratic
ally into unilateral concessions to those who deny her right to
exist."

Despite sharp differences on domestic policy issues with most
American Jews, major Evangelical leaders have called for close and
trusting relations with Israel. In a telegram to President-elect Reagan in 1980, for example, the presidents of the Religious Roundta-
ble, the Moral Majority, and the Committee for the Survival of a
Free Congress, declared, "From our religious, moral, and strategic
perspective, Israel supremely represents our values and hopes for
security and peace in the Middle East."

The National Christian Leadership Conference for Israel, under
the leadership of Father Edward Flannery, has spoken often on
behalf of hundreds of church and community leaders across the
country. On the occasion of the fortieth anniversary of the liberation
of Hitler's concentration camps in 1985, the conference placed ads
in major newspapers with a plea to its fellow Christians, "Give
special consideration to the meaning of Israel in the thought, faith,
and life of Jewish people throughout their long history. It is impera-
tive that all who seek decency and justice among nations show a
concern for the survival and well-being of Israel."

These expressions of support make it clear that Israel's struggle
for independence and security has found a most positive response
throughout the United States—not necessarily for every particular
action, but for the fundamental right of Israel to exist in peace.

Surely and not surprisingly, that response has been particularly
overwhelming in the American Jewish community. How could it not
be? There are 6 million American Jews at this time, the largest
Jewish community in the world. There are only about 8.5 million
additional Jews in the entire world—about 3.5 million in Israel and
about 2 million in the Soviet Union, the rest mostly in western
Europe and South America. This generation of American Jews, still
suffering the pain and memories of the Holocaust, feels a special
responsibility to fellow Jews again threatened. The feeling persists
that if more had been done in the thirties and the forties to mobilize
public opinion and to persuade the Roosevelt administration to take

appropriate action, at least some of the 6 million victims of the Holocaust might have been saved.

American Jews have learned from this experience that they dare not ever again be silent when fellow Jews are threatened. They reject suggestions that crop up every now and then that there is something wrong in having religious or ethnic or nationality groups "meddling" in foreign policy. Former President Gerald Ford gave an eloquent response to any such attitude when he declared:

> Rather than question in any way those who feel deep emotional ties to other countries—whether it be Israel or Ireland or Africa—we should salute this as a manifestation of the genius of our nation. It is one of the things that make both Israel and the United States unique in the world. It is perfectly possible for Americans to hold on proudly to the best elements of their different national heritages and yet be united in common love of our country.

On July 4, 1986, on the occasion of the one hundredth birthday of the Statue of Liberty, I tried to explain, in a *Washington Times* article, why American Jews had a "love affair with America."

"We rejoice as American Jews," I wrote, "not only because we are generally accepted as full Americans, but because we feel free to identify with other Jews who live in other parts of the world under threatening or intolerable circumstances—in Israel, in the Soviet Union, in Latin America."

This is the essence of American pluralism. Every individual or group has the right to appeal to the larger community for what is deemed to be in the public interest. All advocacies are weighed and then a policy is determined by appropriate officials, or the Congress, a policy which they have concluded is indeed in the national interest.

Supporters of present Middle East policies have not been passive; they have worked hard to retain those policies against the efforts of an increasingly active and sophisticated opposition. A range of doubters and critics has worked over the years to change prevailing policy to one euphemistically called a "more evenhanded policy." Some of these advocates are essentially pro-Arab, pro-P.L.O., or anti-Israel; some are truly neutral, objective critics of current policy. All of them, of course, have every right to exercise the same constitutional right to petition the government as do supporters of present policy.

The Jewish Lobby

For about twenty years I was part of the organized Jewish advocacy activities on the Washington scene. While the law did not require that I register formally as a "lobbyist," I happily accepted that designation because I was actively involved in what has come to be known as the "Jewish lobby." For many of those years, I presided over sessions of Washington representatives of all national Jewish organizations. I know how the lobby works; I know its strengths and I know its limitations.

In the narrow sense, the Jewish lobby is a small group of Washington-based professionals performing, within the limits of applicable law, the usual range of duties common to thousands of other representatives of hundreds of American groups or corporations or local political jurisdictions—informing their constituencies of developments important to them, and representing their constituents' interests before the executive branch, the Congress, the courts, and the media.

In the broader and more significant sense, the Jewish lobby is really the whole complex of Jewish organizations, influence, relationships, and community strength across the country. It is the voice— sometimes a single voice around a consensus view, sometimes a range of different voices around an issue—of those Jews who are affiliated with one or more of the many Jewish agencies formed over the years to meet particular needs.

Because of the importance of the Middle East issue, and in order to operate scrupulously within the lobbying and tax laws, the Jewish community has supported the work of AIPAC—the American-Israel Public Affairs Committee. AIPAC is a single-purpose *American* organization, registered under our lobbying law and operating with non-tax-deductible funds, committed to promotion of maximum cooperation between Israel and the United States. It is the heart of what is generally called the "pro-Israel lobby." But most of the other national Jewish organizations proudly consider themselves part of the pro-Israel lobby too, in the sense that they do everything possible, within the law and in the context of their basic mandate, to help Americans understand the historic and emotional ties that American

Jews have with Israel. They deal with the entire Jewish agenda—Soviet Jewry, anti-Semitism, church-state relations, human rights at home and abroad, urban problems, women's issues, immigration, and much more—but proclaim without embarrassment or apology that, except for the welfare and security of America, the security of Israel is the highest single priority for them.

Critics of current American Middle East policy have increasingly resorted to attacks on the pro-Israel lobby rather than on the substance of the policy itself. Their tactics reminds one of the ancients' killing of the messenger when the message delivered was distressing to them. Unsuccessful in refuting the impressive case that exists for continuation of current policy, some critics have made irresponsible, outrageous accusations about the operation of the lobby.

Their central allegation is that a super-powerful lobby has managed to fool/bribe/blackmail/intimidate public officials and legislators into slavish acceptance of a pro-Israel policy for America. Such an indictment is as ridiculous as it is unfair. My short answer to it has always been: *The Jewish lobby is not nearly as strong as its enemies assert, but not nearly as weak as they would like it to be.*

We make no apology for having developed the strength and skills we possess. There's nothing un-American about being effective or successful. We are not the slightest bit defensive about having learned how to participate in the political process—a participation clearly protected in the constitution and available to every other individual or group of Americans.

We remember with anguish that forty years ago we had not yet developed such skills, that we had failed to arouse sufficient concerns in the general public and in the government about the genocide that was being practiced against our co-religionists in Europe. We are tortured with the thought that had we then been able, for example, to persuade 70 or 80 or 90 senators, or 300 or 350 or 400 representatives to insist that President Roosevelt make even one single plane available to bomb the railroad track to Auschwitz, that the ten thousand killings a day might have stopped, at least temporarily.

Yes, the American Jewish community has made every effort to participate effectively in the political process. But it does not fool itself. It knows its limitations. It knows it cannot impose or dictate public policy on the basis of its own numbers or resources. Jews constitute only 2.6 percent of the u.s. population. In most states and congressional districts, there are too few Jews even to get into the statistics.

If on such issues as Middle East policy or the plight of Soviet Jewry, the "Jewish" view seems to prevail, it must mean and it has in fact meant that a very large number of non-Jews concur with those Jewish views. If it is cynically assumed that officials elected in heavily Jewish areas—there are some such areas—vote and act to please their Jewish constituents, how does one explain the support from states like Montana or Oregon or Tennessee or North Dakota? How does one explain the consistency of national polling data?

The answer is as simple as it is gratifying. Americans have understood and accepted the basic premises of our policies. If American Jews have worked hard to help Americans understand, should they be criticized for doing so?

The American people have not been deprived of the opportunity to hear the other side. There is much reporting of the Jewish lobby, much less so of the active, well-financed pro-Arab or anti-Israel lobby which has been operating on many fronts.

Relatively few Arab Americans, compared with the proportionate number of Jewish Americans, are known to be affiliated with organizations actively involved in shaping American Middle East policy. But there are a number of active, efficient, energetic Washington-based national Arab-American organizations. They testify frequently before congressional committees, promote advertising and direct-mail campaigns, and engage in a wide range of public relations activities. In addition, some of Washington's best legal and public relations experts are retained by several of the Arab nations.

The pro-Arab lobby's work is enhanced by numerous Arab and pro-Arab scholars at various Middle East institutes on university campuses and at think tanks, often with direct or indirect financing from Arab governments. Less direct, but important, is the help they get from American corporations with Middle East interests, in the form of "public interest" advertising messages or in direct lobbying. Steven Emerson, in his book *The American House of Saud,* documents the major corporate campaign waged in 1981 on behalf of the sale of awacs planes to Saudi Arabia. The media, both print and broadcast, have been very fair to the pro-Arab side of the debate. Television coverage of hostage situations and other terrorist events usually provides a forum for angry denunciations of Israel and its presumed unfair treatment of Palestinians.

Aware of the deep American commitment to Israel's legitimacy, the Arab-American propaganda campaign does not explicitly challenge that legitimacy. Instead it focuses on four basic themes in an effort to revise American public opinion: (1) Israel's conflict is not with Arab states, but with the Palestinians; (2) Israel is not really a democracy; (3) Israel is not a reliable ally of the United States; and (4) Israel's American supporters are really agents of a foreign power. There is not a single study or poll that suggests significant acceptance of any of these themes by the American people—but each is indeed a serious charge and has required a credible response from the pro-Israel community.

Frustrated, unable to make any real progress based on this propaganda line, pro-Arab forces have made the Jewish lobby the object of much of their efforts. They have zeroed in on the charge that AIPAC and a number of pro-Israel political action committees (PACS) have intimidated Congress into voting the way they do under threat of being defeated for reelection. They point to two or three elections in which, presumably, this is exactly what happened.

One of those presumed victims, former Congressman Paul Findley of Illinois, has written a book—and evidently started a new career—to persuade Americans that the White House and the Congress have surrendered to the Jewish lobby. In several face-to-face debates with Findley, I have asked him whether he really means to charge that every one of our presidents—from Wilson to Reagan—and the many secretaries of state and defense and the hundreds of Congressmen from both political parties who served with him—that all of these public officials had shamefully ignored their better instincts about what would best serve America, in their bowing to the pressure of a Jewish lobby. He ignored that question, as he did the observation that he had had the full opportunity, with at least as many resources as his opponent, to make his case before the electorate, but had simply failed to persuade his constituents that he deserved reelection.

I ask the same question of my opponent in this present debate. Does he, too, challenge the patriotism and courage of every president and member of Congress who does not share his views on Middle East policy? Does he mean to challenge such pro-Israel stalwarts as Ronald Reagan and Bob Dole and George Shultz and Alexander Haig? Are the liberal credentials of Ted Kennedy and Walter Mondale and Alan Cranston less honorable because they are so committed to the U.S.-Israel special relationship?

It is true, of course, that there are a number of PACs operating across the country that are concerned with the single issue of U.S.-Israel relations. Citizens especially concerned with this issue have the same rights as those who have formed thousands of other PACs on other specific issues—labor, environment, taxes, right-to-life, nuclear freeze, etc. Operating fully within the law, these PACs make contributions to candidates with policies compatible with their own. Supporters of the principle of PACs argue that this makes it possible for small contributors to do more effectively what large contributors in the past have always been able to do: to make candidates aware of the issues that are important to them.

I am as concerned with the proliferation of PACs as I am with the mad escalation of campaign costs. I would not be sad to see the end or the serious curtailment of PACism, and the setting of reasonable limits on total campaign costs. I would urge the Jewish community as such not to resist such campaign reforms. But PACs are part of today's system and their legitimate use by citizens concerned with U.S.-Israel relations should not be singled out for criticism.

Within the Jewish community itself, there is a major debate under way about the most appropriate way in which its agenda—its *entire* agenda—should be pursued. There are those who argue that the issue of Jewish security is so critical—especially the security of the only Jewish state—that Jewish resources should be directed almost entirely to the issue of Israel. They argue that other, more universal interests can be pursued in other organizations or coalitions. But I have joined with others who argue that our concerns about Israel cannot and should not be separated from our general concerns, that while Israeli security is indeed our highest single priority, it is not our *only* priority.

Translated into political action, this debate among Jews comes down to the difference between single-issue pro-Israel PACs and multi-issue PACs. At this time, the former is clearly the dominant, but the latter is growing.

American Jews have every right to know a candidate's Middle East views. If the candidate is deemed to be hostile, or even indifferent, to Israel's security needs, the Jewish voter should and will react accordingly. But Jewish voters also want a candidate's views on national and international issues. Candidates offend Jewish voters when they think they need only display their pro-Israel credentials.

During the 1984 presidential primaries, I was embarrassed and disturbed when two otherwise admirable candidates for the nomination, both personal friends, competed for the Jewish vote in New York by overemphasizing the relatively marginal issue of the location of the American embassy in Israel. In a *New York Times* piece on March 30, I appealed to both Walter Mondale and Gary Hart to address themselves to the broader issues of the day. "If basic sympathy for Israel's security is a necessary condition for voters' support," I wrote, "it is not a sufficient condition. . . . Jewish voters will give their votes to the candidate who is most likely to be an effective president or senator or congressman when dealing with the *whole* spectrum of national and international issues. . . .They want candidates to discuss with them how best to use American power in the world; how to assure human rights progress at home and abroad; how to pursue social justice and economic growth goals; how to assure further progress for minorities and women in a truly pluralist society. . . . Jews care very much about the health and strength of America."

The overwhelming, positive reaction to this article was most reassuring. It supported two firm beliefs I had held for years:

■ American Jewish support for Israel and for close u.s.-Israel ties is not a narrowly perceived, parochial interest in the Jewish state. It is part of a broader humanist, democratic, pluralist commitment that Jews share. We have not abandoned our concerns for the best America or best world while engaged in efforts on behalf of a secure Israel.

■ American Jews can feel free to ask other groups to share our concerns about Israel because we have shown we share with them a profound concern about the kind of America and the kind of world we live in.

I recall a precious personal moment that shows the connection between our "pro-Israel" and our "pro-American" interests. In

1975, the United Nations, yielding to the combined pressures of the P.L.O., the rejectionist Arab states, and the Soviet bloc, was considering the outrageous resolution equating Zionism with racism. One of the members of the American U.N. delegation was the late Clarence Mitchell, the outstanding black civil rights leader who for years headed the Leadership Conference on Civil Rights. The American Jewish Committee, which I was then serving as Washington representative, invited Mitchell to report to its Board of Governors on the status of the U.N. resolution. After reciting the situation and reporting the administration's firm opposition to the resolution, Mitchell commented: "It's really quite simple for me. When I'm told that Israel is a racist society, I think of people I know who are devoted to the welfare of Israel. I think of groups like the American Jewish Committee. I know what you have done over the years to wipe out bigotry and discrimination and racism in this country. I just know in my gut that a country supported by groups like yours just could not possibly be racist."

I feel comfortable asserting that the American-Jewish community generally has earned this kind of reputation and credibility. If this has made it easier to win friends for Israel, should we feel guilty or embarrassed? We are an active community. We have much to be active about. We have organized ourselves to be effective in our work. But, to be frank, when it comes to the Israel issue, our strongest asset is that we have an easy product to sell. There is no need for the political intimidation we are charged with. From time to time, there may be excesses in the language or the actions of an overzealous advocate. The single-mindedness of ardent supporters of Israel may disturb some critics, but the record is clear: no charges of illegal or improper conduct have ever, to my knowledge, been successfully pressed against AIPAC, any pro-Israel PAC, or any other Jewish agency. The Jewish community itself will not be intimidated into silence or inaction by irresponsible allegations of impropriety or implications of divided loyalty.

In one of his last major speeches, Hubert Humphrey reacted to such allegations and implications. "Let no one contest the patriotic dedication of the Jewish community in the United States," he said. "From the first days of our Republic, people of the Jewish faith have been in the front lines doing their job for freedom, for justice. . . . They have been thinking about the poor in the country; they've been thinking about the education of our people; they've been thinking about how to make our cities better; they've been thinking about immigration laws; they've been thinking about civil rights and civil liberties and the Bill of Rights and the Constitution."

The former vice president spoke directly to the issue: "If oil producers can spend millions of dollars in their lobbying efforts to get special tax breaks; if sugar companies and shoe companies can seek trade and tariff and quota policies that they think will benefit them; if doctors can work against national health insurance, why can't Americans be concerned about the cultural or physical genocide of their co-religionists and relatives in the Soviet Union and in the Middle East?"

Let the Debate Continue

In stressing the continuing commitment to the basic elements of u.s. Middle East policy—and to the substantial support for such policy by the American people—I do not mean to suggest that American Middle East policy is, or should be, set in concrete. Americans equally concerned about peace in that war torn area can have differing views on how best to use American influence to achieve that peace. They can disagree on what best serves the national interest. Such differences have surfaced frequently over the years even as we have remained united on basic principles.

Should we sell sophisticated weapons to states like Jordan and Saudi Arabia? Should we play a more active role in moving the peace process along? Under what circumstances, if any, should we agree to Soviet participation in the process? How much further can and should the u.s.-Israeli strategic partnership go? These and related questions will have to be faced by American policymakers, in the White House and in Congress. That is one arena for debate. All Americans have the opportunity to contribute to that debate.

Another arena for debate is the American-Jewish community. There is a myth that American Jews are unwilling or afraid to discuss difficult and controversial issues, lest the appearance of division within the community cause Israel embarrassment and give comfort to her enemies. The fact is that, as in Israel, the American-Jewish community is an open, democratic, independent, multi-ideological community. There has always been, and always will be, intensive debate about aspects of Israeli society and Israeli foreign policy. On the central issues affecting Israel's security and legitimacy, the community is solid and is emotionally committed. But again, as in Israel, American Jews are divided on such questions as how best to resolve the Palestinian issue, although they are united in their desire to see justice and maximum self-governance in any final settlement. What advice, in what form, to give to our government and also to our friends in Israel is always on the American Jewish agenda.

There is vigorous discussion on these questions in each of the "mainstream" Jewish organizations. And there have been groups pressing hard for more "dovish" policies (Breira, New Jewish Agenda) and others pressing for more "hawkish" policies (Americans for a Safe Israel, Zionist Organization of America). Dozens of Jewish magazines and newspapers reflect this lively debate inside the American Jewish community.

The principal arena for further debate is, of course, the Middle East. Only there can the parties directly involved in the decades-old dispute finally come to terms on the outstanding problems. In Israel, that debate has never been shut off, even during the years of the Labor-Likud national unity government. Agonizing problems must be faced and resolved. Is territorial compromise on the West Bank still feasible, still possible? Is the demographic danger to the Jewish state as serious as the military threat itself? How does a democratic state deal with Kahanism? Can the religious-secular conflict be contained? Israeli democracy and openness provide assurance that vigorous debate on these and many other questions will proceed, and that the world will know about it.

There will be less debate, and even less knowledge of any, within the Arab world. Fear of violence, including assassination, will undoubtedly continue to inhibit debate. Opportunities for breakthroughs—such as those offered during the Peres years—probably will continue to go unheeded. But nevertheless hope must be entertained that somehow Israel and at least some of her Arab neighbors will get to the negotiating table. Without such hope, there can be no hope at all. But such hope has to be premised—as I have repeated throughout these pages—on Arab leaders, including Palestinians, finally feeling free to say, without ambiguity or conditions, that there is room in the Middle East for the Jewish state of Israel. Every day this indispensable acknowledgment is delayed, it will be more difficult for Israel to respond with the same degree of generosity and flexibility that followed the historic Sadat mission to Jerusalem.

Finally, there is another arena for frank debate. That is the arena in which the co-author of this book plays an important role—the Arab-American community. I have seen little evidence there of the freewheeling, uninhibited debate that goes on in the Jewish community. If Arab Americans have been debating Middle East policy— either that of the United States or that of the Arab states—I have seen little evidence of it. If any of their representatives have spoken out unambiguously about Israel's right to exist, I have not heard them. If Arab Americans are distressed and embarrassed by the proud acknowledgments by the P.L.O. or other Arabs of responsibility for brutal terrorism directed at school children or markets, why are their voices seldom heard? Why, when the largest Arab state made peace with Israel, and the deaths of Egyptian youths stopped after Camp David, did we not hear loud cheers from the Arab-American community?

I raise these questions in sorrow, not anger or with any desire to embarrass Arab Americans. I know that they do not constitute a monolithic group. I know that the intra-Arab tensions of the Arab world are mirrored to some extent in the United States. But their almost total silence can be interpreted as identification with Arab intransigence, with anti-American hostility, with Arab toleration, if not endorsement, of cruel terrorism. Their silence, given the almost daily reporting of intra-Arab violence in the Middle East itself, inevitably suggests fears of personal harm if they should speak out. If indeed such intimidation exists, it is another tragic consequence of the Middle East agony.

Mr. Abourezk knows that I share with him his oft-repeated plea that the tensions and the violence of the Middle East not become part of the American scene. He will recall the calls I made to him, to the director of the American-Arab Anti-Discrimination Committee (ADC), and to the widow of Alex Odeh after her husband had been killed in a 1985 bombing of the Santa Ana office of the ADC. I was one of many Jewish officials to express horror over the terrible incident and to call for a thorough investigation and apprehension of the criminals involved.

On July 16, 1986, on behalf of the American Jewish Committee,

Dr. David Gordis and I testified before the House Judiciary Committee at a hearing on "Ethnically Motivated Attacks Against Arab Americans." Representing an ethnic group that for years has been subjected to countless incidents of terror and desecrations motivated by blind hatred and anti-Semitism, we understood the agony of any group suffering from defamation or physical intimidation. We upheld "the right of every person to be protected from fear, intimidation, harassment, and physical harm which may be imposed upon them by reason of their ethnicity, race, or religion or their political beliefs."

We spoke these words from a witness table at which were also seated Mr. Abourezk, representing the ADC, and David Saad, representing the National Association of Arab-Americans. This joint appearance on behalf of tolerance and civility gave special poignancy to Dr. Gordis' observation, "There is room in this nation for broad differences of opinion on all questions of domestic and foreign policy . . . but there is no room for the kind of heinous crime that took place against Alex Odeh."

It is hard to deny that Arab stereotyping has taken place. It is undoubtedly true that report after report of "Arab terrorists" and "Arab dictators" and "Arab oil embargoes" have had a cumulative impact on American attitudes toward Arabs. None of this justifies group defamation or indiscriminate hostility toward all Arabs. This cannot be overemphasized. Yet, Arab Americans—all Arabs, in fact—must ask themselves whether enough is being done to eliminate or reduce invitation to such hostility.

To put it bluntly—not offensively, I hope—if Arab Americans do not wish to be thought of as Qadaffis or Arafats or Abu Nidals— they cannot remain as silent as they have when terrible crimes are committed in the name of Arab aspirations.

The campaign against stereotyping or violence, moreover, cannot be used as a pretext, the real purpose of which is to defame another group or another country. When a national "anti-discrimination" organization spends its resources, in full-page newspaper ads and in radio commercials, aimed solely at reducing levels of American financial assistance to Israel, it is clear that its principal purpose is not anti-defamation but anti-Israel. When the president of ADC repeatedly accuses Israel of engaging in Nazi-type activities ("the same thing that the Nazis did to the Jews," for example) he shows a pathetic insensitivity as well as a reckless disregard for the truth. It is an example of verbal violence, verbal terrorism.

When this Arab-American spokesman proclaims Yasir Arafat as the appropriate negotiator for peace, American Jews cannot ignore the record of this P.L.O. chief, who, as recently as October 21, 1986, declared in Khartoum that "Palestinian armed struggle will continue to escalate quantitatively and qualitatively. . . . The revolution will forge ahead to achieve all the aims and legitimate rights of our people." What kind of "armed struggle?" Arafat was speaking six days after his agents had lobbed hand grenades at a group of Israeli soldiers and their families congregated near the Temple Mount in the Old City of Jerusalem, the site not only of the Jewish people's most revered holy place, the Western Wall, but also the site of two of Islam's holiest places. Half of the sixty-nine casualties were civilians, including women and children. And American Jews recognized Arafat's words as coming directly from the P.L.O.'s covenant—the basic P.L.O. charter calling for "armed Palestinian revolution" and "rejection of every solution that is a substitute for a complete liberation of Palestine." After years of wishful thinking that Arafat was really a "moderate," advocates of dealing with Arafat were reminded that he had not abandoned his goal of the demise of the Jewish state ("complete liberation of Palestine") and his use of indiscriminate violence ("armed Palestinian revolution").

We have seen too much of violence—verbal and physical—between Arab and Jew. It is incumbent on every American Arab and every American Jew to denounce its use. In his deeply moving book, *Arab and Jew,* David Shipler reveals the pain suffered by both, in Israel, as their respective claims to Palestine/Israel remain unresolved. Personal attractions and affinities between individual Jews and Arabs are overwhelmed by group aspirations and loyalties. Their respective histories of exclusion and suffering provide each with justification for something less than proud behavior. But Shipler, in his scrupulously honest and balanced treatment of the tragedy, adds his personal testimony to what I have always believed: the Jews in Israel, as a people and as a state, do *not* want their children to hate, are not indifferent to any developing racism or bigotry. Their education systems, their television broadcasters, and their public officials accept responsibility to condemn violence and prejudice. There is, for most Jews in Israel and for most Jews around the world, genuine pain that not all Jews adhere to the high moral standards of Judaism. But, Shipler reports, "One looks in vain" for anything comparable to such agony on the Arab side. Too often, hatred and violence are not only accepted, they are praised and hailed by Arab leaders as noble weapons against the enemy.

Whatever the prospects may be for Jewish-Arab understanding and tolerance in the Middle East, one can still hope that in the United States Arabs and Jews will choose tolerance and civility as more appropriate "weapons" in the search for understanding and accommodation. Telling American Jews that they are supporting *Nazi* policies in Israel is a sure formula for disaster.

If this debate does nothing else, it is my hope that it may contribute somehow to such tolerance and civility. The issues are tough enough. They should not be made even tougher to solve by resorting to either physical or rhetorical violence.

J A M E S   G.   A B O U R E Z K

Introduction

*F*or some people, particularly supporters of Israel, retracing the history of the Arab-Israeli conflict is too painful to endure. They argue that discussion of Who-Shot-John is unproductive and that the only relevant subject of debate is the future, or how to end the conflict.

Fine.

I will limit my discussion to the future if, in return, someone in authority will publicly acknowledge that the Palestinians have been betrayed, consistently and viciously, by the world powers, and terribly wronged by the Israelis.

Israel's supporters would rather avoid discussing the historical abuse of the Palestinians. One hears over and over again the endless litany of reasons why Jews feel they were entitled to physically throw out the Palestinians, to take over the land of Palestine and to call it Israel. At various times we hear that Jews lived there two thousand years ago, and at other times we are told it was promised by God. When the occasion calls for it, we hear that the Palestinians left Palestine on their own, and occasionally we are told that most were born outside of Palestine since 1948. (There is no mention of the fact that in 1948, most Jews were born outside of Palestine.)

Those who lay dubious claim to real estate based on Jewish occupancy two thousand years ago also totally deny the much higher rights of Palestinian Arabs who occupied the same land less than forty years ago. The ridiculing of Palestinian claims smacks a bit of racism.

In their most candid moments, Zionists will abandon the pretense of biblical rights, or of Arab wrongs, and concede the kind of chicanery—violent and nonviolent—that was used to take Palestine away from the Palestinians.

The Israeli writer Amos Oz told in his book *In The Land of Israel* of finding such candor during a discussion with a Jewish settler in the West Bank. "Gush Emunim," the settler told Oz, "from the day of its founding, has actually operated by classic Zionist techniques: another stake, another goat, another acre." The technique has not changed and has been used to take the Golan Heights, the Sinai, the Gaza Strip, the West Bank, south Lebanon, and on and on.

Ignoring history is an obstacle to settling the Middle East conflict, to understanding what America's interest really is. Even its slightest revision gives the current status a vastly different coloration. Decision making becomes skewed, unfair, and frequently wrong. American democracy requires full disclosure of both sides of an issue before a fair decision can be made. To date, we have been inundated with the Israeli side of the Middle East story, unfortunately giving rise to the feeling that the other side does not exist. There is an objective history not generally known by members of the public, giving propagandists for Israel the opportunity to distort it. How Israel was created, and on whose land it was created, then, is a necessary antecedent to understanding events today and to answering the question of what is and what is not in America's interest.

The Seeds of Conflict Are Planted

When the twentieth century began, that part of the Arab world known as the Fertile Crescent had been dominated by the Ottoman Turkish Empire for four hundred years. It was just beginning to experience what has been described as the "Arab Awakening," a slowly rising nationalistic fervor. As though coming out of a deep sleep, the Arab world was eager to see the end of the long, culturally sterile Turkish occupation.

Experiencing a different kind of human misery, Jews throughout Europe had been suffering a long history of pogroms and attacks, which resulted in an effort to find them a haven—a place where one could be a Jew without denigration and punishment. The movement organized to establish such a homeland had, in 1896, found expression in a concept called Zionism, which soon gained momentum among Jews all over the world. The catalyst for the movement's founder, Theodore Herzl, was the notorious Dreyfus affair in France. It convinced Herzl that Jews could never find justice at the hands of non-Jews, making a state of their own an absolute necessity. In addition, pogroms against Jews in Czarist Russia created a sense of urgency in Herzl and his followers.

At the outbreak of World War I, Turkey's alliance with Germany compelled Britain to try to keep the Turkish military occupied, decreasing its threat to Europe. Although secret anti-Turkish political activity was stirring among the Arabs, mostly in Egypt and along the Mediterranean coast, the British, interestingly, sought Arab desert leaders to lead an armed rebellion against Turkey. To enlist them for the Allies, Britain played upon the Arabs' desire for independence from colonial rule, promising them freedom once the war ended.

But while pledging independence to the Arabs, the British were trying to satisfy an increasingly active Zionist movement in Britain with promises of support for a "Jewish home" in Palestine. Moving with deftness in British political circles, a leading Zionist, Dr. Chaim Weizmann, and his associates in the British Zionist Federation, obtained a commitment of support for such a home from British Foreign Secretary Lord Balfour. This commitment came in the form of the now famous Balfour Declaration, written to Lord Rothschild on November 2, 1917, stating:

> His Majesty's Government view with favour the establishment in Palestine of a national home for the Jewish people, and will use their best endeavours to facilitate the achievement of this object, *it being clearly understood that nothing shall be done which may prejudice the civil and religious rights of existing non-Jewish communities in Palestine, or the rights and political status enjoyed by Jews in any other country.* [Emphasis added.]

It was a masterful lesson in big power manipulation. Britain made simultaneous promises—of independence to the Arabs in exchange for their valuable participation on their side in the war and of a national home, of sorts, to Jews in exchange for financial support for

the war from England's Jewish community. But their ultimate intention, along with that of France, was to bring the Middle East under
their dominance once it was wrested from Turkey. The manipulation did not end with Britain's conflicting actions. While different
promises were being made both to Arabs and to Jews, representatives
of Britain and France met secretly to divide up the Ottoman Empire
between themselves, intending to consummate the deal once the
war was over.

However, the human dynamics of the area, as well as the growing
fervor of Arab as well as Jewish nationalism, would create more
difficulty for Britain than it could ultimately handle.

Immediately following the war, France and Britain began moving the Middle East toward a "mandate," a euphemism developed
to allow colonization. Syria, part of which eventually became Lebanon, was dealt to France, and Britain was given Iraq and Palestine.
The Balfour Declaration was then made a part of the Palestine
mandate, making it clearer than ever to the Arabs that they had been
lied to, and that the Zionists had been working overtime to influence
British politicians to establish Palestine as a Jewish home. Arab
objections to the failure of Britain to grant the self-determination
they had promised were dismissed as inconsequential.

After the war, in 1918, Jewish immigration into Palestine began
increasing under the observance of the first British high commis-
sioner of Palestine, Sir Herbert Samuel, a pro-Zionist English Jew.
When the terms of the Palestine mandate were announced in 1920,
and they saw the increase in Jewish immigration, the Palestinian
Arabs exploded in anger and violence, sponsoring anti-Jewish riots.
Public announcement of the mandate, combined with increasing
Jewish immigration, made it obvious that the Zionists' ultimate aim
was to create a Jewish state on their lands. They were clearly about
to be robbed of the independence promised them.

The rewards of empire to Britain diminished as it confronted
Arab protests on one side, and continuous political pressures by the
Zionist lobby on the other. The result was a reinterpretation of the
Balfour Declaration in 1922. In a political high-wire effort, the
government issued what came to be known as the Churchill Memorandum. It stated that the Balfour Declaration did not intend an
exclusive Jewish state, but only the "further development of the
existing Jewish community with the assistance of Jews in other parts

of the world in order that it may become a center in which the Jewish people as a whole may take, on grounds of religion and race, an interest and pride."

The memorandum added that the Balfour Declaration did not intend to bring about the "disappearance or the subordination of the Arabic population, language or culture in Palestine."

Britain told the Zionist organization that it must officially approve the reinterpretation before Britain would seek official League of Nations approval of the Palestine mandate. Although the Zionists officially endorsed the reinterpretation, Chaim Weizmann, in later writings, made it clear that no matter what the Balfour Declaration intended, he and other Zionists hoped for the build-up of a Jewish majority in Palestine that would ultimately permit creation of an exclusive Jewish state.

The pressures of nationalism in the Arab world became too great for Britain, which eventually granted independence to its "protectorates," with the exception of Palestine. But as Jewish immigration into Palestine continued to increase, so did violence between the two communities.

The betrayal of promises made by the big powers was bitterly felt throughout the Arab world, resulting in continued riots and uprisings. The intensity of the fighting between the two communities ebbed and flowed over the years. The Palestinian Arabs felt humiliated and frustrated both by their betrayal and by the sponsorship and protection the British gave to Jewish immigration. They fully understood that if immigration were not stopped, creation of a Jewish state would be a *fait accompli.* The violence between the two communities continued.

By 1939, Britain felt increasing pressure from the worsening crisis in Palestine. War with Germany was imminent, and the British Army was apprehensive about tying down its forces to quell the violence in Palestine. To solve its impending problems, Britain issued a new White Paper in May 1939, severely restricting Jewish immigration for the ensuing five years. Afterwards, the new policy provided that the level of immigration would be decided by the Arab majority.

The new British restrictions on immigration directly affected Jews who were trying to flee the Nazis, resulting in the organization of terrorist groups by outraged Jewish militants, primarily the

Irgun Zvai Leumi and its offshoot, the Stern Gang. The Jewish terrorists targeted both the British and the Arabs. At the end of World War II, they were joined by the Haganah, the mainstream army of the Jewish _Yishuv._ They focused initially on assisting the entry into Palestine of hapless Jewish refugees trying to escape Hitler's Europe.

It should be noted here that the powers who have, over the years, contributed the most to fueling the Arab-Israeli conflict—Britain, and later the United States—were two of the countries that refused to accept Jews trying to escape Hitler's persecution during World War II.

By 1947, Britain, already exhausted from its war against Germany, as well as from the terrorist war being conducted against it by Jewish terror groups, announced it would resign its Palestine mandate and hand over the problem to the United Nations for disposition.

In November 1947, the U.N. General Assembly passed a nonbinding resolution partitioning Palestine. Although the Arab population was much larger than the Jewish population, the partition gave 56 percent of the land to the Jewish Yishuv and 44 percent to the Palestinian Arabs. By now, Jews made up less than one-third of the population of Palestine (608,000 Jews as opposed to 1,327,000 Arabs) and owned only 9 percent of the land. The partition plan provided another interesting result—in the part designated as Jewish, there were to be 498,000 Jews and 497,000 Arabs, while in the Arab part, which was 42.88 percent of Palestine, there would be 725,000 Arabs and 10,000 Jews. Additionally, Jerusalem held 105,000 Arabs and 100,000 Jews.

After years of Palestinian frustration, humiliation, and betrayal by Britain and France, with the complicity of U.S. diplomats, the entire Arab world erupted in violent protest over the U.N. vote. So strenuous was the protest that the United Nations refused to go further with the partition plan and began working on a U.N. trusteeship for Palestine, a new plan initially supported and even developed by the U.S. delegate, Warren Austin. While the Zionist organization's military forces prepared for the forcible conquest of a new state, Zionist politicians worked overtime in Washington, D.C., seeking American pledges for diplomatic recognition.

The protests in Palestine broke out in violence, with the right-wing Jewish terrorist groups, the Irgun and the Stern Gang, terrorizing the civilian population. Their objective was to drive the Palestinians from Palestine. Of the hundreds of terrorist operations carried out by the Jewish terror groups, two of the most notorious were the dynamiting of the King David Hotel in Jerusalem by Menachem Begin and his Irgun terrorists, and the intentional massacre of 248 men, women, and children of Deir Yassin village by the Irgun and the Stern Gang in April 1948.

This slaughter was used most effectively by Jewish propagandists to incite fear in the remaining civilian population, speeding their flight from Palestine. In his memoirs, *The Revolt*, Menachem Begin, then leader of the Irgun, wrote of the propaganda value of Deir Yassin.

> The enemy propaganda was designed to besmirch our name. In the result it helped us. Panic overwhelmed the Arabs of Eretz Israel. Kolonia village, which had previously repulsed every attack of the Haganah, was evacuated overnight and fell without further fighting. Beit-Iksa was also evacuated. These two places overlooked the main road; and their fall, together with the capture of Kastel by the Haganah, made it possible to keep open the road to Jerusalem. In the rest of the country, too, the Arabs began to flee in terror, even before they clashed with Jewish forces. Not what happened to Dir Yassin [sic], but what was invented about Dir Yassin, helped to carve the way to our decisive victories on the battlefield. The legend of Dir Yassin helped us in particular in the saving of Tiverias and the conquest of Haifa.

Palestinians fled in great numbers, more than 750,000 of them, enough to change what had been an Arab majority in Palestine into an Arab minority. The result of the terrorism, fighting, and fear was the creation of a new Jewish majority, allowing David Ben-Gurion and his new government to declare, on May 14, 1948, that Israel was now an exclusive Jewish state. There were not enough Palestinians left either to struggle against or to vote against the kind of state created, assuming that they would have been permitted to vote.

To give the new state legitimacy, recognition by the world powers was necessary, especially by the United States. On advice from the State Department, President Harry Truman initially rejected efforts by Chaim Weizmann and his supporters to obtain u.s. recognition. However, Truman's increasing election problems in that presidential year—including a threat from New York Democrats to defeat him for renomination—made him especially attentive to advice to recognize Israel. Although Truman was warned against it by State Department officials, his special assistant, Clark Clifford, advised him that reversing his position on the recognition of Israel would sew up the Jewish vote. Thus, on Truman's order, the United States became the second nation—the Soviet Union was the first—to recognize the newly declared state of Israel.

The argument heard most frequently by Zionist politicians after the Deir Yassin massacre and the bloody fighting in Palestine was that the Arab governments ordered the Arab inhabitants of Palestine to leave, promising their early return after an Arab military victory. This claim is presumably the Zionists' justification for taking the Palestinians' land, as well as the continuing exclusion to this day of those Palestinian refugees who fled for their lives. Aside from the total lack of evidence of any such "order" by Arab governments directed toward civilians, the logic of such an argument is nonexistent. The Palestinians have tried over the years to return, even though there was no "Arab victory," but have, to this day, been prevented from doing so. More logically, no one leaves their home voluntarily.

The authority in Palestine at that time was the British Mandatory Authority, not neighboring Arab governments. It is hardly likely that an outside radio voice could succeed in issuing orders. It is even more unlikely that, assuming such a broadcast took place, people not living under their authority would follow such orders if their safety were not threatened.

The allegation is a fantasy. The bulk of the Palestinians who fled to save their lives were rural peasants, hardly people who owned radios, or who sat around waiting for orders from outside Arab governments. People fled, not in obedience to neighboring governments, but in fear of their lives.

The objective of the terror and violence delivered by Jewish terrorists at Deir Yassin and at other villages in Palestine had been accomplished.

Word spread that Jewish terrorists were coming, and frightened

Palestinians went to Lebanon, to Transjordan, to anywhere providing safety from the fighting in general, and from Menachem Begin's Irgun, Yitzhak Shamir's Stern Gang, and David Ben-Gurion's Haganah in particular.

When the fighting stopped, those Palestinians who tried to return to their homes were prevented from doing so by the Israeli military, which by then had established frontiers along what were formerly the front lines of battle. As a result, an estimated 750,000 Palestinians became refugees.

They, and their progeny, constitute the Palestinian diaspora today.

It is important to examine the justification offered by Zionists as to why the Palestinians left, with special focus on the Zionists' objective of an exclusive Jewish state. Would it have been possible to create, democratically, an exclusive Jewish state while Palestinians were still in the majority? The answer is obvious—of course not.

Had all the Palestinians stayed in their homes during the fighting in 1947 and 1948, there would have been no Jewish majority. It follows that there would have been no exclusive Jewish state, at least not as a result of a democratic election. Since such exclusivity was the ultimate objective of the Zionist movement, it also follows— most clearly—that enough Palestinians had to be driven out of Palestine to give the Yishuv the majority it needed. Democracy in Israel was then, and is now, merely a slogan with no relation to the truth for non-Jews. Israel has become a nation that is partly a fundamentalist theocracy, partly a national security state, and partly a parliamentary democracy with a perpetual occupation over a subjugated population of Arabs. Israel's government has never been forced to choose between calling itself a democracy or calling itself a settler state forcibly repressing the indigenous Palestinians. So far, it has been able to have it both ways, without having to make a choice.

One of the most interesting arguments advanced by Jewish Defense League founder Meir Kahane is that Israel cannot at the same time be a democracy *and* an exclusive Jewish state. His fear, and that of his right-wing followers, is that because the Palestinians produce children faster, they will overtake the Jews in number, gaining a majority, and outvoting them. Kahane's argument that all Arabs must immediately be deported carries an internal Zionist logic, and creates panic among mainstream Zionists, who understand and agree with what he is saying but prefer that it not be said out loud. Kahane frequently tells his audiences, "I say what you think."

What I find interesting is that even those furthest on the left of the Israeli political spectrum, those who demonstrate in the streets demanding peace with the Palestinians, do so *not* so much out of concern for Palestinians living under Israel's brutal occupation, but out of fear that continued occupation will dilute the "ethnic purity" of Israel.

One need only ask what Israel's reaction would be today should Arabs become the majority and vote to make Israel a democratic, secular state—meaning that it would no longer be exclusively a Jewish state. The transparency of Israel's claim of democracy would become immediately evident. There is, in fact, no democracy in Israel for Arabs.

That is why Jewish terrorists had no choice but to drive out enough Arabs to deprive them of majority status.

In his book *Arab and Jew, New York Times* correspondent David Shipler described the orders given to Defense Minister Yitzhak Rabin by David Ben-Gurion during the fighting in 1948. "Drive them out," Ben-Gurion said of the Palestinian population of Lod and Ramle (this confession was removed from Rabin's memoirs by the Israeli censor). According to Shipler, Benny Morris, a *Jerusalem Post* reporter, located documents that recorded Israeli efforts to drive Palestinians out of the Negev region, including whispered threats of attacks and revenge and firing into the air to frighten them. It worked. The inhabitants of the area fled to the West Bank, near Hebron.

The best description of the result of it all was that expressed to me by Ahmed Khalil, a Palestinian whom I met in Amman, Jordan, several years ago. "I was born in Palestine, educated in Cambridge University at the same time that Abba Eban was educated there," he said. "Eban was born in South Africa, but now he is foreign minister of Israel, and I am forbidden to return to the land of my birth."

Khalil's lament is a depressingly accurate summation of what has happened to the Palestinians.

Israel Consolidates Itself

*I*t has been said that the "War of Independence," as Israel has called its war of aggression in 1948, was won *after* the cease-fire agreements of 1949. Once the truce was signed, not only did Israel's forces continue firing on Arabs—both military and civilian—but they proceeded to import more arms and build new fortifications using Arab prisoners of war for labor. They also began the forced relocation of Arab civilian populations for both military and political purposes, in complete violation of international law and norms.

After the truce and cease-fire agreements were signed following the 1948 fighting, Israel moved, with troops and arms, into the Huleh valley below Syria's Golan Heights, forcibly replacing the Palestinian farmers with Israeli kibbutzim. The truce agreements left the Huleh valley as a sort of no man's land, with neither side having sovereignty. That additional land grab by the Israelis prompted intermittent Syrian shelling of the valley from the Golan Heights above. Again, the superior propaganda skills of the Israelis convinced the world that the Syrians were barbaric, firing on innocent civilians. The Syrian reaction is well-known, but the Israeli provocation is not, and without the entire story, a false picture of the behavior of both is drawn.

Although the original partition plan devised by the United Nations conceived of Jerusalem as a *corpus separatum,* the new Israeli government sought to make Jerusalem its capital. As early as mid-September 1948, Israel's Supreme Court was established in Jerusalem. Then, on December 20, 1948, while the war was still raging, the Israeli cabinet officially decided to move "government institutions" to Jerusalem from Tel Aviv. The Knesset, Israel's parliament, held its first session in Jerusalem on February 14, 1949, and three days later Chaim Weizmann took his oath of office there as Israel's first president. Alarmed by these moves and by public calls for establishing Israel's capital in Jerusalem by such firebrands as Menachem Begin, the U.N. General Assembly opened a debate on the issue in its fall session of 1949.

While the debate was going on, Prime Minister Ben-Gurion defiantly declared on December 5 to the Knesset, "We will not consider any attempt made by the United Nations to forcibly re-move Jerusalem from the State of Israel, or to interfere with Israel's authority in the eternal capital. We declare that Israel will never willingly give up Jerusalem. . . ." He had earlier called Jerusalem "an integral part of Israeli history, in her faith and in the depths of her soul. Jerusalem is the 'heart of hearts' of Israel. . . ."

Although Israel and its supporters have frequently cited the 1947 U.N. partition plan as the basis for its existence, the section on Jerusalem, and all the others, they chose to ignore. (Among other things, General Assembly Resolution 181—the partition plan—called for Arab and Jewish provisional governments to be established in each area designated; for the guarantee to all persons of equal rights in civil, political, economic, and religious matters as well as the enjoyment of human rights and fundamental free-doms.)

It was clear that the leaders of Israel had never intended to abide by the partition plan, or any other plan that interfered with their taking as much territory as they could. Israeli cabinet member Dov Joseph admitted as much when he said, "From the first day of the state, we behaved as if Jerusalem were part of Israel. . . ."

In a part of the world where water resources are as precious as life, the new state of Israel made it a point to take as much water from the Arabs as it could. In 1951, backed by its military, Israel began draining Lake Huleh, a part of the Jordan river system, over protests by United Nations forces and the U.S. State Department. Then, in 1953, pursuant to requests from Israel, the United States and the United Nations began working on a unified water plan using the Jordan River and its tributaries, with the aim of irrigating Israeli and Jordanian farms. While the plan was being prepared, American officials were stunned to learn that Israel was secretly, and on a crash basis, constructing a canal to divert much of the Jordan River into Israel. The diversion was in direct violation of the truce agreements, which were noted by the U.N. observer when he asked Israel to stop the project. Israel's response was to speed up its work, expanding the work crews to three shifts.

Secretary of State John Foster Dulles then notified Israel that $26 million in U.S. aid money intended for Israel would be withheld until Israel agreed to stop work on the diversion project. President Eisenhower also conditionally ordered the Treasury Department to remove the tax-deductible status of contributions made to the United Jewish Appeal and other Zionist organizations operating as charities. Israel stopped its diversion of the Jordan River.

In 1956, Egypt's President Gamel Abdel Nasser nationalized the Suez Canal. The culmination of a long-standing dispute between Egypt and Britain, it was done partly as a response to the United States' refusal to provide financial aid for the Aswan dam, and partly as an expression of Egyptian nationalism.

The nationalization was all that was needed by France, England, and Israel. All three countries wanted Nasser toppled, believing a military defeat would accomplish just that.

France saw Nasser as a threat to its influence in Algeria, where an anti-colonial struggle against the French was raging. England had just lost its control over the canal, and Israel, seeing an opportunity to do away with a charismatic Arab leader, joined with the two European powers to invade Egypt.

By the time they invaded, President Eisenhower was in the midst of the 1956 reelection campaign. Despite pressures from Israel's supporters in the United States, he threatened all three countries—Britain, France, and Israel—with economic retaliation if they did not end their military aggression. Britain and France immediately withdrew, but Israel tried to hold on to the Sinai desert, saying it would withdraw its troops from the Sinai, but that it would keep the Gaza Strip. To weaken Eisenhower's influence, in December 1956, Israel staged a propaganda campaign in the United States seeking support for its position in an effort to override Eisenhower's decision. It held on until February 1957, when a frustrated Eisenhower finally went on national television to announce that an aggressor should not be allowed to retain the fruits of its aggression. He suggested that the United Nations pressure Israel to force it to comply with the several withdrawal resolutions passed in that body.

After additional pressures from the United Nations and the United States, on March 16, 1957, Israel finally withdrew. But as it did so, it destroyed surfaced roads, railroad tracks, and telephone lines. At least two villages were entirely destroyed, as well as the military buildings around El Arish.

The invasion of the Sinai, however, was not Israel's last effort at seizing additional Arab territories.

The 1967 War

At the beginning of 1967, the Middle East was experiencing new and heightened activity by Fatah, a new organization of Palestinians joining the struggle to recapture their homeland. Headed by Yasir Arafat, a Palestinian engineer who had been working in Kuwait, Fatah had earlier begun conducting raids against military targets inside Israel. These raids created fear inside Israel but great excitement throughout the Arab world. At the same time, Nasser was chafing under criticism from his many rivals in the Arab world for allowing U.N. Emergency Force (UNEF) troops to be stationed on Egyptian soil. The UNEF forces had remained in the Sinai as a condition of the withdrawal of Israel, Britain, and France after the 1956 invasion of Egypt. Israel had refused to allow U.N. troops on its side of the line, so they remained on the Egyptian side.

In May 1967, Nasser ordered the U.N. troops to leave, and shortly after that, declared the Straits of Tiran closed to Israeli shipping. Technically, both areas were under Egyptian sovereignty, giving Nasser the legal right to close the straits.

But legalities were not the prime mover in the events that followed. On the morning of June 5, 1967, without warning, Israel's air force struck airfields belonging to Syria, Egypt, and Jordan, destroying the air power of all three nations.

The Egyptian troops in the Sinai were without air cover and were no match for the combined air and land forces of Israel. In only six days, Israel chased the Egyptian army out of the Sinai, captured the Wailing Wall in Jerusalem, and by breaking a cease-fire, took the Golan Heights from Syria.

In a direct attack on American interests, on June 8, 1967, Israeli warplanes and torpedo boats repeatedly assaulted a U.S. intelligence ship, the USS *Liberty*, which was steaming off the Sinai coast, killing thirty-four Americans and wounding another 171. The attack involved the use of napalm, rockets, machine guns, and torpedoes. Once the air attack on the ship was completed, Israeli torpedo boats strafed the American sailors trying to put out the fires caused by napalm and rockets. When the *Liberty* put out lifeboats, the Israelis strafed those as well. The Israelis also sent troop-carrying helicopters to finish off any remaining sailors who might be potential witnesses to their crime. Mysteriously, American fighter jets that had taken off from an aircraft carrier in the Mediterranean to come to the defense of the *Liberty* were called back. Under orders from Washington, the American sailors on the ship were left to fend for themselves.

Before they destroyed it, Israeli planes buzzed the ship for at least five and a half hours, during a time when the ship was flying a new flag that flew freely in a light breeze. To the great shame of the United States government, the deliberateness of the attack was covered up in a subsequent Naval Board of Inquiry, and the United States accepted Israel's lame excuse that the deadly assault was an "accident."

Not only did the Johnson administration cover up the *Liberty* affair, but when its members were not prosecuting the war in Southeast Asia, they appeared to have spent much of their time promoting Israel's interests. One can find in the presidential archives staff papers with titles as revealing as: "What We Have Done for Israel," "New Things We Might Do in Israel," and "How We Have Helped Israel." It is no surprise that the permissiveness present in the administration encouraged Israel to take measures no other nation would dare take against United States interests.

The 1967 war marked a dangerous escalation in the Soviet-U.S. struggle. Always protective of its interests and, thus, of its allies in the Arab world, the Soviets could not allow continued humiliation of Syria, Egypt, and Jordan, the Arab states confronting Israel.

Soviet power in the Mediterranean had grown substantially in the intervening years since 1956, and now included about twenty warships with their accompanying vessels and eight or nine submarines. After Israel broke the cease-fire to invade the Golan Heights on June 9, the Soviet Union broke diplomatic relations with Israel— they remain broken today—and activated the "hot line" to the White House to deliver a harsh threat. Premier Alexei N. Kosygin bluntly warned of a "grave catastrophe" if Israel did not stop fighting and said Russia was prepared to take the "necessary actions, including military."

The war resulted in the second massive exodus of Palestinian refugees. An additional 323,000 Palestinians were driven out by the fighting and were piled into refugee camps in other parts of the Arab world already teeming with the three-quarters of a million Palestinian men, women, and children made homeless by the

1948–49 war. For the guerrilla organizations, there could be no better place to recruit fighters in the struggle to regain the Palestinian homeland.

Palestinian guerrilla groups grew rapidly after the 1967 war with thousands of new recruits. The new factions eventually took over the P.L.O., which had been formed in 1964 by Arab leaders to diffuse growing Palestinian frustration with their condition. As head of Fatah, the largest Palestinian grouping, Yasser Arafat was elected chairman of the P.L.O.'s Executive Committee in 1969. The P.L.O. was loosely knit and never came under the total control of Arafat. According to its own reports, overall P.L.O. attacks against Israel grew from a monthly average of 12 in 1967 to 52 in 1968, 199 in 1969, and 279 in the first eight months of 1970.

In the summer of 1967, while the United Nations was trying to end the Middle East conflict, Israel secretly offered Egypt a separate peace treaty—one of Israel's long-term strategic objectives. It offered to return the Sinai to Egypt in exchange for a peace treaty, demilitarization of that territory, free navigation in the Suez Canal, and internationalization of the Straits of Tiran. The offer was quickly rejected by Nasser. Dean Rusk, then secretary of state, who, it seemed, was carrying water for Israel, approached the Egyptians with a similar plan that was also turned down.

Although U.N. Resolution 242 had been advertised as a way out of the conflict, it had immense shortcomings in its application. The Arab countries signed onto 242 after representations by the American ambassador to the U.N., Arthur Goldberg, that Israel, with minor border adjustments, fully intended to withdraw from the territories it had occupied in the 1967 war.

Israel also began establishing settlements in the occupied territories, further humiliating the Arabs, and in particular, Nasser, who was still smarting from Egypt's devastating defeat in the 1967 war.

Not only did Israel show its intention to keep those territories, but it also began building fortifications along the Sinai side of the Suez Canal which were collectively called the Bar-Lev Line. The fortifications were built in reaction to Egyptian shelling of Israeli troops dug in across the canal; but to Nasser, the presence of Israeli troops and the Bar-Lev Line were concrete evidence of Israel's intentions to stay.

The War of Attrition

Nasser's strong, but unfulfilled, commitment to the Palestinians, and his inability to do anything for them, only added to his humiliation when the Israelis showed their hand with respect to withdrawal from the territories occupied in 1967. Golda Meir declared publicly that the Palestinians "did not exist." Nasser became convinced that force was the only way to recover what the Arabs had lost.

Egypt began shelling Israeli positions across the Suez in March 1969, opening what was to be called the War of Attrition. In retaliation, Israel began deep penetration air strikes inside Egypt, as well as commando raids, further humiliating Nasser. Plagued by lack of technical knowledge, in addition to having inferior equipment for defense, Nasser asked the Soviet Union for help. The Soviets acceded to his request and poured Russian troops into Egypt— technicians, pilots, and advanced weapons, including new MIG fighter jets and surface to air missiles (SAM). Once the anti-aircraft missiles were installed, the deep penetration raids by Israel stopped. After a few more months of confrontation between Israeli and Russian pilots, in August 1970, the War of Attrition ended.

A month later, in September, Nasser died. He was replaced by Anwar al-Sadat.

Although Sadat continued to build Egypt's military strength in early 1971, at the same time he moved to try to end the Middle East conflict. He made a detailed offer to Israel that would have ultimately resulted in a peace treaty between the two nations, but that also would have required Israel to withdraw to its pre-1967 borders. Israel refused to link any initial steps to Resolution 242, or any larger concept of an overall peace settlement. Sadat was unable to accept Israel's conditions, and the failure of the initiative brought about a two-year diplomatic stalemate. It was a stalemate encouraged by Henry Kissinger, then director of the National Security Council, who believed that the longer Israel—and the United States—held out for tougher terms, the more likely Sadat would be to give in.

In May 1971, Sadat signed a Treaty of Friendship and Cooperation with Moscow, which provided that Russia would come to Egypt's defense. He continued importing Soviet arms and troops until Nixon's 1972 summit meeting with Brezhnev that, under Kissinger's tutelage, produced a statement on the Middle East designed

to strip Egypt of its Soviet support. When Sadat learned of this new
Soviet attitude, he decided to expel the ten thousand Russian advisers then working in Egypt. Even that failed to get the reaction he
expected from the United States, since Kissinger was not then taking
Sadat seriously. His aim was to achieve "complete frustration" of the
Arabs. He later admitted his policy was shortsighted and "may have
contributed to the October 1973 war." In fact, by the time the
Soviets were expelled from Egypt, the Russian leadership had begun
acting as a restraining force on Sadat, urging him not to enter into
armed hostilities. The Soviet role was irrelevant to the posture both
President Nixon and Henry Kissinger wanted to display—that of
winning what they called "foreign policy victories."

Sadat fell back on the only option he believed remained open to
him—war against Israel.

The 1973 War

Finally, after a prolonged diplomatic drift, exacerbated by Nixon's
involvement in the Watergate scandal, on October 6, 1973, both
Egypt and Syria launched attacks against Israel, taking that country's
military by surprise. Although Israel's intelligence had a few hours'
advance warning, there was not enough time to prepare. The surprise was almost complete, both in Tel Aviv and in Washington,
since Israeli officials—in particular General Sharon and Moshe
Dayan—had been boasting that Israel was militarily so superior that
the Arabs posed no danger.

The armies of Egypt and Syria moved rapidly—the Syrians
through the Golan Heights and the Egyptians through the Sinai.
Golda Meir sent messages to the u.s. government in apocalyptic
terms saying Israel's survival was at stake. Although Kissinger, ex-
pecting a quick Israeli victory, held off sending additional arms for
a time, he eventually ordered a full resupply effort. The Israeli
military turned the battle around, recovering ground on both fronts.
The calls for a cease-fire went unheeded by either side, depending
on who had the military advantage at the moment, but on October
22, both sides agreed.

The next day the Soviets contacted the u.s. government, charging that Israel was violating the cease-fire and was advancing beyond
the lines drawn the day before. Brezhnev threatened to intervene
directly with Soviet forces if the United States allowed Israel to

continue. Seeing the danger in a superpower confrontation, Kissinger bluntly told Israel that the u.s. would not stand for the destruction of the Egyptian Third Army, then completely surrounded by Israeli military forces.

The United States spent the next two years disentangling the forces on both sides, with Kissinger conducting his now-famous "shuttle diplomacy" between the Arab and Israeli sides.

On January 18, 1974, after the Kissinger shuttle, Egypt and Israel signed a disengagement agreement, termed "Sinai I." Israel was to withdraw its forces west of the canal, liberating the Egyptian Third Army, which it had surrounded while breaking the October 22 cease-fire. It would also withdraw its forces fifteen miles east of the Suez to positions west of the Gidi and Mitla passes. A u.n. peace-keeping force would be stationed between the two armies. Both sides also agreed to force limitations.

Syrian-Israeli Disengagement

The Syrian-Israeli disengagement was more difficult, however. Israel had established more than twenty settlements in the part of the Golan Heights that it had occupied in the 1967 fighting, violating the Fourth Geneva Convention of 1949 prohibiting the transfer of an occupier's population into occupied territory. In the 1973 fighting, Israel had expanded beyond what it had taken in 1967.

Now Syrian President Hafez al Assad demanded that Israel not only give up what it had captured in 1973, but that it also withdraw some distance beyond the 1967 cease-fire line.

Golda Meir refused. The situation remained explosive. Because the opposing troops were so close to each other, both sides eventually saw the advantage to disengagement. Incidents were occurring daily, making the situation more and more dangerous. On April 27, fourteen Israelis were killed in incidents in the Golan Heights. The continuing violence, along with the ugly mood inside Israel resulting from the Israeli military's lack of preparation for the war speeded up an agreement.

An offer to increase u.s. aid to Israel was additional incentive in gaining Israel's agreement. As in so many other such negotiations, Israel demanded a price from the United States for doing what it should have done in any event. As so many administrations have done, Nixon's, with Kissinger as the guiding force, lavishly spent

American taxpayers' money on Israel's arms requests, which were then used against the Arabs. Afterwards, more taxpayers' money was spent buying Israel's withdrawal to soothe Arab feelings. A $2.2 billion aid package was voted by Congress after the 1973 war so Israel could pay for the war. Nixon forgave $1.5 billion of it as an incentive to Israel to disengage from part of its war conquests. The years following the 1973 war brought Israel record amounts of u.s. aid money, visibly reaching $5 billion each year, which does not include private, tax-exempt contributions and other enhancements.

Following another Kissinger shuttle between Israel and Syria, an agreement was reached between the two on May 29, 1974, and signed shortly thereafter.

The butcher's bill for the 1973 Middle East war for the Arabs was 8,528 killed and 19,549 wounded; for the Israelis, 2,838 killed and 8,800 wounded.

War in Jordan

After the fighting in 1948, Palestinian refugee camps were established in Lebanon, Syria, and Jordan, and after 1969, each became a center of recruitment for the growing Palestine Liberation Organization. The largest of the p.l.o. factions, Fatah, was headed by Yasir Arafat. After Fatah's spirited defense in 1968 against an Israeli attack on the Jordanian village of Karameh, new recruits flocked to the movement. Using advance information, three hundred Palestinian guerrillas held off fifteen thousand Israeli troops, supported by tanks and helicopters, at Karameh. The inability of the p.l.o. to absorb and train the flood of new recruits led to a plethora of different organizations all with the objective of liberating Palestine. The guerrillas based in Jordan began challenging King Hussein, whose nervousness increased in proportion to the numbers and militancy of the guerrillas operating there.

Forgetting Mao Tse-Tung's dictum against poisoning the sea in which the revolution swims, the Palestinians began setting up roadblocks in Amman, Jordan's capital, and in general threatened the sovereignty of Hussein's kingdom. Some of the p.l.o. factions believed all monarchies in the Middle East should be overthrown as a way to begin their revolution. In 1970, the Popular Front for the Liberation of Palestine, one of the guerrilla groups, hijacked three civilian airliners and landed them in the Jordanian desert. What had been brief skirmishes between troops loyal to King Hussein and the Palestinians broke out in full-scale war in September 1970.

Hussein, buttressed by Henry Kissinger's promise of help, decided to put an end to the Palestinian threat to his throne. The Palestinians anticipated help from Iraq and Syria, but the Iraqi troops still in Jordan from the 1967 war made no move to help. When the Syrian army began moving south to weigh in with the Palestinians, Kissinger requested the Soviets to stop the imminent confrontation with pressure on Syria. Although the Israelis were poised to enter the fighting on the side of Hussein, their intervention did not come about because Soviet pressure eventually stopped the Syrian army from moving all the way to the battle.

Driven out of Jordan, the Palestinians set up their main base of operations in Lebanon.

Civil War in Lebanon

A bloody, cruel, and seemingly endless civil war broke out in Lebanon on April 13, 1975, when Phalangist gunmen opened fire on a busload of Palestinians. Lebanon's internal conflict was centered on the imbalance of power caused by the requirements of the Lebanese constitution that left Lebanon largely under Maronite Christian domination. Although described in the Western press as a "Christian vs. Muslim" religious war, a more accurate description is that it started as a struggle for power between the haves and have-nots. The war has, over the years, caused numerous realignments of loyalties and alliances among the myriad factions.

Under Lebanon's system, the president must be a Maronite Christian. Although positions in the cabinet are allotted to other religions, the bulk of power belongs to the presidency.

In 1970, Israel began bombing south Lebanon hoping to create Lebanese anger toward the Palestinians. The policy worked. The bombing began driving poor Shiite Muslims out of their villages in the south of Lebanon. Beirut was inundated with these new refugees whose misery and discontent added to the already bubbling Palestinian refugee camps there. Although Lebanon's confessional system was created in 1943 when Christians were a majority, the increasing numbers of poor Shiites and Palestinian refugees threatened to upset the old balance of power.

Armed Palestinian fighters angered many Lebanese in the years prior to the 1982 invasion by setting up checkpoints and generally exerting control over unarmed Lebanese citizens, actions which exacerbated the crumbling political structure. Desperate to retain the privileges the French had written into the law for them, elite Maronites adopted the Phalangist philosophy of "drive out the Palestinians." The Phalangists formed an alliance with Israel, which furnished them with weapons, money, and military support.

With the Arab nations in disarray, partly as a result of their internal bickering, and partly because of the Lebanese civil war, which gave expression to the Arab world's own infighting, it remained for Israel, with the help of the United States, to neutralize Egypt with a separate peace.

The Camp David Agreements: Egypt Opts Out

When Anwar Sadat went to Jerusalem in November 1977, he was denounced by several Arab governments—those traditionally called "rejectionist"—for the potential of his visit to sell out the Palestinians.

Less than a year later, when Sadat, Carter, and Begin signed the Camp David accords—a separate peace between Israel and Egypt—their predictions were proved correct.

The agreements signed at Camp David were hyped, unmercifully, by Carter and his administration as a giant step toward peace in the Middle East. But Menachem Begin hardly waited for the ink to dry before he began destroying the parts of the agreement he had not wanted in the first place.

His interpretation of the accords was so narrow that they lost nearly all meaning in their application to the Palestinians and the West Bank.

The accords said that the question of sovereignty of the West Bank and Gaza would be negotiated after five years, but on September 19, 1978, two days after the agreements had been signed, Begin went before the u.s. Congress and declared, "I believe with all my heart that the Jewish people have a right to sovereignty over Judea and Samaria." The following day in New York, he told Jewish-American leaders, "I hereby declare the Israeli Defense Forces will stay in Judea, Samaria, and the Gaza Strip to defend our people and make sure Jewish blood is not shed again. I hereby declare they will stay beyond five years." As for the phrase "legitimate rights of the Palestinians," used in the agreements to acknowledge Palestinian concerns, Begin declared that it "has no meaning." He had accepted the phrase only to please Carter and Sadat, "and because it does not change reality."

President Carter claimed Begin had misled him on the issue of a moratorium on settlements. Carter perceived the agreement between Begin and himself to be a moratorium on settlement activity on the West Bank during negotiations for autonomy, meaning that there could be no new settlements for a minimum of five years. Carter believed, as they terminated the Camp David negotiations, that Begin had agreed to the five-year period. But Begin claimed his agreement was only for three months, a deadline Carter had set for signing a formal peace treaty between Egypt and Israel.

It became obvious to everyone that Begin had no intention of accommodating the Palestinians, and that he had intended the Camp David agreements to neutralize Egypt and nothing else.

Reaction by the Arab governments crystallized into strong opposition to the Camp David accords, including that from Saudi Arabia and Jordan, two countries where Jimmy Carter made a special effort to get endorsements. Egypt became totally isolated in the Arab world.

To further shove the distasteful results down President Carter's throat, in November, Begin asked Carter for a grant of $3.37 billion. Otherwise, he said, Israel could not afford to sign the peace treaty with Egypt requiring it to withdraw from the Sinai.

The centerpiece of Camp David was the separate treaty to be signed between Israel and Egypt. Also to be formed was an Administrative Council in the Arab territories occupied by Israel, consisting of representatives of Egypt, Israel, Jordan, and the Palestinians. The council was to move the Palestinians in the occupied territories toward "autonomy," a term deliberately left vague by the three negotiators.

As Edward Said has stated repeatedly, somehow the Palestinians are never allowed to speak for themselves. There is always someone else to speak for them. In the case of Camp David, three governments—Israel, Egypt, and the United States—not only spoke for, but made major decisions on their behalf and without their agreement. The result was, of course, another in a long line of big power abandonments of the rights of the Palestinians. Nowhere in the Camp David accords was there language adequate to preserve the Palestinians' right to self-determination, or for withdrawal of Israel as their occupiers. Nothing in the agreement prevented Israel from retaining indefinite control over the West Bank and Gaza. The Camp David accords were a sham—a device that served the purposes of each of the parties participating, but did nothing for a comprehensive peace. Carter got a badly needed public relations boost as someone who could accomplish "big plays in foreign policy"; Begin got Egypt out of the way, an aim Israeli leaders had desperately wanted for years; and Sadat received badly needed American aid money, which is still being pumped into Egypt today. It is money whose basic purpose is not to help Egypt economically, but to help Israel militarily by removing any military threat on its Egyptian border. It's more than obvious that if Egypt were to cancel its treaty with Israel, American money would stop flowing to Egypt. The money is nothing more than a bribe paid by the United States to Egypt to keep it neutralized, and as such, should properly be counted as part of American aid to Israel.

The principal problem with the Administrative Council was that it required unanimity to decide any matter before it. When President Carter and Secretary of State Cyrus Vance briefed members of Congress on the Camp David accords at the White House, I asked them what they thought would happen if the Arab members of the council voted an independent Palestinian state in the occupied territories. While Carter listened, Vance flatly stated, "It would most likely be vetoed by Israel. And we would agree with that. Our position is that we're against an independent Palestinian state."

During all the hype of the Camp David matter, no one in the U.S. government cared—even if they understood—what would happen in the Middle East if Egypt—the most powerful Arab country—were removed from the Arab bloc. Israel, already militarily more powerful than all the Arab countries combined, would now have virtually no opposition to its objectives.

Since it is militarily the most powerful country in the Middle East, and perhaps the fourth or fifth most powerful in the world, Israel sees no need to negotiate a return of territory taken by force of arms. So long as the United States serves as its financier and protector, its policy of intimidation will continue to be the basis of Middle East policy.

Thus, after Egypt was, as they say, co-opted out of the Middle East equation by the Camp David accords, and corrupted out of it by American aid money—now some $2.5 billion each year—there remains no combination of Arab countries with enough military power to curb Israel's aggressive tendencies.

We have seen, since then, more evidence than we need of Israel's continuing aggression.

Instead of making Israel more peaceful, once unleashed from the threat of an Egyptian front, its rulers:

■ formally annexed Jerusalem on July 30, 1980, and declared it Israel's united capital.

■ using u.s.-made planes, bombed a civilian nuclear reactor near Baghdad on June 8, 1981, under the pretense that it had the potential to make nuclear weapons. This was done although Iraq has permitted inspections by the International Atomic Energy Agency of its facilities; interestingly, Israel has never permitted such an inspection of its Dimona nuclear facility, where it manufactures nuclear bombs.

■ terror-bombed Beirut's Fakhani district on July 17, 1981— primarily a civilian area, under the pretense that the p.l.o. headquarters was there. More than three hundred civilians were killed in that air raid, which lasted only twenty minutes.

■ on December 14, 1981, declared the Golan Heights were under Israeli civil law, in effect annexing the Syrian territory.

■ invaded Lebanon in the summer of 1982 with its military, concluding with the siege of Beirut and ultimately slaughtering eighteen thousand civilians, wounding more than thirty thousand, and destroying the homes of more than three hundred thousand. The invasion was done under one pretense—that Shlomo Argov, the Israeli ambassador to the United Kingdom, was shot by the p.l.o. Without waiting to learn who had pulled the trigger, on June 4, General Ariel Sharon ordered the Israeli Air Force to attack "p.l.o."

targets in Lebanon, killing forty-five people, and wounding one hundred fifty more. The P.L.O. retaliated against this violation of the cease-fire, which it had observed since July 1981, by shelling settlements in northern Israel. Two days later, on June 6, 1982, Sharon ordered the invasion of Lebanon. It was learned within a day or two that Argov was shot by an anti-P.L.O. group, after which the Israeli excuse for the invasion changed from revenge for the Argov shooting to putting an end to the cross-border shelling by the P.L.O. in northern Israel.

The public learned, belatedly, that the P.L.O. had scrupulously observed an eleven-month cease-fire in the southern Lebanon-northern Israel area, while at the same time Israel violated the cease-fire hundreds of times in an effort to try to draw the P.L.O. into conflict. There was no question that Sharon and Rafael Eytan, the Israeli Army's chief of staff, were doing their best to find an excuse to invade Lebanon. Although unstated at the time, they had two major reasons for the invasion—to destroy the growing P.L.O. influence in the West Bank; and to install Bashir Gemayel as president of Lebanon. The most dangerous threat to Israel was not P.L.O. guns, but P.L.O. diplomacy. The fact that Arafat was moving his constituency in the direction of dialogue and diplomacy and away from armed struggle was a political danger to those in Israel who would stop at nothing to hold on to the West Bank and the Gaza Strip. The slaughter in Lebanon then followed.

Such big gun diplomacy, destructive even for big powers, is even more disastrous when played by a regional power such as Israel—disastrous for the Lebanese and Palestinians who were its victims.

None of the aggression on the part of Israel, and its financing by the United States, could have been possible without the aid of a racist campaign against Arabs and people of Arab descent.

Racism as an Aid to Conquest

*I*sraeli propagandists have had a number of great successes over the years. Numbered among them has been the creation of a series of myths about Arabs and Jews.

One of the most repeated myths about the Arab-Israeli conflict is that it is age-old. "They've been fighting for thousands of years, and they'll fight for thousands more" is the cliché I've heard most often. The fact is that the Arab-Israeli conflict is relatively recent. Before the creation of the Zionist movement around the turn of this century Jews lived more harmoniously with Arabs than with any other ethnic group. Most notably, Arabs were the champions of human rights for Jews as far back as the Spanish Inquisition, welcoming them into their countries as they tried to escape persecution.

Advancing the notion that it's an old fight, and that "you can't do anything about it" is a wonderful way to make Americans throw up their hands and let someone else worry about the problem. This pox-on-both-your-houses attitude permits the Congress and the administration to operate in a political vacuum with respect to the Middle East. The tragedy of this attitude is that the government is so heavily influenced by the Israeli lobby, that, rather than providing a solution, it contributes to the problem.

One of the more enduring myths about the Arab-Israeli conflict is that "little" Israel stood against the might of the combined Arab armies in 1948, eventually defeating them. At the termination of the British mandate in May 1948, the Arab military forces inside Palestine and on its borders totaled thirty-three thousand men. Opposing the Arab units were more than forty thousand full-time Jewish troops supported by fifty thousand militia. But the myth of a "miracle victory" has been extremely important for Israel's public relations in the United States, where most people choose to side with the underdog.

"The Arabs have threatened to drive the Jews into the sea," goes the old story, evoking strong emotions from anyone who hears it. And well it should, that is, if it were true. As a propaganda weapon, it is a magnificent statement.

The most direct response to this allegation is that provided by Christopher Mayhew, a former British member of parliament, who is now a member of the House of Lords. In his letter to the editor of the October 19, 1986 London *Sunday Times*, Mayhew wrote:

> How did you come to inform your readers [front page, October 5] that "hostile Arab governments . . . have sworn at various times to try to destroy Israel and sweep its people into the sea?" This myth was first disseminated by Zionist propaganda in the late 1960s, and has long since been discredited.

In 1973, I made an offer on television and in the House of Commons to pay £5,000 to anyone who could provide documentation for it. A number of eager claimants wrote in, and I would write back explaining that their chosen statement was a misquotation or mistranslation, or straight invention, as the case might be, but always inviting them, if they disagreed, to take me to court.

Eventually, a young Jewish lawyer did take me to court, (Bergson v. Mayhew 1974 No. 8264). His lawyers sent mine a blood-curdling, genocidal statement by Azzam Pasha, a former secretary general of the Arab League. My lawyers replied with the original text in Arabic, showing that the claim was based on a grotesque mistranslation.

At this, my adversaries tried to withdraw, but I refused, and had them declare in open court that after considerable research they had been unable to discover any evidence of any eligible statement by any Arab leader.

Zionist arguments against Israel making peace with the Palestinians are equally subject to historical misinterpretation. Because the real origins of the conflict have been distorted, Americans are susceptible to the argument that Palestinians are not entitled to political and civil rights. With this belief firmly implanted in the American mind, whatever the Arabs do or say is easily put down as not serious, or unworthy of consideration either by Israelis or by Americans.

If we accept the proposition advanced by Zionist apologists (most notably author Joan Peters, who wrote *From Time Immemorial*, and her claque) that the Palestinians never existed in Palestine, then we would feel no moral compulsion to return land taken from them. We also fall prey to other arguments designed to allow Israel to retain land it has taken illegally by force. For example, "we cannot allow the West Bank to be made into a Palestinian state, since it would endanger Israel, because geographically it would become too narrow at that point, making its defense too difficult." This so-called security argument was offered after the American public, and even some government officials, refused to accept the fallacious biblical reasons offered to justify Israel's retention of "Judea and Samaria."

Israel's supporters argue that Israel was created by the United Nations. This myth has been spread both by those who know better, as well as by those who do not. There is a straightforward historical fact here that cannot honestly be refuted. The United Nations did not create Israel, and when it did not, Israel then created itself by force of arms.

When, in November of 1947, the United Nations General Assembly voted the partition plan, it was never ratified by the U.N. Security Council. Because a General Assembly vote is non-binding, the plan was never adopted. If we accept that General Assembly votes are binding, then we would expect that Israel would abide by the dozens of such votes taken since 1947 which call on Israel to withdraw from the occupied territories; to allow the Palestinians to return; to stop building settlements; to stop bombing civilians; and on and on and on. Because the vote was toothless, and because the Arabs vehemently objected to it, Israel then announced its own creation in May 1948, holding its guns ready for the expected violent reaction from the Arab world.

And it came.

But the propaganda skill of the Israelis, assisted by the major American and European media, made what was nothing more than a naked land grab appear to be a "fight for independence," an interesting euphemism for what really happened.

Political decisions made by Americans over the years have been based, in part, on seriously distorted public images created about Arabs and Israelis. Because Arabs generally have eschewed Western public relations efforts, employed with great effectiveness by Israel and its supporters, no one should be surprised that Israel has, by and large, created a "good guy" image for itself, and a "bad guy" image for Arabs. But one must ask if the image matches reality. Is it humanly possible that all Arabs are bad, as we are told, and all Jews are good? Common sense, of course, tells us that it is not possible, yet the image promoted by the Israeli propaganda machine, and advanced by the American media persists.

The consequence of such image making is that journalists, and others, find it easy to ignore the sufferings of Arab people, encouraging the notion that the life of a Jew is worth more than the life of an Arab.

Americans get the distinct impression from the media that Arabs have violence in their genes. In most cases, "Muslim," "Arab," of late, "Shiite," and occasionally, "Palestinian," are used interchangeably. Most Israeli politicians such as Menachem Begin, former Israeli ambassador to the United States, Moshe Arens, and Israel's U.N. Ambassador Benjamin Netanyahu have never missed an opportunity to call a Palestinian, or a south Lebanese, a "terrorist."

Albert Speer, Hitler's industrial organizer in the Third Reich and one of the more experienced practitioners of racism, once said in a *Playboy* interview, "If I had to draw one single lesson from the horrors of World War II, it would be not to depersonalize your enemy. Once this happens—whether it is a case of a Nazi or a Jew, Communist or a Capitalist or Black and White—the greatest crimes are not only feasible but inevitable."

Anti-Arab racism became official in the United States when the F.B.I. set up its first "sting" operation in 1980, which it called "Abscam." An Italian-American F.B.I. agent dressed himself as a gulf Arab, in white robes and kafiyeh, then proceeded to bribe a number of congressmen in exchange for supposed flavors. Although there had never been a case where an Arab was even suspected of trying to bribe a U.S. official, the director of the F.B.I., William Webster, explained that they had to pick some symbol of corruption convincing enough to fool the members of Congress targeted. So they picked Arabs.

Webster was expressing a view presumably held in silence by the public. He was prescient. The congressmen trapped in bribery by the F.B.I. believed it, and most of the public believed it. A cab driver in Philadelphia, commenting on the Pennsylvania congressman caught in the F.B.I.'s trap said, "He shouldn't have taken the money from those Arabs." The stereotype of a corrupt and corrupting Arab became institutionalized. Instead of the U.S. government combatting such racism, it has contributed to it, and continues to do so to this day.

The effort at dehumanization has proceeded at full pace, with people of Arab descent now fully branded with a one-dimensional, negative image. Arabs are portrayed in the American media, mostly in feature films and television, as anonymous, kafiyeh-hooded, evil, violent, womanizing, spendthrift people. They have been accorded no positive attributes by those who purvey fiction, or ostensible fact, to the American public.

We have been made to understand what propels the Jewish psyche in a hundred films and in a thousand books to the point that no human being with even the slightest bit of sensitivity can avoid knowing how Jews feel about their condition.

Everything that has been said by and about Soviet-Jewish dissidents in the American press—and it has been plenty—would be even more appropriately said about Palestinian dissidents in the occupied territories. It is more appropriate because the Israelis are guilty of gross violations of the Palestinians' rights as occupiers of other people in their own land.

It is no less necessary for Americans to know that Arabs are also sensitive, to learn what drives them, whether they are working class Arabs who resent the oil sheikh image, or Palestinian nationalists who resent being labeled terrorists.

As though to confirm the point, and to make certain that only Israelis are qualified to give the Palestinians' point of view, the u.s. government will permit travel in the United States by p.l.o. diplomats and other spokesmen only if they make no public statements. It is not a question of security. The State Department allows their presence here, but not their opinions. This, in a country which jealously protects freedom of speech even for spokesmen from the Soviet Union, a country always defined as the principal threat to the United States.

A spate of exploitation feature films have been made in recent years, vilifying Arabs, Muslims, Palestinians and Shiites to the applause of those who go to the movies. A new dimension to some anti-Arab exploitation films is their production in Israel, with the Israeli military willingly lending its locations and facilities—American-made jet fighters and personnel—to the filmmakers. Thus, the American taxpayer pays part of the bill for films designed to propagandize him, presumably so he will send more of this taxes to Israel to combat the "Arab terrorists" portrayed in the films.

Movies that would otherwise be very entertaining, such as *Back to the Future,* somehow find it necessary to insert a "Libyan terrorist" totally out of context, a clearly gratuitous bit of racism given to us by the film's producers.

The result is the negative image of Arabs, which is a perfect setup for them to become political targets.

The campaign has worked.

When President Reagan needed to make what he considered a political statement following two terrorist incidents in Europe, he

120 *Through Different Eyes*

took advantage of the ongoing campaign of vilification against Qaddafi's Libya and ordered a bombing raid on its capital, Tripoli. Citing
solid "evidence"—never produced—of Libyan responsibility for a
bombing in Germany, Reagan received widespread public support
for the raid, despite the fact that a number of innocent civilians were
killed, including Colonel Qaddafi's daughter. No press report on the
raid since that time has ever failed to mention that the death of
Qaddafi's daughter is a "reported" death, and not, apparently, a real
one, presumably in an effort to soften the effect of what was clearly
an act of terrorism by President Reagan.

Downplayed in the press following the raid were several reports
that perhaps it was not Libya which was responsible for the terrorist
incidents, but maybe Syria.

Arnaud de Borchgrave, the hard-line editor of the *Washington
Times,* ran two front page stories citing an interview with French
Premier Chirac, who was in turn told by West Germany's Helmut
Kohl that an attempted bombing of an El Al 747 in London in 1986
was the work of Israel's covert operations network, the Mossad,
along with disgruntled Syrian intelligence agents. The German mag-
azine, *Der Spiegel,* carried an article in November 1986 quoting
West German security forces who made the same judgment. The
two Jordanians convicted of the West German bombings and the
El Al attempted bombing were double agents working for the
Mossad.

And in the fall of 1986, pronouncements leaked from the White
House warning of more Libyan "terrorist attacks." It was later disclosed that the leaks from the administration were deliberate plants,
phony stories given to the press to "warn" Qaddafi against any future
terrorist actions. There were no questions about whether any of the
other accusations against Arab countries were also disinformation.
And there was no clarification, no follow-up by the media, and no
apologies to Qaddafi for the naked attempt to assassinate him, or for
the slaughter of the civilians. That the build-up of hatred toward
Libya worked was evident when a friend who lives in California told
me, "We kind of thought Qaddafi had it coming."

The pace of anti-Arab racism was set much earlier by Golda
Meir, who had even less sympathy for Palestinians than Menachem
Begin. She said in 1969, "When was there an independent Pales-
tinian people with a Palestinian state? It was either southern Syria

before the First World War, and then it was a Palestine including Jordan. It was not as though there was a Palestinian people and we came and threw them out and took their country away from them. They did not exist."

Prime Minister Meir almost exceeded that statement when she told Barbara Walters during a "Today Show" interview that Israelis were different from the Arabs. Israelis, she said, were respectful of human life, which was why they tried to avoid involvement in wars. Arabs, on the other hand, were indifferent to human life, which was why, she said, they were so aggressive and started so many wars against Israel. Her statement was never challenged by Walters, or by anyone else on the network.

When Menachem Begin announced to the world the Israeli bombing of the Iraqi nuclear reactor in 1981, he said that the raid was timed for a Sunday, "on the assumption that the one hundred to one hundred and fifty foreign experts employed at the reactor would be absent on the Christian day of rest." Begin's statement continued by saying, "This assumption proved to have been correct. No foreign specialists were hurt."

Similarly, the 1981 Israeli bombing raid on the Fakhani district in central Beirut which killed more than three hundred people, was in, as Begin said, "only the Palestinian area" in Beirut.

Not to be outdone, General Rafael Eytan, who was Israeli Defense Force (I.D.F.) chief of staff during the 1982 Israeli invasion of Lebanon, said in a speech to the Knesset, "If there are more than one hundred settlements between Nablus and Jerusalem—and there will be—then the Arabs can run about like drugged cockroaches inside a bottle."

Official racism against Arabs has, of course, spilled over into the Israeli public.

When Amos Oz undertook his travels through Israel, he found, apparently to his surprise, a great deal of anti-Arab racism by Jews he encountered in the settlements of Bet Shemesh and Tekoa.

In his book *The Land of Israel,* Amos Oz quotes a Moroccan Jew living in Bet Shemesh:

What did they bring my parents to Israel for? I'll tell you what for, but you won't write this. You'll think it's just provocation. But wasn't it to do your dirty work? You didn't have Arabs then, so you needed our parents to do your cleaning and be your servants and your laborers. And policemen too. You brought our parents to be your Arabs.

If they give back the territories, the Arabs will stop coming to work, and then and there you'll put us back into the dead-end jobs like before. If for no other reason, we won't let you give back those territories. . . . Look at my daughter: she works in a bank now, and every evening an Arab comes to clean the building. All you want is to dump her from the bank into some textile factory, or have her wash the floors instead of the Arab. The way my mother used to clean for you.

Meron Benvenisti, the former deputy mayor of Jerusalem, wrote in his book, *Conflicts and Contradictions,* that the Arabs in Israel were always perceived there as an "integral part of the scenery though never as a legitimate entity in their own right, with their own national consciousness and aspirations." Many abandoned Arab villages, Benvenisti writes, are meticulously preserved with due attention to setting and scale, but empty of Arabs and designated as "artists' colonies."

Literature about Jewish settlers in the West Bank is replete with remarks like this one quoted in David Shipler's *Arab and Jew,* "We can get along with the Arabs so long as they understand this is our land and that we are the rulers here."

Israeli propagandists have done their work so well that American journalists and politicians, ordinarily sensitive to racism of this nature, have completely blanked out both the racist intent and concern for the victims themselves.

The racist dehumanization of Arabs which has spilled over from Zionist strategy carries serious implications both for America and for Arabs, wherever they might be. If using racist images can create enough public anger toward an ethnic group, political and military decisions that might once have been difficult, become much easier to make. Two examples follow.

■ Although it occurred in the United States, the assassination of Alex Odeh was largely ignored by the press because he was an Arab American, while at the same time, the murder of Leon Klinghoffer during the *Achille Lauro* hijacking was played in a major way.

■ Because of the inaccurate oversimplification of how Lebanon has been portrayed in the press over the years—Muslim vs. Christian—President Reagan was permitted to send American Marines there in 1983 with orders to effectively side with the Phalangist factions (Reagan must have believed he was helping the Lebanese government). This action, and the merciless shelling of Lebanese villages by the uss *New Jersey*, caused so much anger that the United States, once thought of as a friendly power by the Lebanese, has become a pariah. Not only have Americans been kidnapped with regularity, but 265 Marines were killed when their barracks were destroyed by a suicide bomber in 1983.

Racism does indeed make anything possible, and also inevitable. Tragically, it can also work to justify state terrorism.

Terrorism and the Media

*I*n his most recent book, *Pirates and Emperors*, Noam Chomsky relates a story credited to St. Augustine, concerning a pirate captured by Alexander the Great, who asked the pirate, "how he dares molest the sea."

"How dare you molest the whole world? Because I do it with a little ship only, I am called a thief; you, doing it with a great navy, are called an Emperor." It describes perfectly the perspective from which the American media and American politicians view the Middle East conflict.

In 1985 the Israeli Ministry of Foreign Affairs issued a white paper entitled "The Threat of p.l.o. Terrorism" which flatly states that since February 1969, when Yasir Arafat became chairman of the p.l.o.'s executive committee, "the p.l.o. has perpetrated some 8,000 acts of terror, causing the deaths of over 650 Israelis, and the wounding of thousands more."

The grisly business of body counts was popularized during the Johnson administration as evidence of who was winning the Vietnam War—their side or ours. The trouble with an inventory of dead bodies is that it eventually numbs the listeners' sensitivity to death. During the Vietnam War, body counts of Vietnamese dead fell on mostly indifferent American ears, although our military was credited with killing millions, mostly civilians. We were treated each day with a new body count, ever higher, and so long as it was "one of them," a subhuman, one who had been properly depersonalized, there was little objection in the United States.

But when we started counting bodies of our own, the Vietnam War quickly became an issue commanding our attention. It eventually tore apart the fabric of American society, establishing a new and unwanted culture and politics of polarization. There was little grief directed toward the "brown people" we were killing by the thousands in Southeast Asia. We never knew how their families felt. If there was any comment at all, it was similar to the one General William Westmoreland made—recorded in the film, *Hearts and Minds*—that life is cheap in Vietnam. We were told not to care about the lives we snuffed out over there because they were not like us. We may never know the grief suffered by the families of those we killed and maimed in Southeast Asia, but we will never forget those of our own who died.

Body counts, however, are simply too abstract to allow us to associate sympathetically with the victims. We need names, families, places, pictures to build anger against the commission of violence by humans against humans.

One of the reasons we know, without the Israeli Foreign Ministry telling us, that the P.L.O. is responsible for the deaths of 650 Israelis is both the quantity and quality of press coverage they got. We saw on television, night after night, the grieving families, the vows of revenge, and the funeral marches for the Israelis killed.

In addition to the Israeli civilians killed by the P.L.O., we were informed, on a day-to-day basis, exactly how many Israeli soldiers were killed by Lebanese resistance fighters during the occupation of south Lebanon by those resisting the occupation. We were given their names and we watched their funerals in the print press and on network television.

We know precisely how many Israelis have been killed. But we may never know how many Arab men, women, and children have died at the hands of Israeli pilots, gunners, and infantrymen, murdered with the use of American weapons, American money, and American political protection, allowing Israel to conceal the crime. Conservatively, more than twenty-two thousand Arabs have been killed by Israeli state terrorism since 1969. Many more were killed by Jewish terrorists before 1969. We never saw their funerals or grieved along with their families because American television and American newspapers for some reason chose not to cover them. No one ever counted the thousands more killed as Israeli jets indiscriminately bombed Palestinian refugee camps overflowing with civilians.

When it is Arabs who are being killed and mutilated and whose families are grieving it doesn't seem to matter.

This double standard is without question grounded in racism. How else does one explain the way the Middle East conflict is covered in the American press, or the hypocrisy of u.s. officials, such as President Reagan and Secretary of State George Shultz, who respond in vastly different ways to the same kind of violence, depending on who is responsible?

Six hundred fifty Israelis killed over a seventeen-year period averages slightly more than thirty-eight people killed each year—in the scheme of things, not very many; that is, unless you happen to be one of those killed, or one of their family members.

In 1985, when Palestinian terrorists murdered Leon Klinghoffer, President Reagan repeatedly denounced those responsible. Hardly a day went by without a statement from him about the murder announced in apocalyptic terms by the media. Reagan telephoned Klinghoffer's family. New York Senator Alfonse D'Amato suggested the Congressional Medal of Honor for the unfortunate Klinghoffer. Newspaper and television outlets described for us the lives from birth of Klinghoffer and his family. At the end there was little we did not know about this tragic victim.

At the same time, in October 1985, a Palestinian American, Alex Odeh, was assassinated in Reagan's home state of California by unknown assassins, later identified by the f.b.i. in its 1985 annual report on domestic terrorism as "Jewish extremists." (It was one of five acts of terrorism in the United States the f.b.i. said were committed by Jewish extremists, out of a total of seven during 1985.) Neither Reagan nor Shultz commented on this act of terrorism in their own back yard. There was nothing but silence. Eventually an anonymous, written handout was issued from the White House deploring the killing. It received virtually no coverage. Reagan never bothered to telephone Mrs. Odeh and her three small children left fatherless by the assassin's bomb.

Although the Congressional Medal of Honor most likely would have amused Alex Odeh's family, even amid the sadness of his passing, there was no gesture of sorrow, or of compassion, either by the administration, or by Odeh's two U.S. senators, Pete Wilson and Alan Cranston. Aside from a sympathetic story about Odeh by *Washington Post* reporter Jay Matthews, newspaper reports of the assassination were small blurbs, describing the death of a "P.L.O. supporter." The *Des Moines Register*'s headline over the story of Odeh's murder was, to say the least, descriptive: "Arafat Man of Peace—Boom."

The article referred to a television interview Odeh had given the night before his death in which he denounced the *Achille Lauro* hijacking, but also described Arafat as a Palestinian leader who wanted peace for his people.

Is the life of an Arab American worth less than the life of a Jewish American?

Is the life of an Arab worth less than the life of an Israeli?

Because of the headlong rush to please Israel and its supporters in the United States, have we created a racist atmosphere designed to minimize Arabs and Arab Americans as human beings? The evidence is overwhelming that we have.

When Americans become targets of angry Palestinians or Lebanese, we are surprised, and ask ourselves why is it happening to us? We do not make the connection between the devastation of Israel's bombing of civilians in Lebanon and the furnishing of planes and bombs by the United States because the media chooses not to tell us of the connection. And when we are kept ignorant of what is being done in our name, we do not try to stop it. As in the case of so many foreign policy mistakes, the victims of our weaponry are fully informed of who is furnishing the bombs, but it is kept from those of us who are held responsible by the victims. And it is average Americans who pay for the careless foreign policy disasters, not those who are so irresponsible in making policy. Sometimes, as in the case of the marines in Beirut, they pay with their lives.

The following is only a partial catalogue—a counter-body count—of terrorism conducted by Israel since 1969, the same period surveyed by the Israeli Foreign Ministry:

■ January 6, 1969: Israeli artillery and helicopters fired on the village of Safi, Jordan killing three civilians and wounding five.

■ March 26, 1969: Israeli jets attacked a resthouse near al-Salt, Jordan, killing eighteen Jordanian civilians and wounding twenty-five.

■ August 11, 1969: Israeli jets bombed near Mt. Hermon in south Lebanon, killing four civilians and seriously wounding three.

■ February 12, 1970: Israeli jets launched a bombing raid on a Cairo suburb, al-Khanka, dropping a bomb on a scrap metal plant, killing seventy Egyptian civilians and wounding ninety-eight.

■ April 8, 1970: Israeli jets bombed Baqr al Baqr village in Egypt, killing thirty children when their bombs struck a school.

■ May 25, 1970: Israeli jets bombed Bint Jubayil village in south Lebanon, killing twenty civilians and wounding forty.

■ July 8, 1972: Israeli agents in Beirut planted a bomb in the car of Ghassan Kanafani, a Palestinian novelist and editor, killing him and his sixteen-year-old niece.

■ September 16, 1972: Israel invaded southern Lebanon after two Israeli soldiers were killed the previous day in an ambush on the Golan Heights. Instead of hitting Syria, an Israeli force of three thousand troops protected by tanks and air cover invaded fifteen miles into Lebanon, looted and marauded for a day and a half. Israel said "at least sixty" guerrillas were killed; the Palestinians reported thirty-five guerrillas, eighteen Lebanese soldiers, and twenty-three civilians killed. Israeli forces deliberately destroyed more than 150 homes in sixteen villages.

■ September 17, 1972: An Israeli tank deliberately drove over a taxi with nine passengers, killing all of them.

■ December 8, 1972: Israeli Mossad agents installed a remote-controlled bomb in the Paris home of Mahmoud Hamshari, a Palestinian leader and intellectual. Hamshari lost his leg in the explosion and subsequently died on January 8, 1973.

■ February 22, 1973: The Israeli Air Force shot down an unarmed Libyan airliner which had mistakenly flown over the Sinai, killing 108 innocent civilians on board.

■ April 6, 1973: Israeli agents gunned down and killed Dr. Basil al Kubaissi, an Iraqi political science professor, on a Paris street.

■ June 29, 1973: Israeli agents installed a bomb in the car of Mohammed Boudaiah, an Algerian poet. The explosion killed Boudaiah instantly.

■ July 21, 1973: Israeli agents gunned down Ahmed Bouchiki, a Moroccan waiter in Oslo, Norway. In the subsequent trial following the capture of the Israeli agents, it was disclosed that they killed Bouchiki when they mistook him for Ali Hassan Salameh, alleged by Israel to be a leader of the Black September organization. During the court proceedings, information was disclosed linking the Israeli agents to the murders in Europe of Wael Zuaiter, Mahmoud Hamshari, and other Palestinians.

On March 15, 1978, Israel launched an invasion of southern Lebanon with twenty thousand troops. "Operation Litani" resulted in the death of more than a thousand civilians. Two hundred fifty thousand Lebanese became temporary refugees.

In a rare burst of candor at the time, Israeli Chief of Staff General Mordechai Gur, when asked by an Israeli newspaper whether efforts had been made to avoid civilian casualties, replied: "I am not one of those people who have a selective memory. Do you think that I pretend not to know what we have done all these years? What did we do to the entire length of the Suez canal [during the War of Attrition]—a million and a half refugees. Really, where do you live? We bombarded Ismailia, Suez, Port Said, and Port Fuad—a million and a half refugees. . . . Since when has the population of south Lebanon become so sacred?"

In further response to the question of whether Israeli attacks were not in retaliation for attacks on troops, Gur said, "Please be serious. Did you not know that the entire valley of the Jordan had been emptied of its inhabitants as a result of the War of Attrition?"

■ August 10, 1973: Israeli warplanes forced an Iraqi Airways passenger jet with seventy-four passengers, en route from Beirut to Baghdad, to land in Israel in the expectation that PFLP leader George Habash was aboard; he was not and the plane was allowed to fly on. The incident brought another unanimous condemnation of Israel from the U.N. Security Council, and a question by Foreign Minister Abba Eban as to whether his "government was still in full contact with international reality."

And on and on and on it goes.

Over the years, America experienced a kind of domestic terrorism against blacks in the South. In the 1960s, the self-styled White Citizens Council, a marauding band of white racists protected by local police complicity and indifference, roamed through black neighborhoods destroying property, assaulting defenseless blacks, and, in general, terrorizing the black community.

■ In behavior identical to that of the White Citizens Council, Jewish settlers, over the years, have terrorized Palestinian Arabs in villages in the occupied territories. For example, in June 1980, they committed the horrendous crime of planting bombs in the cars of West Bank mayors Bassam Shaka of Nablus, Karim Khalaf of Ramallah, whose legs were blown off, and of Mayor Ibrahim Tawil of El Bireh, who escaped. The Jewish terrorists responsible for the bombings were caught, tried, and convicted, but in every case where the courts had leeway, the sentences were made lighter, giving the strong implication of community and official approval of the crimes. Arabs committing the same crimes consistently receive the maximum sentence allowed under the law.

If we value human life, we cannot help but grieve for the death of the 650 Israelis, and, beyond that, for the innocent Jews who were senselessly murdered in the Istanbul synagogue in 1986, and for innocents everywhere.

And we must remember—so it will not happen again—the madness of Hitler's extermination of approximately six million Jews prior to 1945 throughout Europe. But it is important to know that it was not the Palestinians who committed this horrible crime. They should not be made to pay—with their land and with their lives—for crimes perpetrated by the Nazis. The horrors of the Holocaust should not justify committing similar crimes against the Palestinians, with seemingly total absolution by the Western world.

■ During a twenty-minute bombing raid on the Fakhani district of Beirut, more than 300 Lebanese and Palestinian civilians were killed by the Israeli Air Force. Once we have vented our rage at the killing of 650 Israelis, is it possible for us to be outraged by the wanton murder of Arabs as well?

■ In an ultimate act of terrorism in the summer of 1982, more than eighteen thousand Lebanese and Palestinian civilians were killed by the Israeli military; and more than thirty thousand were wounded when they invaded Lebanon. During the siege of Beirut, the Israelis poured into the heavily populated center of the city phosphorus bombs, napalm, and cluster bombs—each inhumanly destructive in its own way. When it comes into contact with the skin, phosphorus from the bombs burns inward, making it almost impossible for physicians to treat or to ease the pain and suffering of those who survive the initial impact of the bomb. The cluster bombs the Israelis dropped in Beirut mutilated and killed untold numbers of civilians. Many were small children, who, with normal childlike curiosity, died or were mutilated when they picked up unexploded bombs. To add to the suffering of the bombing casualties, Israel refused to allow medical supplies and water into the city for long periods of time, making it impossible for medical people to treat their victims.

■ In the fall of 1982, hundreds, perhaps as many as three thousand—the exact figure is unknown—helpless Palestinians in the refugee camps of Sabra and Shatila were murdered by heavily armed right-wing Lebanese Phalangist militiamen who were dispatched into the camps by the Israeli military.

Israeli tanks surrounded Sabra and Shatila camps about noon on September 15, 1982. Residents of the camps approached Israeli soldiers manning their positions around the camp exits expressing fears that armed Lebanese militiamen would try to enter the camps. The Israelis told them not to be afraid, then ordered them to return to their homes. Israeli General Amos Yaron, Israel's Beirut commander, provided aerial maps of the camps to his Phalangist allies, assisting them in finding ways to enter the camps. Later, during the night, the Israelis lit up the area with floodlights to assist the Phalangists in their butchery.

Israeli journalist Amnon Kapeliouk, the first journalist in the camps after the massacre, described it as follows:

> From the beginning, the massacre assumed huge proportions, according to those who escaped. Throughout those first hours, the Phalangist fighters killed hundreds of people. They shot at anything which moved in the alleys. Breaking down the doors of the houses, they liquidated entire families in the middle of their supper. Residents were killed in their beds, in pyjamas. In numerous apartments, one would find children of 3 or 4 years, also in pyjamas, wrapped up in blood-soaked blankets. But, often, the killers were not content just to kill. In very many cases, the assailants cut off the limbs of their victims before killing them. They smashed the heads of infants and babies against the walls. Women, and even young girls, were raped before being assassinated with hatchets. Sometimes, [the killers] left one single member of the family alive, killing the others before his eyes, so

that this unfortunate could afterwards tell what he had seen and been through.

When Palestinians tried to flee the slaughter in the camps, the Israeli soldiers surrounding the camps forced them back inside. At one point a group of about five hundred people tried to escape and an Israeli tank aimed its gun directly at them, forcing them to go back in. Kapeliouk estimated approximately three thousand people were slaughtered in the camps. This is a much higher figure than the seven hundred to eight hundred given by the Israelis.

■ In December 1985, sixty-eight people were killed and twenty-eight were wounded when Israeli jets flew all the way to Tunisia to bomb "P.L.O. headquarters," an act which incredibly drew a statement of approval from President Reagan. The statement was drafted by State Department legal adviser Abraham Sofaer, calling the bombing an appropriate response to an act of terror. Of course, he did not bother to specify for which act of terror the "response" was approved.

■ The number of bombing raids on Lebanon and on Palestinian refugee camps filled with women and children cannot be counted, but they have occurred regularly since 1970, and continue to this day. Although the average American may not make the connection, the knowledge that the terror delivered from the skies by the Israelis comes from American bombs dropped by American-made jets is not lost on those in Lebanon who are targets.

Israeli terror did not begin, however, in 1969. It was clear to the Zionists that establishing the state of Israel would require something extra—something other than diplomacy. That something was terrorism, and its success was manifested in the driving out of their homes of three-quarters of a million Palestinians, and the establishment of the exclusively Jewish state.

■ Before 1969, the major acts of Jewish and Israeli terrorism recorded include the sinking by Haganah terrorists of the ss *Patria* in November 1940. The ship carried helpless Jewish refugees to whom the British had refused entry into Haifa harbor. More than two hundred Jews lost their lives.

■ More than seven hundred Jewish refugees from Rumania were killed in February 1942, when Haganah terrorists blew up the MV

Struma in the Black Sea. The Jewish Agency declared it another act of mass protest, as it did when the *Patria* was sunk.

■ In November 1944, terrorists from the Stern Gang assassinated Lord Moyne, the British resident minister of state in Cairo. All the blustery rhetoric about terrorism heard from the Israeli government can be summarized in just one of its recent acts: In 1975, twenty-seven years after the Moyne assassination, Egypt returned to Israel the bodies of two terrorists who had been caught and executed for the crime. The remains of the two, Eliahu Hakim and Eliahu Bet-Zuri, were given full military honors in Israel, which included lying in state in the Hall of Heroism, and burial in that part of Israel's military cemetery reserved for heroes and martyrs. The president of Israel, the prime minister, and the minister of religious affairs were in attendance at the burial.

■ In July 1946, Menachem Begin's Irgun blew up the south wing of the King David Hotel in Jerusalem, killing and wounding more than two hundred people, including, according to Begin's memoirs, fifteen Jews.

■ Jewish terrorist groups introduced letter bombs in the Middle East. Many were sent to British politicians in London whom the terrorists considered enemies of Israel.

■ On April 9, 1948, the Irgun and the Stern Gang, operating together, massacred the inhabitants of Deir Yassin, a village in Palestine, killing at least 254 people. The two terrorist groups planned to evacuate the village by using loudspeakers, telling the villagers to leave. However, the initial gunfire between the terrorists and the villagers defending their homes drowned out the announcements.

The Jewish terrorists tossed grenades into houses filled with families, all of whom died. The terrorists then dynamited each house in Deir Yassin, one by one, firing on anyone who tried to escape. They shot a group of residents who had surrendered toward the end of the battle. The few survivors of the massacre were herded into trucks and paraded through the streets of Jerusalem before being released. Historians have speculated that by doing so the terrorists were sending a message of doom to Palestinians who did not flee Palestine.

■ On September 17, 1948, members of the Stern Gang assassinated Count Folke Bernadotte, the U.N. mediator in Palestine, during a visit to the Israeli-controlled section of Jerusalem. Then under the leadership of Yitzhak Shamir, now Israel's prime minister, the Jewish terrorists objected to Count Bernadotte's plan calling for Jordanian sovereignty over Jerusalem. They also objected to his proposal to allow 300,000 refugees to return to their homes.

■ In April 1950, in Baghdad, Iraq, the first of three bombs exploded, this one hurled from a passing car at a coffee shop where young Jewish intellectuals were gathered. The bomb, thought to be the work of Iraqi extremists, spread enough fear in the Iraqi Jewish community to cause a number of Jews to plan emigration to Israel. Not long afterward, another bomb exploded at the u.s. Information Center, where many young Jews came to read. Although Jewish registrants asking to emigrate to Israel had tapered off after the first bomb, there was another rush following the second bombing. Then, as March 1951 approached, the deadline set for renunciation of Iraqi citizenship, a third bomb exploded, this time killing a young Jewish boy and badly wounding the eyes of a man standing near him. The rush to emigrate reached panic stage, and when it finished, only five thousand Iraqi Jews remained in Iraq, out of 130,000.

Then the shocking news came that the bombings were the work of a Jewish underground group called "The Movement," which sought to frighten Iraqi Jews into emigrating to Israel. Those responsible were caught, tried, and convicted of the crimes.

■ In October 1953, a specially trained terrorist unit of the Israeli Defense Force—Unit 101—under the command of then Major Ariel Sharon, attacked the Jordanian village of Kibya in what was called a "reprisal" raid. The terrorists used automatic weapons and grenades first to blast through the village's defenses, then to force the villagers to hide in their homes. Afterwards they dynamited forty-one residences and a school building, killing fifty-three civilians.

Moshe Sharett, in his diary, noted his strong objection to the planned Kibya raid. The Kibya operation was ostensibly in reprisal for a minor incident along the Jordanian border. This pretext lost its credibility when Jordan publicly condemned the incident, and Jordanian representatives on the Mixed Armistice Commission promised that such incidents would be stopped. Sharett became convinced that the raid was an effort by Ben-Gurion to draw Jordan into a war with Israel. For his part, Ben-Gurion wanted the Israeli government to publicly blame the Kibya raid on outraged Israeli villagers along the Jordanian border. Ben-Gurion's position was incredibly cynical with respect to any Palestinian reprisals for the Kibya raid. By falsely blaming Israeli villagers living on the Jordanian border for the Kibya massacre, he unnecessarily put them in great danger.

■ In July 1954, Israeli agents undertook sabotage operations against Egyptian, British, and American targets in Cairo, Egypt. In what appeared to be a clumsy attempt to disrupt Egyptian-U.S. relations, the Israeli terrorists set fire to the U.S. Information Agency offices in Cairo and Alexandria, the Alexandria post office, the Cairo post office, and a British-owned theatre. Some of the terrorists were caught, some escaped to Israel, but the entire ring was broken. A great deal of controversy surrounded what came to be known as the "Lavon Affair," centering mostly on charges that the cover of the terrorists was deliberately blown by some Israeli government officials, upsetting attempts by Prime Minister Moshe Sharett to reach an accomodation with Egypt.

■ The first skyjacking in history was conducted by Israel's government December 12, 1954, when Israeli warplanes forced a Syrian civilian plane to land at Lydda airport in Israel. The passengers and crew were interrogated for two days until international protests forced their release. Moshe Sharett recorded in his diary part of a letter he wrote about the skyjacking to Foreign Minister Lavon:

> It must be clear to you that we had no justification whatsoever to seize the plane, and that once forced down we should have immediately released it and not held the passengers under interrogation for 48 hours. . . . What shocks and worries me is the narrow-mindedness and the short-sightedness of our military leaders. They seem to presume that the State of Israel may—or even must—behave in the realm of international relations according to the laws of the jungle.

■ On October 10, 1956, Israeli troops made a nighttime raid on the Jordanian village of Qalqilia, killing forty-eight Jordanian civilians.

■ On October 29, 1956, on the eve of Israel's invasion of Egypt's Sinai, the Israeli Army ordered all Israeli-Arab villages near the Jordanian border placed under curfew—from 5 P.M. until 6 A.M. the next day. The order said that there were to be no arrests and that any Arab found on the streets was to be shot. Israeli border policemen were given strict orders that no mercy was to be given, even to those Arabs who, because they were working in the field, did not know of the curfew.

Forty-seven Arabs were killed in cold blood by the Israelis before the slaughter ended, Arabs who were innocently returning to their village after a day's work. All were Israeli citizens.

No one—neither officers nor enlisted men—spent more than three-and-a-half years in jail for their crimes. In fact, David Ben-Gurion had urged substantial reductions in their original sentences.

According to David Shipler's account of the massacre in *Arab and Jew,* Colonel Yissachar Shadmi, the officer who gave the order, denied that he ordered no mercy be given. He was not prosecuted, but promoted to brigadier general. In 1982, he was an honored guest at President Yitzhak Navon's reception for soldiers wounded in the Lebanon invasion. He was described in an article in the *Jerusalem Post* as a "near-legendary figure in the army," which neglected to mention his part in the massacre at Kfar Kassem.

Major Shmuel Malinki, his subordinate, was sentenced to seventeen years in jail but was released after three years. He was reinstated as an officer and given a senior security post at the Dimona nuclear power plant.

Similar honors were given to Israeli Major General Amos Yaron, the Israeli commander in charge of Beirut when the Lebanese Phalangists massacred innocent Palestinian men, women, and children in Sabra and Shatila refugee camps in 1982.

Yaron was found by the Kahan Commission that investigated the affair to have tacitly approved the massacre of the civilians, and it was recommended that he be reprimanded and stripped of his command.

According to testimony given the commission, Yaron stood on the rooftop command post and allowed the Phalangists—murderers bent on revenge—through the Israeli lines and into the camps. He overheard the Phalangist commander, Elie Hobeika, give orders to kill Palestinian women and children. Yaron made no effort to stop Hobeika. Nor did he report to his superiors the slaughter that went on into the next day.

Although stripped of his command, Yaron was appointed chief of the Israeli Army's manpower branch and later promoted to major general. In August 1986, he was named military attaché in Washington, D.C., the most prestigious post for any Israeli officer.

■ December 28, 1968: Israeli commandos landed at Beirut International Airport, destroying thirteen civilian planes belonging to Arab airlines. The attack was in retaliation, the Israelis said, for a Palestinian attack on an Israeli El Al jetliner two days earlier in which one passenger was killed.

Books have been written about the operation of Jewish and Israeli terrorists and the tens of thousands of people they have killed and wounded over the years. Yet the man on the street invariably associates terrorism with Arabs. The Israeli catchword, "Arab terrorism," has made its way into everyday parlance, compliments of the U.S. media, allowing Israel to escape responsibility for its heinous crimes under the pretext that it is either "self-defense" or "retaliation."

When an Arab is killed or terrorized by an Israeli Phantom Jet, is it somehow different? Is death delivered from a distance more benign than death delivered in person? The complete blacking out by the press of the vast numbers of deaths of Arabs at the hands of the Israelis is, without question, racist in character, and dangerous in result.

Experience has shown that when the media covers up Israel's terrorism by calling it "retaliation" or a "search for terrorists," it only encourages more of the same. This journalistic double standard allows the Israelis to camouflage state terrorism with euphemisms.

The censorship by the press of the numerous deaths of Arabs at the hands of the Israelis is racist and repercussive. Israeli terrorism will continue if no one knows about it, but publicity will dampen it. For example, when several black clergymen visited south Lebanon in 1979 to publicize the Israeli bombing there, the bombing stopped for more than a year, saving untold numbers of lives during that time.

At this point, it's only proper to state my own position on terrorism. I am opposed to violence in any form. I strongly believe in freedom for people living under occupation. I'm convinced that in the long term the most practical resistance to occupation is nonviolence. It is a tactic which often can cause more suffering to those resisting, but it is more lasting. I am not one of those who can sit in the comfort of my home in Washington, D.C., and applaud violence being committed elsewhere.

I can distinguish, however, between the occupied, who by definition are the weaker of the two parties, and the occupiers, who are the stronger. The case of the Israelis and the people whose land they occupy is much like any occupation. Israel has done everything within its power to humiliate the Lebanese in south Lebanon, the Syrians in the occupied Golan Heights, and the Palestinians in the occupied territories. Israel has done everything in its power to make them into subhumans, to frustrate their nationalist dreams, to subject them to deportation, to economic injury, to imprisonment, to torture, and to death. It has prevented the Palestinians from expressing themselves either in the West Bank and Gaza, or in the United States, the country which writes the ticket for Israel's oppression.

Perhaps even worse than terrorism itself is the hypocrisy of the morality play acted out by people such as Reagan, and Ambassador Benjamin Netanyahu of Israel, in their shrill denunciations of "Arab terrorism." Is there a difference between a lone Palestinian placing a bomb in a Jerusalem marketplace, and the president of the most powerful country in the world in a tantrum-like frenzy ordering the bombing and shelling of Lebanese villages, or financing and training the Contras who specialize in raping women and killing children in their efforts to terrorize the Nicaraguan government? If the hijacking of an Israeli bus by Palestinians is terror, then how should we label Netanyahu's government when it orders the deliberate destruction of the USS *Liberty* or the shooting down of an unarmed Libyan passenger plane or the hijacking in 1986 of a small Libyan passenger jet with Syrian officials aboard or the bombing of civilian centers teeming with innocent people or the multitude of other acts of state terror that demagogues never mention? Calling such state terror "self-defense" cannot take the edge off the massive commission of such state terrorism. Individual Palestinians strongly believe—with better reason—that every act of violence committed by them is "self-defense" against aggression by the Israelis.

When the Israeli Air Force devastates a Palestinian refugee camp in Lebanon, the attack has nothing to do with "retaliation," but everything to do with intimidation. Such actions are taken whether or not there has been a prior act of violence directed toward Israel. Israel has worn out its traditional excuse that it is constantly under threat and such aggression is necessary. The P.L.O. has never been a military threat to Israel, but it has certainly been a political threat, which explains the overriding concern with it. Were it not for the protective cover given Israel by the media, its aggression would be seen for what it is—the bullying of a weaker people, and it is unseemly for the United States to support it.

One might wonder why the American public is silent about foreign aid to Israel. Providing American tax money—especially as an outright grant—for the indiscriminate slaughter of civilians and for the forceful taking of their territory would be unthinkable if it were done by any other country. Why, then, is there no public outcry when government belt-tightening is seriously damaging various segments of American society? The desperation of American farmers grows each year as they face foreclosure, eviction, and bankruptcy. Students wishing to attend college can no longer find government loans, preventing all those except the children of the wealthy from attending.

The public simply does not know how much or what kind of aid the U.S. Treasury is funneling to Israel. Those in Congress who vote for such aid do so partly because of a near-total press vacuum. While support for Israel from members of Congress is cemented with campaign money from supporters of Israel, the media have succeeded in keeping the public in the dark about sins committed on a daily basis by Israel with American taxpayers' money.

The pervasive bias in Middle East news coverage has always raised a question of motive and of responsibility. There seems to be no shortage of self-serving, self-congratulations by the news media for their responsibilities and their self-proclaimed fairness. Readers are regularly treated to editorials—print and electronic alike—smugly celebrating press freedoms in the United States.

How, then, does one explain the severe imbalance in coverage of the conflict in the Middle East? It is, in my view, a combination of several factors: Journalists are afflicted with what author Timothy Crouse once described as "pack journalism," a fear of being different from mainstream journalists; many news editors, especially at major newspapers that define and influence the news for the rest of the nation, such as the *New York Times* and the *Washington Post,* for many different reasons, are ardent supporters of Israel. During the Israeli siege of Beirut in 1982, when *New York Times* reporter Thomas Friedman sent a dispatch describing one day of heavy bombing and shelling of Beirut by the Israeli military as indiscriminate, his editors removed the word "indiscriminate" from the report on grounds that the Israelis could never bomb indiscriminately.

I once asked two journalists who had covered Lebanon—one from the Associated Press and one from the *Washington Post*—why they had never sent in stories reporting on the devastation from Israeli bombing of southern Lebanon over the years. Both responded that they had regularly sent in such stories, but that their editors had never used them. Only Israeli military communiqués routinely describing the terror bombing campaign in south Lebanon as a "search for terrorists" were read in the American press.

The images created by the media are basically of "good guy" Israelis, and "bad guy" Arabs. One expects little else after decades of heavily biased coverage, concealing Israel's flaws and magnifying those of the Arabs.

Even labels and basic terms of reference for events in the Middle East are, not surprisingly, set by the media. Thus, the civil war in Lebanon came to be known as a "Christian-Muslim" conflict. Although the bulk of the Phalangist forces contained Maronite Christians, there were also Orthodox Christians as well as Muslims and Druze. The same was true for those militias who challenged the Phalangists. Most were Muslim and Druze, but many were also Christians, including approximately 35 percent of the Palestinians. While it may have been easier in terms of reporting to call it a religious war, it was anything but that. The damage such labeling does is incalculable.

Both the Phalangist forces, whose leader, Pierre Gemayel, received his political inspiration from the Nazis when he attended the 1936 Berlin Olympics, as well as the Israelis, used the public's press-created misconception to their advantage. Menachem Begin grew overly fond of stating publicly that he saw it as his duty to "protect the Christians" in Lebanon. It was more than obvious that he meant "protect the Phalangists" who were his allies there, and who happily kept the Lebanese pot boiling to Israel's benefit. Because of the importance of American public support for Israel, the confusion created by Begin and Bashir Gemayel over who was Christian and who were the Christians' enemies enabled them to more comfortably continue their slaughter in Lebanon.

While the press regularly overemphasizes negative stereotypes about Arabs, it also omits virtually anything positive about them. During the entire civil war in Lebanon, the p.l.o. protected the American embassy in Beirut, as well as the Jewish quarter there, defending both from attack. When American dependents were evacuated from Lebanon at one highly critical point during the internal fighting, the p.l.o. protected the evacuation, ensuring that no one was harmed. But so far as Americans are concerned, it was as though it had never happened. I have no question that American journalists posted in Beirut reported these actions, just as I have no question that news editors in the United States quashed the stories written.

Israel maintains what it describes as a "security zone" in south Lebanon, roughly six miles deep reaching from its northern border into southern Lebanon. The press had informed the world that this zone is held by an "Israeli-backed Lebanese militia," or, as the media sometimes refer to it, a "breakaway" Lebanese Christian faction. In fact, the militia is quite simply made up of mercenaries, commanded by Israel, in their pay, and in any other context would be counted as part of their army. They have no ideology other than their paycheck. And far from being a Christian militia, its religious breakdown is Druze, Muslim, and Christian.

The most dangerous terminology that the American press corps has established, under the tutorship of Israel's propagandists, is that of defining anyone who opposes Israel as a "terrorist." The word has a legitimate usage, but when it is carelessly attached to anyone who is an enemy of Israel, it is in danger of losing its meaning.

If we were to accept the Israeli definition, then the word "terrorist" would be given to George Washington and his revolutionaries, to Robert E. Lee and the Confederate army, to the Afghanistan rebels, and on and on.

The label has, incredibly, been attached to Palestinian soldiers seeking to liberate Palestine—their homeland—from the Israeli, to the Lebanese resistance in south Lebanon trying to get the Israelis to leave their country, and to anyone else who opposes their territorial acquisition by force of arms. It is truth stood on its head.

Israel's occupation of Lebanon following its 1982 invasion brought fierce resistance by the Lebanese. Various resistance groups, including Amal, the largest Shiite Muslim organization in Lebanon, began fighting back against the Israeli occupation.

But anyone who simply reads press accounts of the resistance movement without knowing anything else would come away angry at the Lebanese for committing acts of violence against what has been portrayed as a righteous occupation. Israel's attempt to crush the resistance came to be called the "Iron Fist." It was not unlike the methods used by the Nazis during the occupation of Europe during World War II. In response to Lebanese resistance against the Israeli occupation, the Israeli military has swept through Lebanese villages, kidnapping "suspects," dynamiting homes as collective punishment, killing anyone who resists, and torturing those who they believe can give them information.

But press reports have focused only on Israel's injuries, ignoring the devastating effect of the occupation on the Lebanese. There was never any talk of the right of the Lebanese to resist the occupation, only the death toll of Israeli soldiers killed by Lebanese "terrorists" during acts of resistance. As David Shipler wrote, "Between 1982 and 1985, a total of 654 Israeli soldiers died in Lebanon to prevent Palestinian guerrillas from continuing attacks that had cost a total of twenty-nine lives in northern Israel in the four years from June 1, 1978, to June 5, 1982. Fifteen of the twenty-nine were Israeli soldiers.

We knew, on a daily basis, and with great precision from the *Washington Post* and the *New York Times*, how many Israeli soldiers had lost their lives. We learned nothing of the suffering of the Lebanese who lived under the Israeli boot, because the mainstream American press had no interest in publishing it.

We have been consistently treated with discussion, both in articles and in books and even in an Israeli Army training film, of the tragedy of Israel's 1982 invasion of Lebanon—but only of the tragedy befalling Israel. There was nothing said of the devastation visited upon the Lebanese and Palestinians, presumably because they don't feel, they don't care, and, obviously, they don't count. The invasion failed, we are told, because it was the first war Israel was not forced into fighting. (No mention is made of Israel's 1956 invasion of Egypt, as well as other aggressive invasions.) There are reams of written material on the negative effect of the war on Israel's society. It has been convenient for supporters of Israel to write that it was actually Arabs who killed Arabs at Sabra and Shatila, drawing attention away from the Israeli government, which controlled and assisted the killers.

Discussion of the effect of the invasion on the Lebanese and Palestinians is nonexistent. Perhaps the deliberate slaughter of more than eighteen thousand civilians by Israel during the invasion does not mean much—if they're Arabs, that is. The wounding of thirty thousand more is not worth discussing, nor is the fact that Lebanon's economy, which withstood seven years of bitter civil war, was finally destroyed during the Israeli occupation of Lebanon.

During the scorched earth policy conducted by Israel in south Lebanon from 1970 until 1979, we were treated to heavily emotional press accounts—both in print and on television—of Israelis killed or wounded by rocket attacks, or by Palestinian guerrilla raids inside Israel. We were never shown Arabs mourning for their dead children, killed in Israeli air raids by Israeli cluster and phosphorus bombs, leading unsuspecting Americans to believe that life is cheap in the Arab world. But mourn they did, in numbers far, far greater than those who mourned in Israel. To their misfortune, the Arabs have been mostly ignored by the American media, confirming the one-dimensional image already established by the press.

What, then, is the American public to think of a people who do not rate even a few lines in the *New York Times* or the *Washington Post?* Can Arabs be taken seriously if their suffering, or their legal rights, or their hopes and aspirations are not worthy of discussion in the major American media?

Again, the answer is obvious—of course not. That is why the campaign to dehumanize Arabs was initiated in the first place. Those in the United States who try to argue the case against Israeli occupation suddenly find themselves the target of the same kind of depersonalization, the result being that neither they nor their arguments are taken seriously.

The traditional and typical means of attacking those who speak

out in behalf of Palestinian rights, or of Arab rights in general—
attack the person, but avoid debating the issue. Make them into a
pariah so their words and thoughts are discredited, but avoid discussing the substance. In this way, a debate on the correctness or incorrectness of u.s. policy in the Middle East can be avoided.

Both the American Israel Public Affairs Committee (aipac) and
B'nai B'rith Anti-Defamation League have published lists of those
whom they identify as enemies of Israel. They are nothing more
than thinly veiled political hit lists with ominous implications for
free debate and for American principles.

The imbalance in the Arab-Israeli story is not restricted to television and news organizations, however. American writers who try to
write objectively about the Middle East conflict find publishers
almost impossible to locate. Those who succeed in publishing find
it even more difficult to avoid being trashed by the *New York Times
Review of Books*, a magazine whose approval publishing houses
deem critical to decent book sales. In a rare interview, the former
owner of Grove Press, Barney Rosset, disclosed that he asked his new
superior at Grove, George Weidenfeld, "what can't we publish?"

"You can publish anything, my boy," Weidenfeld answered,
"but I'd appreciate it if you wouldn't publish anything too anti-Israel
or too pro-Arab."

Rosset told Weidenfeld he could live with that restriction, since
Grove press was not dealing with such books anyway. But, Rosset
said, one of the books cut from the fall list at Grove Press was an
Israeli novel, *The Road to Ein Harod*, which was critical of the
Israeli government. A writer I know who has published two books
on the Arab Israeli conflict so far, and who has had great difficulty
finding a publisher for the third in his series, read the Rosset statement and told me he was relieved, since he was beginning to think
the problem he was having with publishers was caused by his own
failings.

The cumulative effect of *ad hominem* attacks on writers, or of
completely ignoring their writings altogether, is that the public
believes that only pro-Israeli writers are to be taken seriously.

People who come to the United States from Europe react with
amazement when they read American press coverage of the Middle
East conflict. It is the dramatic difference in coverage which shocks
the senses. Outside the United States, the public is told of the

violence emanating from both sides in the conflict. In the United
States, the awareness is only of Arab violence, while that committed
by Israel is either ignored altogether, or justified.

Occupation

One frequently hears, by way of justification, that Israel's occupation of the West Bank and Gaza has greatly benefited the
Palestinians living under it. Their living standards are
greater, so the story goes, and they are better off now than when they
were living under the Jordanians.

To lift the rhythm of a phrase from Gertrude Stein, an occupation is an occupation is an occupation is an occupation.

Trying to justify the forced occupation of other people and their
land is like trying to explain the benefits of dying by cancer as
opposed to being shot. This has been the burden of those whose
business it is to make excuses for the Israeli occupation of the West
Bank, the Gaza Strip, the Golan Heights, and, of late, southern
Lebanon.

Israel's occupation of those lands is both illegal and immoral, and
no amount of apologia can mask the horrendous wrongs being committed daily by its continuation.

What is nearly worse than the occupation itself is the continuing
cynical violation of high American principles of self-determination.
As it has with so many other issues involving Israel, the American
government and the American press have chosen to look the other
way because the occupation is Israel's, rather than, say, the Soviet
Union's.

The brutality suffered by the Palestinians and Lebanese living
under the Israeli boot is no different than that suffered by South
African blacks. Yet depressingly absent is the sense of American
outrage over the deportation, imprisonment, torture, murder, destruction of homes of innocent people, confiscation of land and
water rights, and the myriad other crimes committed against people
who have no defenses against the brutality of the Israeli occupation.

Although without a sense of outrage, some Israeli leaders, such

as Abba Eban, see nothing but a dead end in continuing the occupation. Eban wrote in the *New York Times* on November 9, 1986:

> The Palestinians live without a right to vote or be elected, without
> any control over the Government that determines the conditions
> of their lives, exposed to restraints and punishments that could not
> be applied against them if they were Jews, permitted to cross into
> Israel to work, but without permission to sleep overnight. It is a
> bleak, tense, disgruntled, repressed existence, with spurts of vio-
> lence always ready to explode. There is no precedent for believing
> that this condition can long endure without explosion.
>
> Israel lives in a state of structural incoherence. If we were to hear
> that the Netherlands was imposing an unwanted jurisdiction on
> four million Germans, or that America proposed to incorporate 80
> million Russians into the United States against their will, we would
> assume that they had taken leave of their senses. Yet, some people
> still talk of Israel ruling a foreign population that accounts for 33
> percent of its own inhabitants as though it were a serious option.

Eban quoted the Labor Party's positions of 1984 and 1986 which
resolved that permanent Israeli rule over the entire area of Judea and
Samaria and Gaza would "contradict the Zionist character of the
state, undermine its moral and democratic foundations and thwart
any hope of peace in the future."

But the settlement policy pursued by both the Labor Party and
the Likud coalition—is designed to continue the occupation. It is a
deliberate political act on the part of Israel, leaving violence as the
only alternative for the Palestinians living there. While not the
majority, the core of the settlers who have moved into the West
Bank consists of hard-line members of the religious movement,
Gush Emunim, who are convinced that they belong in the West
Bank and the Arabs do not.

The repetitious claims of Israeli "democracy" by its supporters
and apologists in the United States ring terribly hollow when confronted with reality. What is real is that Jewish settlers in the West
Bank have an excess of democracy, and the Arabs who live there
(and who have for a millennium) have none. Stripped of its propaganda cover, it is the relationship of colonizers to colonized.

New York Times reporter David Shipler wrote in *Arab and Jew,*
"For most of the six years that Menachem Begin was prime minister,

Jews could kill Arabs on the West Bank with impunity. Arrests were sometimes made, prosecutions sometimes begun. But somehow the cases rarely came to trial."

When four eighteen-year-old Palestinians hijacked a bus in the Gaza strip in 1984, resulting in the death of an Israeli woman soldier who did not keep her head down during the Israeli commandos' assault on the bus, two were killed and two were taken prisoner. Shin Beth agents beat the two prisoners to death under orders from the head of Shin Beth, Avraham Sholom, then lied, saying they had been killed during the storming of the bus. The affair was covered up for a time, but exposed when an Israeli photographer broke press censorship by publishing photos of the two prisoners being led away from the bus in handcuffs, at that point very much alive. The Israeli government eventually pardoned every one of several Israelis involved in the murders, first using security pretexts, then reasons of fairness, claiming that if some were pardoned, then all should be.

In the same way as do South African blacks, Palestinian Arabs, who are the majority, must live under a set of laws different than do Jews in the occupied territories. The most frequently used laws under which Palestinians must live are the day-to-day regulations issued by the Israeli military commander. Next in frequency are the British Mandatory Defense (Emergency) Regulations of 1945, the same set of laws that the British used against both Jews and Arabs during the mandatory period. Then, Jordanian law is invoked when convenient. In the West Bank and Gaza Strip, both military and civil courts operate. The civil courts have jurisdiction whenever the military feels the case has no interest for them. Lea Tsemel, an Israeli lawyer who defends Palestinians in the occupied territories provided an example of the military taking jurisdiction over a case in which one Jordanian killed another. The accused murderer was a collaborator for the Israeli military, which, fearing he would be convicted in the civilian court, took jurisdiction of the case and acquitted him.

Palestinian workers from the West Bank cross into Israel to find work. Those who do are in a legal gray area, unrepresented by the Histadrut (the Israeli Labor Federation) and exploited by Israeli employers. Meron Benvenisti reports that Palestinian workers receive half the pay Israeli workers receive for the same kind of work. It is illegal for West Bank Palestinians to stay overnight in Israel, but many are forced to do so to avoid long commutes or to work longer hours. They sleep on tables in restaurants where they work, or crowd into cellars and attics. They are searched and arrested by the Israeli authorities on an average of twice a week. Yet the Histadrut collects what it calls, "organization fees" from the Israeli Employment Service, deducted from West Bank employees "to look after their professional interests."

The occupation overall has been an economic boon to Israel, since the occupied territories are a protected market and provide a plentiful supply of cheap labor—a condition which a good socialist country such as Israel would never trumpet. But in virtually every area, including that of political freedoms, the Palestinians have a difficult time. Education of Palestinians has decreased, primarily because the Israeli authorities continue to close Palestinian schools when they display sentiments of Palestinian nationalism. The Palestinian standard of living, although higher than when Jordan occupied the West Bank, is measured as one-fourth of that of Israelis.

Public expenditure by Israel in the West Bank is also disastrously low. Expenditures for public services in Israel is 6.6 times that expended in the West Bank. If the contributions by the U.N. and other private organizations are added in, the ratio drops slightly to 4.5 to 1, and is 75 percent of what the Jordanians spent on public services during that period. When money is sent into the West Bank by the U.N., or by private voluntary organizations, Israeli authorities block its use in most projects except those that improve existing services. In 1949, to prevent a repeat of Hitler-like actions by occupying powers, Israel successfully pressed for international agreements that prohibit deportation of natives from, or settlement of their own population in, occupied territories. In this case, under Article 49 of the Fourth Geneva Convention of 1949, Israel is prohibited by international law from moving Israeli citizens into the West Bank and Gaza. Yet Israeli settlers are moved into the occupied territories every day, and the United States government, which speaks in glowing terms of international law and self-determination, pays the bill.

The occupation in the West Bank and the Gaza, as well as that in southern Lebanon would draw consistent banner headlines here—that is, if it were an occupation of any other country in the world. The brutality of the Israelis easily matches that of the South

Africans, but the difference in media treatment can be explained only in terms of racist attitudes toward Palestinian and Lebanese Arabs.

The minority government in South Africa has gotten what it deserves by way of American press coverage, the result being a more or less informed American public, and, consequently, a shifting of American attitudes against South Africa's policy of apartheid. Because the media spent a great deal of time and space covering the evils of the South African apartheid system and the resulting violence committed by the minority white government against the majority blacks, the u.s. Congress, in the fall of 1986, first passed a bill imposing sanctions on South Africa, then overrode President Reagan's veto of the bill. Although apartheid, and its attendant violence, had been around for years, the publicity it garnered brought enough public support for the sanctions legislation.

There is, by contrast, virtually no coverage of the crushing Israeli occupation of Palestinians and Lebanese. Almost on a daily basis the Israeli authorities arrest Palestinians without charging them with a crime and administer collective punishment, usually in the form of dynamiting the homes of anyone even suspected of resistance to the occupation, or "terrorism," as the Israelis call it. The destruction of homes occurs whether or not the remainder of the suspect's family lives there. Palestinian prisoners are routinely tortured by their Israeli captors. Lebanese citizens are taken from their homes inside Lebanon and removed to Israel, in unquestionable violation of international law and of treaties agreed to by the United States and by Israel, according to *The Iron Fist,* an ADC Research Institute report.

The United States denies weapons to South Africa, and has for years, because its government uses them against the people it governs. If that policy is in the interest of the United States, how is it in our interest to furnish weapons to Israel to do exactly the same thing? By paying the bill and furnishing the weapons, we are, in effect, co-occupiers with Israel.

Torture of Palestinians

No matter how cooperative the American press has been in preventing the publication of news embarrassing to Israel, reports continue to appear documenting a policy of torturing Palestinian throughout the West Bank, although such reports have great difficulty finding their way into the columns of major newspapers such as the *New York Times.* The *Washington Post* did, on one occasion in 1979, publish a story co-authored by T. R. Reid and Edward Cody on Israeli torture. However, both the *Post* and the *New York Times* refused even to mention a major investigation on Israeli torture published by the *London Sunday Times* in 1977, essentially hiding the fact of torture from the American public, which, undeniably, has a major stake in what the Israeli government does, partly in the name of the United States.

The *London Sunday Times* 1977 report on Israeli torture documented case after case of torture of Palestinians in the West Bank. The reporters questioned forty-nine Palestinians of whom forty-four alleged ill-treatment at the hands of the Israelis. Twenty-two agreed to be named. Response to the torture allegations by the Israelis was sharply limited, and in most cases, off the subject. They addressed only six of the twenty-two cases that were named in the *Sunday Times* with arguments that did not challenge the allegations with substantive arguments, but only with straight denials or by raising peripheral issues.

The human rights group Amnesty International has consistently challenged the Israeli government's administrative detention practices, but just as consistently has received only stonewalling responses from Israel. Amnesty International's concern was with torture of Palestinian and Lebanese prisoners, as well as the broad formulation of the occupation law governing administrative detention, which makes no distinction between violent or nonviolent political behavior. Amnesty International investigated several cases of administrative detention in the occupied territories, asking the Israeli authorities for details of the specific use of violence of those Palestinians detained. No details were given to them by the Israelis.

In one example, two Palestinian field workers for a human rights group called, Law in the Service of Man, Ghazi Shashtari and Zahi Jaradat, were imprisoned under the administrative detention laws, the stated reason being that they had tried to set up a terrorist infrastructure in the occupied territories, and that Shashtari had contributed to the preparation of terrorist actions. However, while in prison, neither of the two were interrogated about such activities, but were questioned *solely* about their human rights work on behalf of Law in the Service of Man, an entirely legal activity. They were not allowed to appear before a normal court to allow refutation of evidence against them.

Amnesty International has reported a number of cases of such detention, most of which are unquestionably for political purposes rather than for security, but few of which receive publicity in the United States.

Additionally, Israel's mercenaries in southern Lebanon, the South Lebanon Army (SLA), hold Lebanese prisoners in a prison in Khiam, in the so-called security zone. In August 1986, the SLA held about two hundred Lebanese in Khiam, which is operated by the SLA with the assistance of the Israeli Security Service. Amnesty International reports that some of the prisoners are held as hostages to encourage informants among their relatives. The prisoners are not only Palestinian and Lebanese men, but include teenagers, women, and old men. Some have been held for more than a year, and others for several weeks until their interrogation is completed. There are no administrative or court procedures of any kind for those imprisoned in Khiam. In all cases, whether in Khiam, or in the occupied territories, prisoners are held incommunicado for long periods of time without families, friends, or lawyers being able to see them. Reports of torture are the most prevalent in Khiam. In 1986 Amnesty International interviewed one ex-prisoner who described his interrogation in graphic detail. During most of the six or seven days he was being interrogated in Khiam, he was "hooded with a thick black canvas bag with his hands tied behind his back. He was kicked all over the body and beaten with fists and with a thick electric cable. On a number of occasions he was taken from his cell and, still hooded and handcuffed, stripped and soaked with water and subjected to electric shocks. Electrodes were applied to all parts of his body, including the testicles [but not his face.]" He reported losing consciousness from the intensity of some of the electric shocks. The shocks were administered by members of the SLA, but supervised by Israelis who asked questions and gave instructions. After the shock treatments, he was taken outside several times and suspended by his wrists, which were handcuffed together, from a crossbar. His toes barely touched the ground and he was left in that position for three to five hours, during which time he was kicked, beaten, and soaked with cold water. The hairs on his chest and arms were pulled out, his nipples were squeezed, and his skin was burned with cigarettes.

Because confessions comprise the main body of so-called evidence against accused Palestinians and Lebanese in the occupied territories, there is great incentive to torture prisoners to obtain them. Beginning in 1981, the confession of a third party was allowed in trials against Palestinian defendants. The most notorious case of the use of third party confessions was that of Ziad Abu Eain, who was arrested in Chicago by the F.B.I. while visiting his sister there. A bomb had gone off in Tiberias, and a suspect in the bombing, Jamal Yasin, was picked up and interrogated. Knowing Abu Eain was in the United States, Yasin implicated him in the bombing. During Abu Eain's extradition hearing in the United States, his lawyers were prevented from offering evidence of his alibi. At he time of the bombing he was at a hospital in Ramallah—some three and a half hours away—where his sister was delivering a child. Israel demanded his extradition and he was handed over to the Israeli authorities in the middle of the night by Assistant Secretary of State William Clark—a ploy to avoid pressure from several Arab ambassadors—then put on trial in Israel. (Israel's double standard came into sharp focus when it refused to allow extradition to France of William Nakash, a French Jew convicted in absentia in France for the murder of a French Arab.) Yasin renounced his confession, testifying that it had been obtained under torture, adding that he had named Abu Eain because he thought he was safe in America. Despite Yasin's testimony, Abu Eain was convicted and sentenced to life. The U.S. State Department made a special effort to accede to Israel's wishes in the Abu Eain case. The tainted evidence used against Abu Eain would never have been allowed in an American court. Requirements of due process here prohibit the use of third party confessions, particularly when they are obtained forcibly as in the case of Yasin. Yet, the State Department even sent one of its officials to testify against Abu Eain in the extradition hearings in Chicago. It was clearly an effort by the State Department to send Israel a Christmas present in the form of Abu Eain.

The American Arab Anti-Discrimination Committee, which had taken on Abu Eain's case as a cause, asked several American lawyers to attend his trial as observers. They were former U.S. Attorney General Ramsey Clark, New York ACLU representative Henry Schwarzchild, and Detroit lawyer Abdeen Jabara, all of whom reported that not one shred of evidence was presented at the trial to show Abu Eain's guilt, except for Yasin's recanted confession. It was a confession written in Hebrew, a language which Yasin could not read, speak, or write, and was obtained under suspicious circumstances—weeks after Yasin's arrest when he was denied access to counsel, family, or friends.

Abu Eain lost his appeal to the Israeli Supreme Court. He was later made part of a release program under which Israeli prisoners of war were traded for Palestinian prisoners, although the first of such trades did not go through when the Israelis held him back at the last minute. After being released during the second exchange in 1985, Abu Eain remained at home in the West Bank and was again picked up under the administrative detention laws, without charges being made against him, and at this writing is still in an Israeli prison.

Abu Eain was never a security risk in Israel or in the West Bank. But he was a political organizer, which is apparently more of a threat to Israel than are bomb throwers. He is not the first organizer to have been imprisoned or deported using security as a cover, nor was he the last. In 1986, a well-known Palestinian newspaper editor, Akram Haniye, was deported, and Mohammed Shadid, a Palestinian intellectual, was barred from teaching at a West Bank university; neither of the two were ever charged with a crime. Both Israeli and Arab human rights activists charged that the two men were being punished without trial because of their beliefs, and not their actions.

Historically, and for obvious reasons, evidence of torture has been difficult to gather, whether in Latin American dictatorships, or Israeli "democracy." When the evidence does become available, it is devastating.

In most documented cases the same methods of torture have been used, with the same lack of coverage in the United States media. One very brief, one-day exception, however, was the case of Ghazi Dabaja, an American citizen from Dearborn, Michigan. Dabaja, accompanied by his eight-year-old son, went to the village of Bint Jebail, in south Lebanon on February 11, 1986, to visit his parents. He was picked up the next day by members of the SLA and imprisoned for thirty days before the U.S. embassy in Israel learned of his imprisonment. During the time he was held, Dabaja was tortured by the SLA, with Israeli officers present at the torture sessions. He was interrogated and beaten by the Israelis while SLA members applied the instruments of torture to his body.

Quoting from Dabaja's affidavit, which he provided to the U.S. embassy in Israel:

> The second day one Israeli whose name is Yaaki (an Israeli officer) started beating me on my face and all over my body. I was also subjected to electrical shocks on all parts of my body, including my penis and testicles.
>
> I was handcuffed with hands behind my back and hung from the ceiling naked, my feet and toes barely touching the ground. Cigarette burns were applied to my hands and stomach, water was poured over me and my body hair on my chest and arms were pulled by some people while Yaaki supervised.
>
> A hood was placed over my head. I was also beaten repeatedly across the back and legs with electrical cables . . ."

In one cable sent by the U.S. embassy in Israel to the State Department in Washington, members of the embassy staff reported that they had seen the handcuff marks and cigarette burns on Dabaja's hands and wrists.

U.S. embassy officials in Tel Aviv contacted the Israeli Foreign Ministry eleven times asking for information about Dabaja, but except for confirming his arrest, Israeli authorities refused to provide any other relevant details to the United States.

Finally, after more than a month of detention and torture, and an angry challenge by U.S. Ambassador to Israel Thomas Pickering, Dabaja was released in Metulla, Israel.

One wonders why there was no rhetoric flowing from the White House, or from Congress, on such gross and wanton violations of the human rights of those tortured by Israel. Such mistreatment by any other country, especially of American citizens (except for Arab-American citizens), holds the prospect of President Reagan ordering an air strike or, at a minimum, ordering a SWAT team to avenge such mistreatment. Instead, there is silence, and except for the April 15, 1986 *Washington Post* story, nothing happened. There was no outrage, no follow-up, no speeches by Secretary of State Shultz, who is capable of unlimited outrage toward Arabs. In short, nothing. That is why Israel continues its violation of human rights with impunity, and, it seems, with ever greater rewards from the United States Treasury.

Taking Water and Land

In the semi-arid climate of the West Bank, a water supply is critical to survival. It is a resource that has been preciously conserved over the centuries to ensure the continuation of agriculture by Palestinian farmers.

Since the occupation of the West Bank and Gaza by the Israelis, water is gradually being denied to Palestinians, and its use is being shifted to Israeli settlers. Palestinians cannot drill new wells for irrigation purposes, despite the fact that Jewish settlers have drilled where they please, primarily near existing Arab wells, siphoning the water from them and denying the Arabs the use of irrigation water. The new "Jewish wells" cannot be used by Arabs.

Israel has adopted a time-honored technique used by settlers in other times and other places to steal land from native Palestinians in the occupied territories. It has developed a number of ways to make the land grabbing routine, such as severely restricting construction by Palestinians; expropriation of abandoned land (a euphemism for grabbing land after chasing out those Palestinians who lived on it); expropriation for public use; and requisition for military purposes.

One of the techniques used by the Israelis, described to me by a Palestinian woman whose family still lives in the West Bank, is that of declaring uncultivated, unregistered land as "State Land." My friend comes from an old line Palestinian family, which has farmed land on the West Bank for centuries. The Israelis have repeatedly denied them full use of the water resources available to their farm. In 1984, her brother was told he must reduce the use of water for cultivation, which forced him to plant fewer acres of crops. He was then told by the Israeli authorities that because he was not cultivating that part of his land, it was declared "State Land" and confiscated.

Israeli Meron Benvenisti, the former deputy mayor of Jerusalem, who runs the West Bank Data Base Project, has, perhaps, expressed more pessimism about the future of the West Bank than anyone. He believes the point of no return has been reached in the West Bank, that is, the Israelis have consolidated control over every aspect of life there—the land, the infrastructure, the economy, and the people. The Israeli political center, which includes the Likud coalition and the Labor Alignment, is satisfied with the status quo and intends to maintain it as long as possible, since it does not believe it is possible for the Palestinians to change anything from this point onward.

Benvenisti's 1986 report reveals the principal strategy of the occupiers in the West Bank:

> Not only are Palestinians prohibited from exploiting the growth potential concealed in empty "State Lands," they are forbidden to use their own land if it is situated in the vicinity of Israeli settlements. "Closed areas," are closed for Palestinians only, and open for Israelis. Entire settlement regions are declared "prohibited for building," but only Palestinian land is affected. Israeli settlements on requisitioned land are exempted from building prohibition by virtue of a special order which applies only to Israelis (Order 997, 1982).
>
> Palestinian regions, and land use are regarded as constraints. Land control methods are intended both to encircle Arab areas and penetrate them by long strips of "prohibition on building" areas. Road networks are designed to bypass Arab population centres, but also to fragment and dissect Arab settlement regions. In fact, the orders prohibiting building confine the Palestinian population to rigid "boxes" which prevent natural expansion. In Israeli directives this strategy is described as "prevention of uncontrolled expansion of (Arab) townships and villages" and "creation of Arab shanty towns."

Through the use of the various land-grabbing techniques, Israel now controls about 52 percent of all land in the West Bank.

Israeli Settlements

Israeli policy has been, for a number of years, to encourage and even to subsidize the construction of Jewish settlements in the occupied territories. By the end of 1986, the last year for which figures are available, sixty thousand Jewish settlers had moved into the West Bank. This figure includes about seventeen thousand who moved in between December 1984 and November 1986, a time when there was presumably a freeze on settlement activity during the term of Shimon Peres. But during this period, eleven new settlements were established, settlements that were previously paramilitary posts. Only four hundred of the seventeen thousand new settlers were what can be called pioneer Zionists, that is, members of the right-wing Gush Emunim. The remainder were what are termed Israeli Yuppies, members of the liberal left, Peace Now, and others, who have taken advantage of subsidized West Bank housing provided by the Israeli government. What began as an effort to provide space for settlers in what Menachem Begin called "Judea and Samaria," has come to the point where the West Bank is no longer a place for pioneering Zionists, but a low-cost, subsidized bedroom area for commuters to Tel Aviv and Jerusalem. The settlers who consider themselves pioneers are the religious right wing, such as Gush Emunim, many of whom are Jews who have emigrated from America in search of an identity they were unable to find in the United States.

The location of the settlements is clearly designed to encircle Arab villages, to prevent their expansion, to cut them off from each other, and to encourage emigration by making life difficult for the Palestinians who live there.

The World Zionist Organization's first five-year plan for settlement in "Judea and Samaria" stated:

> The best and most effective way of removing every shadow of a doubt about our intentions to hold on to Judea and Samaria forever is by speeding up the settlement momentum in these territories. . . .The purpose of settling the areas between and around the centers occupied by the minorities [meaning the Palestinian majority] is to reduce to the minimum the danger of an additional Arab State being established in these territories. Being cut off, by Jewish settlements, the minority population will find it difficult to form a territorial and political community.

For Eban, and others in the Labor Alignment, the possibility of despoiling Israeli "democracy" and moral values constitutes only a moral dilemma. It is sufficient to agonize over, but there is no requirement for a political decision to be made on ending the occupation. Both Jordan and the United States support the status quo as well—Jordan, because the occupation prevents Palestinians from spilling over into Jordan, and the United States, because Israel wants it that way.

Perhaps the best capsule description of Jewish settlement psychology was provided by the Jewish woman protesting the return of the Sinai to Egypt, and the planned destruction of the settlement of Yamit, where she lived. "I didn't come all the way from Miami Beach to become an Egyptian," she complained to an NBC news camera crew.

In *The Fateful Triangle* Noam Chomsky has documented the staging, for public relations purposes, of the withdrawal from the Sinai settlement of Yamit, quoting Israeli General Chaim Erez, commander of the Yamit evacuation: "Everything was planned and agreed from the beginning" with the settlers to offer a show of resistance. Israeli writer Amnon Kapeliouk has described the Yamit affair as "one of the largest brain-washing operations conducted by the [Israeli] government in order to convince the Israeli people that they have suffered a national trauma the effect of which will be felt for generations" and that will "create a national consensus opposed to similar withdrawals in the remaining occupied territories."

The American press, of course, cooperated fully with the Israeli public relations specialists, and made the evacuation a lead story. We were treated to "heart-rending" accounts of Jewish settlers forced to leave their homes in the Sinai. There was, as Chomsky pointed out, absolutely no coverage of the manner in which the former Arab settlers had been driven out by the Israelis when they decided to build the Sinai settlements. The Arabs who had lived on the land where Yamit was built by the Israelis believed they would be able to move back into Yamit and take advantage of the billions of dollars (provided by the United States taxpayers) used to make the town a modern one. They were prevented from using even the water pumping station that had been built there. When the Israelis withdrew, they totally destroyed the town, making it uninhabitable for the former residents.

Is it possible to understand the Palestinians' point of view that each Jew who immigrates into Israel from the Soviet Union, or from the United States, or from anywhere else, displaces a Palestinian? The situation must be thought of in terms of the diaspora. Palestinians, like Jews throughout history, now have no place to go once they are driven from Palestine. It is specious to argue that the Arab countries should take them in, or that Palestine exists in Jordan. Such arguments refuse to take into account the Palestinians' feelings and are clearly designed to remove the burden from the shoulders of Israel, which is solely responsible for the Palestinian diaspora, not the Arab countries.

Israel's Iron Fist Policy in Lebanon

U.S. Special Envoy Philip Habib, with the help of Saudi Arabia, in July 1981, arranged a P.L.O.-Israeli cease-fire along the border between Lebanon and Israel. During the following eleven months the Israelis tried hard to provoke the P.L.O. by breaking the cease-fire themselves. From August 1981 to May 1982, the Israelis violated Lebanese airspace 2,125 times, and Lebanese waters 652 times. The P.L.O. did not respond, holding to the cease-fire even though Palestinians were killed by the Israelis. Then, on June 3, 1982, an Abu Nidal agent shot Israeli Ambassador Shlomo Argov while he was walking on a London street. It was known shortly afterward that members of Yasir Arafat's P.L.O. were also on the hit list found in the assassin's pocket. Defense Minister Sharon had found his pretext. He ordered the bombing of Palestinian and Lebanese targets in Lebanon. More than two hundred Palestinians and Lebanese were killed in the vicious raids, including those in a hospital, and civilians in the Sabra and Shatila refugee camps. Finally the P.L.O. responded by shelling Israeli settlements in northern Israel, and on June 6, the Israeli invasion began in earnest.

There seems to be little question that Sharon and Begin had planned to go to Beirut from the beginning. Wars of invasion are planned ahead of time. Only the most gullible would believe that Israel was forced to move to Beirut at some point in time after its announced forty-kilometer limit was reached. Stopping forty kilometers north of its border with Lebanon—as Israel said it would—could not adequately serve the purposes of the invasion. How could Prime Minister Menachem Begin install Bashir Gemayel as president of Lebanon unless Israeli troops were in Beirut? How could the P.L.O.'s political influence over the West Bank be destroyed unless the P.L.O. was destroyed? And how could the P.L.O. be destroyed unless the Israeli military went into Beirut after them?

An ancillary benefit to the 1982 invasion was Israeli control over the Litani river, which flows north to south in Lebanon, and into the

Mediterranean before it reaches Israel. The Israeli "security zone" in southern Lebanon takes in part of the Litani. Immediately after the I.D.F. went into Lebanon, they confiscated all the hydrographic charts and documentation relating to the Litani. In 1983 the Israelis conducted seismic soundings and began construction on the river. They then performed work upstream on the Wazzani river, which does flow from Lebanon into Israel, designed to increase their flow of water. Evidence of any continued drainage of Litani water is difficult to gather, since the I.D.F. refuses to allow observers into the area where they are suspected of stealing water from the Litani river. The existence of an old Zionist plan, however, first made public in 1919, which included the waters of southern Lebanon as part of the area to be included in a Jewish national home, combined with the activities of the I.D.F., have convinced most Lebanese that the water of the Litani is indeed being stolen and sent into Israel.

In the 1960s, Lebanon's government began construction of an irrigation dam on the Wazzani, but were unable to continue after Israeli air attacks on the construction workers. The project was abandoned and the Lebanese farmers in the mostly arid region of the south were forced to stay with the hardscrabble farming that has kept that part of Lebanon poor.

Following the Israeli invasion of Lebanon, and the resulting massive devastation of civilian life, culture, and economy, Israel played another destructive game with the people of Lebanon. The I.D.F. recruited a number of mercenary militias from the various communities in Lebanon, then withdrawing further south over the following three years, it did so in a manner designed to promote internecine fighting between the communities, creating more death and destruction. But it has been the actual Israeli occupation of Lebanon since 1982 that has destroyed so much of the country.

In spite of the murderous civil war that has flamed up and out, then up again since 1975, the Lebanese economy held up reasonably well, that is, until Israel began dumping its own goods into the Lebanese economy, an act which ultimately ruined the value of the Lebanese pound, as well as the country's economy.

The Israeli strategy of restricting the transport and sale of Lebanese products, and, concomitantly, the dumping of its own goods, has destroyed Lebanese tobacco, citrus, banana, and other export crops. Perishable items being taken to market by Lebanese farmers were held up in their trucks by the Israelis for several days until they rotted. In order to create a demand for Israeli goods, the I.D.F. systematically destroyed whatever Lebanese goods would have competed with them. At one point in 1984, the I.D.F. maintained only one checkpoint open for transport from the south into the rest of Lebanon. By September 10, 1984, closure of the checkpoint resulted in one thousand five hundred trucks stranded there waiting permission to enter south Lebanon.

In his monograph, *The Iron Fist*, Joseph Schechla has compared the Israeli operations in south Lebanon to the pacification program run by U.S. counter-insurgency experts in Vietnam. Because the Lebanese chose not to like Israel's occupation of their country, a resistance movement sprung from those living in the south. Resistance from the Lebanese brought harsh repression from the Israelis. They raided Lebanese villages after first sending in fifty to sixty members of their internal security police, the Shin Beth, to seal the exits. Then armored personnel carriers and bulldozers entered the village. If a Lebanese attempted to run, he or she was summarily shot, then identified as a terrorist if the press was there to ask questions. Lebanese homes were destroyed by bulldozer, with no real reason needed, except that the Israeli commander on the scene had determined that a suspected "terrorist" had lived in it. Whenever a Lebanese village is raided in this manner, the men are usually rounded up and taken to prisons, either in the Israeli security zone in Lebanon, or in Israel, a transfer of civilians that completely violates treaties signed by Israel, and international law.

Villages have been looted by the Israelis, leaving already poor villagers in a desperate condition after their departure.

When the I.D.F. entered Beirut in 1982, one of its first objectives was the Palestine Research Center in Beirut, a repository for Palestinian history. All of the documents maintained there were stolen and taken into Israel by the Israeli military. In south Lebanon, Israeli troops looted historic and religious collections and have defaced archaeological artifacts considered precious by the Lebanese.

The southern Lebanese refused to be cowed by the brutality of the occupation, deciding to sacrifice their lives in an effort to drive out the Israelis. Week after tragic week saw reports in the American press of Lebanese suicide missions, of young Lebanese strapping explosives to themselves, then colliding with patrolling Israeli troops. We were told by American newspapers and television precisely how many Israeli soldiers had been killed each day during resistance to the Iron Fist policy, but no one counted the Lebanese, especially in the American media, giving the impression that their lives were of little or no value.

The loss of Israeli soldiers became a political detriment to the government, which finally decided to withdraw to the six-mile "security zone" in the south, where they remain today. Aside from the continued Israeli presence on Lebanese soil, raids into Lebanon north of the "security zone" have continued. Villages continue to be destroyed, Lebanese men continue to be taken prisoner, and, in sum, very little has changed, except that Israel has withdrawn from most of its former positions, and is now using its Lebanese mercenaries, the South Lebanon Army (SLA), to do most of its dirty work.

It is an occupation that is extremely brutal in its execution, but, like the Israeli occupation of the West Bank and the Gaza Strip, has been ignored and forgotten by the rest of the world.

Unquestioning Support for Israel: The Impact on America

Americans are outraged when their own government is caught selling arms to Iran or to dictatorships in Latin America. It is reflected in speeches by members of the House of Representatives and the Senate, in editorials in major newspapers, and in heavy coverage of criticism of such sales by television network news programs. Yet Israel has been selling arms to dictatorships for years, and American arms to Iran, despite an official embargo on such shipments by the United States. Although President Reagan was caught red-handed doing the same in 1986, including sending arms to Iran through Israel, Reagan argued he did so to improve relations with "moderates" in Iran, and to free the American hostages held in Lebanon. We do not know, however, the extent of the monetary profit Israel made on its arms shipments to Iran. Israel's arms customers include Guatemala, Haiti, Honduras, Nicaragua while Somoza was in power, the Philippines under Marcos, and Pinochet's Chile. Arms sales by the United States to these same dictatorships produced loud complaints from some Americans, but those who complained the loudest about America's involvement are silent about Israel.

Similarly, Moscow received heavy criticism from American politicians when Russia invaded Afghanistan. There seemed no end to the denunciations, the sanctions, speeches, and editorials directed at the Soviet Union for its aggressive actions—and they continue to this day. But when Israel invaded Lebanon in 1982, violating every international standard of morality and legality, American politicians and American entertainers lined up to make speeches of approval in the u.s. they traveled to Lebanon—behind Israeli lines, of course— singing the praises of the invasion. These were no mere conservatives with long histories of interventionist machismo. They were repre- sented by the likes of Tom Hayden, Jane Fonda, Senator Alan Cranston, Senator Christopher Dodd, and many more such folks who, not long ago were waving a different flag—against wars and aggression and bullies. The power of money flowing from the Israeli lobby to American politicians comes into sharp focus when we learn that they find it easier to criticize a president of the United States than a prime minister of Israel.

And, of course, none of these defenders of human rights would brook a country torturing prisoners. But we hear no speeches on human rights on the Senate floor when Israel is exposed as a major torturer of Palestinians and Lebanese. There are no amendments offered to cut off aid to Israel because of its inhumane practices.

When Turkey used American arms to invade Cyprus in 1974, Congress was quick to enforce the Foreign Military Sales Act, which prohibits using American weapons aggressively against a third party. Over the years, Israel has used American airplanes, cluster bombs, phosphorus bombs, napalm, tanks, and ammunition to devastate Lebanese, Syrian, Egyptian, Jordanian, and Palestinian civilians. The administration has never come close to certifying to Congress that American weapons were used in such a manner, and Congress has never bothered to enforce the prohibition in the law with respect to Israel.

The u.s. State Department has done its best to cover up the spy scandal in which Jonathan Pollard, an American citizen, was recruited and paid by the Israeli government to steal classified military secrets from the u.s. Navy. As hard as the State Department has tried to conceal the affair, it will not go away because of resistance from law enforcement professionals in the u.s. Department of Justice.

The Israeli embassy in Washington as well as the Israeli mission at the United Nations have been used as control offices for those stealing secrets from the United States. Yet all Americans were crudely patronized by the State Department's legal officer, Abraham Sofaer, who went to Israel to "negotiate" the return of the documents stolen by Pollard and sold to the Israelis. Sofaer announced that the documents were returned, Israel had apologized, and the case was closed. Incredibly, this fantasy sailed through the American media without critical comment. Sofaer had accepted the fiction offered by Israel that the Pollard affair was a "rogue" operation, meaning that it had not been approved by the Israeli government. Yet nothing changed when it was revealed that the Israeli charged with running the u.s. spy network, Rafael Eitan, was promoted to chairman of one of Israel's largest state-owned concerns, Israel Chemicals, and Colonel Aviam Sella, who controlled Pollard in the United States, was promoted to brigadier general and put in charge of one of the largest air bases in Israel.

When Pollard was arrested trying to seek asylum in the Israeli embassy in Washington, the Israelis immediately began trying their case in the press, leaking a number of different reasons for the spying to reporters, hoping to find one that would sell. They began by saying the spying was done in order to collect intelligence on Arab countries friendly to the United States, or, Pollard was working for an "anti-terrorism" unit in Israel, always a good rationale for whatever sins are committed. In the end, Israel relied on u.s. government officials to help cover up the scandal, although there have been suspicions voiced that the Israelis were gathering information to sell to other countries. Those suspicions may never be confirmed, since as a result of a deal cut, there was no public trial, and little public information disclosed regarding the extent of the affair.

Even before his sentencing, American citizen Pollard told an Israeli writer, Wolf Blitzer, that he "tried to do his best for his beloved Israel," lamenting the fact that the Israeli embassy had refused to give him asylum when the F.B.I. arrested him. Blitzer, who once worked for *The Near East Report,* the newsletter of the American-Israel Public Affairs Committee, wrote in the *Jerusalem Post* that Israel should pay for Pollard's legal fees, then "consider using its political clout with Washington to free [him] and to help him fulfill an earlier dream of moving to Israel. . . ." Blitzer included in his commentary that Pollard's blunder "stemmed from his background as a Jew and Zionist."

Even more serious than spying on its benefactor is the theft by Israel in the late 1950s and early 1960s of weapons grade nuclear materials from the NUMEC plant in Apollo, Pennsylvania. Little has been done about the theft, and the U.S. government has never called Israel to account for it, although it is public knowledge that Israel now has one hundred to two hundred nuclear weapons in its arsenal. Although a U.S. Senate delegation, led by Connecticut Senator Abe Ribicoff, attempted—without success—to visit Israel's Dimona facility in 1976, Congress has remained silent as well. Israel has not signed the Nuclear Non-Proliferation Treaty, and thus is not subject to international inspection. In 1986, however, Mordechai Vanunu, a disaffected former worker at the Dimona plant disclosed to the *London Sunday Times* both the story and the photographs of the Dimona facility manufacturing nuclear weapons. Following the disclosure, Vanunu was kidnapped by the Mossad and taken to Israel in October 1986.

Again, in 1985, it was disclosed that Israel illegally purchased 810 krytons—nuclear switches—through an American named Richard Smyth. Smyth was indicted for violating the Arms Export Control Act by smuggling the krytons to Israel between 1980 and 1982. When the matter became public, according to the *Washington Post,* Israel said it would return the unused switches to the United States. Smyth has disappeared and is believed to be hiding in Israel, but no effort has been made to find or extradite him. And nothing has been said to Israel about its violation of U.S. law.

The Israeli lobby, generally headquartered in Washington, D.C., is the name applied to a grouping of pro-Israeli organizations which concern themselves with one issue—doing what Israel wants done in the U.S. capital. Its umbrella organization is the American-Israel Public Affairs Committee (AIPAC), but it also includes such organizations as the B'nai B'rith, the American Jewish Congress, and the American Jewish Committee, and it operates with the help of a network of Jewish synagogues throughout the United States. Its single-minded effort to make certain that aid to Israel remains at a high level has turned the u.s. Congress into something resembling a small-state legislature. Operating with the help of Jewish campaign contributors, the lobby has become expert at twisting political arms to get its way.

There are an estimated ninety or so pro-Israeli political action committees, PACs, whose sole purpose is to collect and contribute money to candidates who will vote the way they want on issues affecting Israel. The result has been that politicians literally stumble over themselves trying to please the Israeli lobby in order to get on the "approved" list of candidates eligible for such contributions. The pandering by national office-holders just before election time is sometimes embarrassing, but it accomplishes precisely what the Israelis want—accession to their wishes by the u.s. government, whether or not those wishes coincide with American national interests. In that respect, it is a lobby for a foreign country that has gotten completely out of hand.

Americans are learning to turn their heads away from major crimes committed by Israel in America's name, principally because very few opinion leaders in the United States have the moral or intellectual courage to protest what is happening. If Americans are in danger of giving up the high moral ground because of permissiveness vis à vis Israel, American Jews who actively support u.s. policies toward the Middle East have even more to lose.

Less than a generation ago, American Jews were in a position of absolute leadership in the struggle for civil rights throughout America, were against the unreasonable build-up of arms, and helped to lead the fight against the strong and powerful taking unfair advantage of the vulnerable and weak.

Since the creation of Israel on land where the Palestinians once lived, a fiction has been created by Jews to justify the horrendous wrongs committed against Arabs, beginning before 1948 and continuing to this day.

The Arabs left voluntarily, they repeat over and over, as though this lie has made it all right to take over their homes, their crops, and their land.

The Arabs are all terrorists, we are told, again and again, by those who hope that Israel's own terrorism either will be overlooked or rationalized as self-defense.

Israel must sell arms to dictators, and it must do business with South Africa, because, its apologists say, it has very few allies in the world.

Occasionally it all becomes too much for some American Jews who grew up with different values, values that demand humanity and concern, and who can no longer close their eyes, or turn their heads while Israel cynically violates every tenet known to the liberal spirit. But each time Jews try to gather in protest of the killing, of torture, of land grabbing, they are cut down—politically and financially—by self-described leaders of the Jewish community—those who brook no dissent from the line laid down by Israel and followed by its professional apologists in America—those whom writer Earl Shorris would define as "Jews without mercy," as Shorris has titled one of his books. A group called Breira once existed as an alternative to the increasing militancy of organized Jewry, but faded into obscurity when its contributors learned of its mild opposition to some of Israel's more egregious crimes. The New Jewish Agenda has since attempted to offer the same kind of alternatives, as has a new Jewish journal called *Tikkun.* The efforts to exert peer pressure on these dissenters are enormous, the result of which is to ensure that other dissenters think long and hard before breaking ranks.

Most rank and file Jews in America have a strong feeling for the concept of a Jewish state, often offering blind unquestioning support. A class of American Jews has come into view who have learned that the route to political and financial power in America lies in using broad Jewish support for Israel as a club to enhance their own power. It includes Jews who have made a profession of championing the arms build-up by the United States, who provide needed public support for the incursions of a warlike Ronald Reagan in Grenada, Nicaragua, and Angola.

The New Republic, once a fount of liberal thought in America, now editorializes in terms tending to discourage détente with the Soviet Union, and concedes that arms sales are acceptable, because Israel needs arms. It is joined by the likes of Norman Podhoretz and his wife Midge Decter. Some of these spokesmen have made it into the higher reaches of the u.s. government—Richard Perle, former assistant secretary of defense; Max Kampelman, chief arms negotiator; Richard Schifter, assistant secretary of state for human rights and humanitarian affairs; Morris Abram, vice-chairman of the u.s. Civil Rights Commission; Abraham Sofaer, legal counsel to the State Department; and Elliott Abrams, formerly an assistant secretary of state for human rights, and now for inter-American affairs. (The irony of shifting a supposed human rights advocate to the handling of the Contra war in Nicaragua may have escaped the president, but such is the progress of human rights in the 1980s.)

Nathan Yalin-Mor, a former leader of the Stern Gang in the 1940s, once remarked to me that professional Zionists in America and the leadership in Israel had created a sort of escalating round robin. As American Zionists expressed their militancy in increasingly shrill terms, Israelis then increased the volume of their militancy, which in turn demanded even more volume from American Zionists. Yalin-Mor's view was that at some point the cycle had to be broken in order for a chance to end the conflict.

As an idea to create a haven for Jews trying to escape historic racism directed against them by host countries, establishing a Jewish state seemed to offer the answer. The problems arose when the Zionist movement chose a land already inhabited by people who desired their own independent state. Because of this, the effort to find justice for Jews has created great injustice for Palestinians, as well as others around them. The concept of Israel—a settler state forcibly implanted in the midst of a group of Third World nations— has created many more problems than it has solved.

In their zeal to do Israel's bidding, American Jewish leaders, instead of standing firm against it, have chosen to look the other way even in cases of racism against Jews in the United States. Clearly, caving in on such an important principle has more to do with protecting Israel than with protecting Jews, as several examples have shown. Jesse Jackson, always suspect in the eyes of Zionist leaders, was hammered unmercifully for labeling New York "Hymietown." But it was different when Republican Congressman Robert Dornan took to the floor of the u.s. House of Representatives to attack a Soviet spokesman, Vladimir Posner, as a "disloyal, betraying little Jew who sits there on television claiming that he is somehow or other a newsman. Its an affront to decency and dignity and to Jewish people all around the world." Jews who saw Dornan's outburst on television told me his tone and manner were "frighteningly anti-Semitic." Labeled by the *Washington Post* as a long-time critic of the Soviet Union and an ardent supporter of Israel, Dornan told a reporter that a pro-Israel group had called him and said he had no reason to apologize for his remarks. Because of his support for Israel, he was publicly forgiven by two of his pro-Israeli, Jewish House colleagues, Representative Steven Solarz of New York and Representative Tom Lantos of California. Lantos joined Dornan at a press conference called to soften the anger of American Jews around the United States who had seen him making the statement on television. Lantos said Dornan had "made a slip of the tongue. We all do." Solarz sent a statement to the press conference in which he said, "A misspoken phrase in a moment of heated debate should not be allowed to overshadow Bob's long history of support and involvement with Israel, Soviet Jewry and other Jewish causes."

The view of some who were concerned with anti-Jewish racism was not as forgiving as Lantos, Solarz, and the unnamed pro-Israeli group. One letter writer in the March 5, 1986 *Washington Post* called Dornan's remarks a racial slur worthy of Joseph Stalin, and went on to say, "Hypocritical apologetics aside, Representative Dornan's behavior was itself an 'affront to the decency and dignity of Jewish people around the world.' We will not be used to advance the political agenda of anyone, including congressmen."

Indifference to racism so long as the racist supports Israel is not restricted to members of Congress, however. When Menachem Begin gave the Reverend Jerry Falwell the Jabotinsky Award in 1980, it marked formal recognition of a relationship that had been developing for a number of years—that between Zionists and Christian fundamentalists. (Vladimir Jabotinsky, for whom the award was named, was the leader of the Revisionist Zionist Movement. His biggest fan and follower has been Menachem Begin along with the Herut party. Jabotinsky was opposed to the partition of Palestine and wanted the Jewish state created in all of Palestine, which, according to his belief, included Jordan as well.) Television viewers are hard put to find a fundamentalist minister who does not, at one time or another, preach the gospel of support for "tiny little Israel," as it is described. And Zionist organizations for years have worked the fundamentalist community, developing it as a grass-roots support group for Israel. Many fundamentalist television sermons are produced in Israel during tours which they have sponsored, using the Mount of Olives as a backdrop.

On the surface, there should be nothing wrong with Zionists seeking alliances with American Christians who also happen to believe in the fundamental interpretation of the Bible. But it is disturbing to a great many Americans, Jews and non-Jews, especially those raised in the liberal tradition. It chafes not only because many of the fundamentalist ministers have preached hatred against Jews in the past ("God does not hear the prayers of Jews," said one such minister), but also because they have favored enforced prayer in schools, are opposed to abortion, and in particular, because of evangelical support for an arms build-up. The alliance has great potential for seriously heating up the nuclear arms race.

The evangelicals are most anxious to see the final battle—Armageddon—occur in order to pave the way for the return of Jesus and his salvation of the world. According to fundamentalist theory, Armageddon will take place in its supposed biblical location of Meggido, Israel, and will constitute a nuclear holocaust that will kill most of the Jews before Jesus undertakes salvation. Those Jews remaining will be converted to Christianity and will, at once, begin preaching the gospel of Christ.

A catalogue of alliances built up by Zionist leaders has created a distinct pattern, extremely disturbing in its result. Zionist leaders will befriend anti-Jewish racists so long as they support Israel. Israel will support South Africa because South Africa supports Israel, despite South Africa's crimes against humanity. Israel will sell arms to Iran to prolong its bloody war with Iraq because Iraq is an Arab enemy. Where are the human values in this policy? Where is the symbiosis with the liberality of American Jews, or non-Jews for that matter? Why are Israel's objectives (rather than Israel's survival) more important than the safety of individual Jews? Again, where is the United States interest?

American politicians, because of the enormous amount of money poured into their campaigns by Jewish contributors, long ago decided to give Israel its free ride, not only in terms of excessive American aid money, but in terms of political and diplomatic protec-

tion when Israel's victims seek formal censure of Israel for its violations of international law.

I know U.S. senators who, just prior to attending fund raisers for
their campaigns in New York or Los Angeles, have made either
anti-Arab, or pro-Zionist speeches on the Senate floor, making certain to have them reproduced from the *Congressional Record* for
distribution to Jewish contributors. That seems harmless. But it
leads to demagogic escalation in the form, at times, of amendments
offered on the Senate floor piling on extra dollars from the American
taxpayer to be sent to Israel. Many such amendments are unasked
for either by Israel or the U.S. State Department, and a few have
been done in such a pandering manner they have even embarrassed
the Israelis.

One of the more embarrassing instances of pandering to Israel
took place over the past several years concerning the Lavi airplane,
a plane developed by Israel with virtually all American funding and
American technology. In his August 6, 1986 *Washington Post* article on the Lavi, Charles Babcock said, ". . . virtually all of it, every
rivet, every microchip, paid out of nearly $2 billion in U.S. aid money
earmarked for the plane's development. Although no mention of it
was made that night, Israel is operating on the assumption that the
United States will spend billions more on the fighter's production
costs." Going beyond military aid for ostensibly defensive purposes,
the Lavi was announced as a boon to the Israeli arms industry—
designed not for Israeli use, but for export to other countries. An
amendment in the U.S. House of Representatives in 1985 seeking to
stop the use of American money and technology for the plane was
soundly defeated, the sponsor of the amendment receiving not more
than forty-one votes. There was an incredible silence on the part of
the American airplane industry, which will lose business, and the
labor unions which will lose jobs, as the Israelis begin to market the
Lavi.

There used to be a standing joke in the Senate Democratic
cloakroom in the 1970s when so many U.S. senators were lined up
to challenge Richard Nixon and later, Gerald Ford for president.
We knew, from the nature of the speech being given on the floor
of the Senate—suddenly pro-Israel or anti-Arab—that the senator in
question was making ready his campaign for the presidency.

In 1985, the campaign manager of a congressman who was

preparing to run for the Senate called to ask if I thought American Arabs could raise more money for his candidate's senate campaign than American Jews. My answer was no, that Jews obviously could raise much more. Not more than two weeks later I saw in the *Congressional Record* a speech inserted by the congressman that clearly marked the beginning of his fund-raising effort. For the first time in his career he made a speech on the House floor calling for increased emigration for Jews from the Soviet Union.

All that seems harmless as well, except when it comes to the divergence of American and Israeli interests, a condition that occurs more frequently than anyone likes to admit. Senators and congressmen cannot, of course, admit publicly that the u.s. credit card that they've handed Israel is a direct result of the money Israel's supporters pour into their campaigns. A credible, public reason is necessary to explain such blind, unquestioning support. As a consequence, their rationale comes in a great many other forms, many of them most ingenious.

"Israel is the only democracy in the Middle East." The Palestinians in the West Bank should be asked about this.

"Israel is the only bastion of support against Soviet aggression in the Middle East." However, in the unlikely event that the Soviets moved troops beyond the buffer states on their borders, and into an Arab oil country, it is even more unlikely that Israel would sacrifice even one soldier to challenge it, or that it would be able to make a difference if it did.

"Israel is America's strategic ally." After years of using this excuse, of taking money, of keeping America in hot water with allies in the Arab world, Israel finally had a chance to prove its value as a strategic ally during the hijacking of twa Flight 847 in the summer of 1985. Those holding the American passengers hostage were demanding the release of the Lebanese hostages held by Israel in Israeli prisons. Defense Minister Yitzhak Rabin, when asked by a journalist if Israel intended to do so, flatly stated that the hijacking was America's problem, and not Israel's. Israel eventually agreed to release the Lebanese hostages they were holding, but not until the American hostages and their families, and, in fact, the entire country was held in anguish. So much for Israel's value as a strategic ally.

After years of stumbling around trying to find some credible public reason why we continue to pour billions of taxpayers' dollars into Israel, their apologists have finally settled on citing Israel's intelligence value to the United States. It is a good choice, since one can neither document nor disprove the claim. It's classified, you see.

Several books have been written about the Mossad, most of them creating a mystique of infallibility, raising the suspicion that they must have been written by Mossad publicists, particularly after the assessment delivered by former C.I.A. Director, Admiral Stansfield Turner, who said, unequivocally, that the Mossad's best work was in promoting its own image. (One wonders, however, if Israel's intelligence is so good, why was it necessary to turn Jonathan Pollard into a traitor to his own country, paying him to steal information which Israel boasts about giving to us in the first place.)

When Abba Eban was foreign minister of Israel, his song to American audiences was give Israel weapons and money and it will hold off the Soviet Union for you. It is an amazing claim, but one that found an audience in American politicians eager to please the Israeli lobby.

But after all the lame excuses are given, one fact remains unchanged: Israel pursues its own interests whether or not they are damaging to the United States. It is naive in the extreme to think otherwise.

It was disclosed in 1986 that the Israelis convinced Ronald Reagan that arms shipments to Iran would free American hostages there. Israel had been shipping arms to Iran since the beginning of the Iran-Iraq war in 1980. Since the U.S. had asked for an arms embargo against Iran, Israel obviously felt more comfortable if it could get the United States to join—secretly—in its adventure. Reagan agreed, and the resulting scandal when the shipments were disclosed gave Reagan more trouble than he wanted.

What is interesting is that Reagan has been one of Israel's best friends, making it ironic indeed that Israel's self-serving actions created Reagan's first real presidential crisis.

Israel's history of pursuing its own interest began long before the Iran arms scam, however. Its destruction of the U.S. Navy intelligence ship, the USS *Liberty*, was done to prevent the United States from overhearing Israel's radio traffic just prior to its invasion of Syria in 1967.

Israel and South Africa

Before it built up its arms industry, South Africa relied in great part on Israel to provide it with weapons and technology. The two countries have had a military alliance dating back to the mid-1960s, during which time they have traded arms, equipment, military know-how, and advice on how to maintain control over a repressed majority.

To defeat the first U.N. arms embargo in 1963, South Africa purchased missiles, anti-tank weapons, and small arms from Israel. After the 1967 war, when France ended its arms supply to Israel, South Africa provided spare parts for the Mirage jets that Israel had purchased from France. The Mossad had earlier stolen the blueprints for the French Mirage III engine which Israel then sold to South Africa.

Following an agreement signed in 1976, arms sales from Israel to South Africa increased dramatically. Israel ignored U.N. General Assembly Resolution 418, passed in 1977, which forbade arms sales to South Africa, continuing its shipments, but publicly denying them.

The high point of the military alliance came when Israel and South Africa jointly tested a nuclear weapon over the south Atlantic in 1979. Since then, Israel has accumulated between one hundred and two hundred nuclear weapons, and South Africa boasts that it is capable of producing two such weapons each year.

When Congress passed anti-apartheid legislation in 1986, the *Jerusalem Post* wrote that the legislation was "clearly a threat to Israel," because of language it contained forcing a cut-off of U.S. military aid to Israel should it be found to be supplying South Africa's military.

The relationship has created a serious problem for supporters of Israel, especially those who are dedicated to ending apartheid in South Africa. The dilemma rests in the great similarity between the two countries—both are settler societies sitting on usurped land belonging to others; both have decided on military aggression as a response to the political problems created by their occupation; both practice apartheid; and both are basically unstable societies whose instability results from the churning unrest of those they rule. Israel's supporters generally respond to questions about South Africa with the answer that Israel has such few friends in the world that an alliance with anyone is reasonable. Providing the means for each other's ongoing internal repression and external aggression is an alliance which violates any kind of reason. *One can find no American interest whatever in the South Africa connection.*

Impact on the United Nations

In the United Nations, the u.s. government has, over the years, distinguished itself by lending its veto power in the Security Council to support some of the most reprehensible acts ever committed by another country, all in an effort to protect Israel from formal criticism. By the end of 1986, the United States used its veto a total of twenty times on resolutions, most of them condemning Israel for its illegal actions.

The first veto ever cast by the United States was in March 1970, against a resolution dealing with southern Rhodesia.

■ The next veto—the first on Israel—was cast on September 10, 1972, on a Security Council resolution condemning Israeli attacks inside Lebanon and Syria. The vote was thirteen to one in favor, with one abstention.

■ July 26, 1973: The u.s. vetoed a Security Council resolution affirming the rights of the Palestinians. The vote was thirteen to one in favor, with China not participating.

■ December 8, 1975: The u.s. vetoed a Security Council resolution condemning Israel's attacks against southern Lebanon. The vote was thirteen to one in favor, with one abstention.

■ January 26, 1976: The u.s. vetoed a Security Council resolution calling for self-determination for the Palestinians. The vote was nine to one in favor, with three abstentions.

■ March 25, 1976: The u.s. vetoed a Security Council resolution deploring Israel's changing of the status of Jerusalem and ordered it to stop establishing settlements on Arab land. The vote was fourteen to one in favor.

■ June 29, 1976: The u.s. vetoed a Security Council resolution affirming the "inalienable rights" of the Palestinians. The vote was ten to one in favor, with four abstentions.

■ April 30, 1980: The u.s. vetoed a Security Council resolution calling for the right of self-determination for the Palestinians. The vote was ten to one in favor, with four abstentions.

■ January 20, 1982: The U.S. vetoed a strong Security Council resolution demanding Israel's withdrawal from the Golan Heights. The vote was nine to one in favor, with five abstentions.

■ April 2, 1982: The U.S. vetoed a Security Council resolution condemning Israel's occupation policies. The vote was thirteen to one in favor, with one abstention.

■ April 20, 1982: The U.S. vetoed a Security Council resolution condemning the shooting by a berserk Israeli soldier of eleven Moslem worshippers on the Temple Mount, the Haram al-Sharif, in the Old City of Jerusalem. The vote was fourteen to one in favor.

■ June 8, 1982: The U.S. vetoed a Security Council resolution that would have imposed sanctions on Israel if it did not withdraw from Lebanon. The vote was fourteen to one in favor. This was two days after the Israeli invasion of Lebanon. The U.S. effectively endorsed the invasion with this vote.

■ June 26, 1982: The U.S. vetoed a Security Council resolution that would have imposed sanctions on Israel if it did not withdraw from Beirut. The vote was fourteen to one in favor.

■ August 6, 1982: The U.S. vetoed a strong Security Council resolution that would have cut off all economic aid to Israel if it did not withdraw from Lebanon. The vote was eleven to one in favor, with three abstentions.

■ August 2, 1983: The U.S. vetoed a Security Council resolution condemning Israeli settlements as a serious obstacle to peace. The vote was thirteen to one in favor, with one abstention.

■ September 6, 1984: The U.S. vetoed a Security Council resolution deploring Israel's violence in southern Lebanon. The vote was fourteen to one in favor.

■ March 12, 1985: The U.S. vetoed a Security Council resolution condemning Israel's "iron fist" policy in southern Lebanon. The vote was eleven to one in favor, with three abstentions.

■ September 13, 1985: The U.S. vetoed a Security Council resolution condemning Israel's human rights violations in the occupied territories. The vote was ten to one in favor, with four abstentions.

■ January 17, 1986: The U.S. vetoed a Security Council resolution "strongly deploring" Israeli violence in southern Lebanon and urging Israel's withdrawal. The vote was eleven to one in favor, with three abstentions.

■ January 30, 1986: The u.s. vetoed a Security Council resolution condemning Israel's provocative actions toward the Moslem religious shrine Haram al-Sharif in the Old City of Jerusalem. The vote was thirteen to one in favor, with one abstention.

■ February 6, 1986: The u.s. vetoed a Security Council resolution condemning Israel's hijacking of a Libyan passenger plane two days earlier. The vote was ten to one in favor, with four abstentions.

With time left to go, the Reagan administration already has broken the record previously held for Security Council vetoes, protecting Israel with thirteen vetoes.

We have witnessed an attack, over the past several years, conducted by Israel and its apologists in the United States aimed at destroying the United Nations. Always masked in terms that the u.n. is dominated by "Arab" sympathizers, the efforts to discredit and destroy the world body are made by Israel solely to allow it to evade criticism for its illegal adventures.

Supporters of Israel are almost too quick to point out that the General Assembly vote in 1947 was the instrument that created Israel. It was not, since General Assembly votes are non-binding. If they were, the Middle East would be more stable than it is now, and, of course, the Palestinians would not be sitting in refugee camps. There is a plethora of General Assembly votes dealing with the Arab-Israeli conflict, virtually all of which have tried to right the wrongs committed by Israel against the Palestinians. There are twenty-five General Assembly resolutions generally condemning those Israeli practices and policies which are in violation of international law; eight that demand Israel's withdrawal from land it took militarily in 1956; five that demand Israeli withdrawal from the occupied territories; nine that call for repatriation and compensation to the Palestinians for their property losses; eight reaffirming Arab/Palestinian rights to natural resources in the occupied territories; three condemning Israeli military aggression in Lebanon; four expressing concern for the living conditions of those living under

Israeli occupation; fifteen calling for the Palestinians' right to self-determination; six condemning Israeli economic practices in the occupied territories; thirteen seeking to establish a nuclear weapons free zone in the Middle East, including condemnation of Israel's raid on the Iraqi nuclear reactor; four condemning the relationship between Israel and South Africa; one dealing with the status of the Palestinians in relation to the Camp David accords; and one condemning the deportation of elected Palestinian mayors from the West Bank.

Small wonder that Israel and its supporters want to destroy the credibility of the United Nations.

There is no escaping the consequence of Israel's anti-u.n. campaign—it is destructive of efforts made by the u.n. to make our world more peaceful and a bit safer for everyone. Those who are running the campaign against the u.n. have effectively offered American Jews a choice—either Israel or the u.n. It's a tragic dilemma for Jews who would like to support both, leading many reluctantly to choose Israel. But the choices given are dishonest ones. A more honest choice would be between the u.n. and Israel's illegal activities—a choice which would allow Israel's continued existence as a state, but one that keeps Israel within the boundaries of international law, traditions, and customs.

But how credible is the United States when it challenges the Soviet Union in the u.n. for employing double standards? How can the United States explain the fact that its closest allies on the Security Council consistently vote to censure Israel's illegal activities? How is it in America's interest to isolate itself diplomatically in the world community—to earn the dislike of Third World countries who see our vote as an attack on their aspirations?

Effects on the Media

Certain components of the American media are faced with the same problem—that of journalistic honesty. A perfect example is the schizophrenia forced on the *New York Times*, a newspaper that aspires to eternal greatness, but which fails miserably when it comes to honest reporting about Israel. Jacobo Timmerman's exit from Argentina and his comments and writings after leaving there commanded virtually daily stories in the *New York Times*. But since he wrote his impassioned criticism of the Israeli invasion of Lebanon,

Timmerman has completely disappeared from the pages of the *Times*. The op-ed pages seem to belong solely to those with a Zionist point of view, with articles written from a Palestinian slant being few and far between. There is a great reluctance to run news stories embarrassing to Israel, such as Israeli spying in the United States, or Israeli arms deals with Iran and other countries. The stories eventually appear in the *Times*, but only in a seemingly forced fashion after appearing on television network news shows or in other major newspapers.

Only since the Israeli invasion of Lebanon in 1982 have the television networks evidenced a semblance of balance and fairness in their reporting of the Middle East conflict, although they still have a long way to go. At the beginning of the invasion, the press, as well as the networks, were simply regurgitating communiqués issued by the Israeli military, that the Israeli Army once again was involved in the valiant task of weeding out terrorists. The networks were becoming willing partners with Israel in its propaganda war. Because a war has great visual impact, and because the network television crews were sending back thousands of feet of videotape recording the destruction of lives and property during the siege of Beirut, the urge to broadcast it as news overcame the urge to protect Israel. Even the sanitized footage shown on the nightly news was too much for the public to take, causing President Reagan to tell Prime Minister Begin to call it off. Had the networks shown everything from the beginning, unsanitized, Reagan's phone call would have come weeks earlier. Despite the attack on the networks by the Israeli lobby for actually showing Israel's bloody work, they have now become somewhat accustomed to publicizing Israel's more heinous crimes.

The most glaring omission, with respect to press coverage, is the brutality of the Israeli occupation in Lebanon and the West Bank. It is a journalistic void that has never been filled, but should be.

Had the American media been more fair at the start, had it reported both sides of the story and allowed the American public to make a decision based on all the facts, we would not face today's dilemma and protecting America's interest would be easier.

Searching for America's Interest

*T*he official statement of u.s. Middle East policy issued by the State Department has a principled sound to it. But beyond the rhetoric, the reality obviously is to allow Israel a free hand in the Middle East, giving it whatever financial, political, and military support necessary to do whatever it wants to whomever it wants.

Currently, Israel's relationship to the United States emphasizes the worst aspects of our overall foreign policy, in much the same respect as our relationship to Guatemala, the Contras, Jonas Savimbi, and others. There is a pretense that Israel exists in the middle of the Arab world to do our bidding, to act as our agent there. It is only a form of rhetoric used by Zionists and their supporters to keep American aid money flowing. It's all too clear that Israel's interests are more often than not antithetical to ours.

Our interests lie in doing justice, for whatever meaning remains in that word, and in bringing peace. To do so it is necessary for us to maintain an honest relationship with all the parties to the struggle, avoiding unreasonable bias in favor of Israel, or of the Arabs for that matter. No one, whether in the Arab world or elsewhere, rationally expects the United States to end its support of Israel. But it is much more in our interest to stop supporting Israel's territorial objectives, which we can do, and still be seen as a fair and just interlocutor.

In considering how to end the Arab-Israeli conflict, we are faced with either an ideal resolution, or a pragmatic one. Ideally, the Palestinians driven out of Palestine when the Israeli state was created should be allowed the right to return and the right to vote on what kind of government they want. It's obvious that Israel would never allow it to happen. Ideally, a Jewish homeland should have been found that did not create more suffering than its creation was intended to remedy. Since events have by-passed the ideal, we are left with a pragmatic response, which means the United States either continues its present policy or changes it in a way that is least damaging to people in the Middle East.

We are constantly reminded that Israel's and America's policies are identical. The logical question then is: who benefits from a continuation of the present policy—Israel or the United States?

Every official statement, every governmental action makes it clear that Israel's objective is to retain the West Bank, the Gaza Strip, south Lebanon, and the Golan Heights as long as possible. A change in u.s. policy would require Israel to give up those occupied lands in exchange for a peace treaty. While Israel does not see in its interest a comprehensive peace in return for territory, it is very much in the interest of the United States.

A static u.s. policy means a contination of the occupation by Israel; of a military build up; of expenditures for armaments at the expense of human and resource development; of the gross violations of the human rights of those Palestinians, Lebanese, and Syrians forced to live under Israeli occupation; of huge appropriations of American taxpayers' money for Israel and for tribute to Egypt on account of its separate peace; of the continued debasing of America's veto in the u.n.; and of the ever present threat of nuclear confrontation between the United States and the Soviet Union.

Now that Israel has in its arsenal some two hundred nuclear weapons, we should not be surprised if the Arab countries tire of being on the receiving end of Israel's aggression, and develop or buy their own nuclear arsenal. And no one is certain that the Soviet Union will not weigh in on the side of Syria in some future war. There is talk that Israel is developing—as crazy as it sounds—an icbm capable of reaching the Soviet Union.

From a combined perspective—both moral and pragmatic— Israel cannot continue to occupy the West Bank, the Gaza, and south Lebanon in perpetuity. An uprising in the occupied territories would make nuclear weapons useless, and who knows when the American press will actually start covering the brutality there, causing Israel, like South Africa, to lose its support in the United States?

By the end of fiscal year 1987, the u.s. government, using American taxpayers' money, has poured $40 billion ($39,716,700,000) into Israel since its founding in 1948. The bulk of this money started flowing in the late 1960s, and has reached record proportions now of over $3 billion each year—more than $8 million each day of the year. In fiscal year 1987 Israel's direct aid is 22 percent of all u.s. foreign aid, and with Egypt's included, is 39 percent of all u.s. aid. Not only does the amount increase each year, but since 1985, it has been converted to total grants, making it no longer necessary to pretend that Israel must repay it. The figure of $39.7,167 billion is conservative because it does not include the hefty, individual charitable gifts, exempt from u.s. taxes, sent to Israel in great quantities each year, and advance payments which enhance the grants even further. This advance payment scheme allows Israel to earn interest on the money until it is used, while the u.s. is required to pay interest on it because it is borrowed.

The United States should, without more delay, use its considerable financial and moral influence on Israel to reach an accommodation with the Palestinians and with its Arab neighbors. Instead of taking the lead in moving Israel toward a settlement, the United States government adjusts its own policies to fit the desire of Israel. Since Henry Kissinger in 1975 foolishly promised the Israelis the United States would not talk to or recognize the p.l.o., we have effectively shut out all the diplomatic initiatives made by the p.l.o. since then. Our government spokesmen claim they refuse to talk to the p.l.o. because they are terrorists, but that excuse is only one more lie in a long series of lies about the Middle East. President Reagan has dispatched his staff to talk to Iran, and Secretary of State George Shultz has met with the head of the African National Congress, which, like the p.l.o. in the Middle East, is engaged in armed struggle to liberate South Africa.

It is unrealistic to think, as both the Israeli government and the State Department do, that Jordan can be convinced to sign a separate treaty, followed by Syria, à la Anwar Sadat's Egypt. In the unlikely event that such separate peace agreements were to come about, the Palestinians would still be under occupation.

Such an accommodation must include the return of all of the Arab lands forcibly taken by Israel after 1948. The West Bank and the Gaza Strip should be given to the Palestinians specifically for the purpose of creating an independent Palestinian state. Jerusalem can be used by both Jews and Arabs as their capital, since there is an Arab Jerusalem and a Jewish Jerusalem. An agreement allowing the free movement of all religions, Christian, Muslim, Jewish, whatever, in all parts of Jerusalem must be a part of the overall settlement.

I've heard many times over the multitude of arguments that hold that Israel needs the West Bank and Gaza Strip for its security because Israel is a very narrow country without them.

The argument is specious and without foundation.

Israel is a very narrow country *with* them, and with today's destructive military technology, the width of the West Bank cannot prevent missiles either from the ground or the air. Holding the West Bank only guarantees more danger, not less. Genuine security derives from neighbors who are not hostile, and not from occupying or threatening others, as the Soviet Union is learning the hard way. And interestingly, the premise of the security argument—that Israel needs security—seems to have been stood on its head. There is no Arab country sitting on Israeli land, but clearly Israel is sitting in its entirety on Arab land—more evidence of how the images of the Middle East have been distorted beyond recognition. In honesty, after years of Israeli expansion, it is the Arabs who require security arrangements.

The entire task of making peace presupposes that negotiations over the conditions of peace must take place. Obviously, a peace treaty must be signed before any territory can be transferred. I have full confidence that Israeli negotiators are competent enough to insist on terms that would protect their own security. I have no doubt that the superpowers, once involved with the treaty signing, would ensure the security of all of the parties to the agreement.

For a peace conference to be successful, it must include all the Arab countries involved in the conflict, the Palestinians, and the Soviet Union as well as the United States. Secretary of State George Shultz discovered, much too late, the difficulty of cutting deals without all the parties to the conflict being present. When he negotiated the infamous May 17th agreement between Israel and the puppet regime in Lebanon, ignoring the role Syria plays in the Arab world, not only Shultz, but the entire United States as well, learned a bitter lesson.

We have witnessed the devastation caused by the separate treaty signed between Israel and Egypt, a folly which would be multiplied many times over if it is attempted again with any single Arab country.

Israel has consistently resisted a comprehensive peace conference that includes the P.L.O. and the Soviet Union. That resistance is the only real obstacle to ending the Arab-Israeli conflict. A comprehensive peace conference is a progression which Israel does not want to see taking place. It would begin with the P.L.O. giving up its armed struggle against Israel, and Israel giving up the territories it occupies. Excluding the Russians from a Middle East peace conference dooms it to failure before it starts. But that is the major reason for Israel's objection to including the Soviets—it guarantees that a conference will not be held.

This is not to say that Israel does not seek peace—it does, but only on its own terms, which include keeping the land it has taken from others. As the Palestinians have pointed out more than once, that would not be peace, it would be surrender, an alternative not currently contemplated by any of the parties.

Israeli spokesmen continuously say they will not talk to the P.L.O. because it has vowed the destruction of Israel. How has any nation ever made peace with an adversary bent on its destruction—by talking with allies? The answer, of course, is obvious. Since the struggle is basically between the Israelis and the Palestinians, and since the P.L.O. represents the Palestinians, logic would require that they be a party to a peace negotiation.

Israel and its supporters insist that the P.L.O must recognize Israel's right to exist before its government will talk to the P.L.O. Since Israel is the stronger of the two parties, and since the P.L.O. has no other negotiating card, would it not make more sense to stop the killing and begin negotiating, saving the formal recognition of each other for a treaty? Doesn't the fact of sitting down across the table from each other constitute recognition?

Israel further says that it will not deal with the P.L.O. leadership, but instead will talk with other Palestinians, a position supported by the United States. Only in the movies would Israel and the United States be able to choose the negotiators for the other party—in this case for the P.L.O. It is patently ridiculous to believe that rank and file Palestinians would support a peace settlement signed by someone other than their own chosen representatives —in this case the P.L.O.

Those who opt for retention of America's current Middle East policy have become practiced at self-delusion. It amounts to nothing more than ordering and paying for the continuation of the daily misery and suffering resulting from our present policy. We are only now beginning to measure how America's standing has declined both in the Arab world and the rest of the Third World as well. Americans, once universally respected, are increasingly becoming the targets of those victimized by our policy of blind support of Israel's expansion and brutality.

We need only to calculate the enormous economic, moral, and human cost to the United States until now, and into the future, to understand that our policy must be changed.

REBUTTALS

HYMAN BOOKBINDER

I regret that Mr. Abourezk has chosen to state his case in a
manner more appropriate for a P.L.O. rally than for the kind of
thoughtful readership we had both expressed a desire to address.
From the first page ("racism") to the last ("brutality") the Abourezk
argument is filled with sweeping indictments and characterizations
of Israelis and Jews, charging them with all of the worst possible
national and human traits—without reflecting any of the subtleties
or nuances or ambivalence that even critics of Israel ought to have
the grace to acknowledge.

How can one take seriously an analysis that—among many other
distortions and defamations—repeatedly refers to Israeli actions as
"Nazi-like" or declares that both South Africa and Israel practice
apartheid? Such vitriol would indeed get cheers at a P.L.O. rally, but
it makes more difficult—rather than facilitates—the search for understanding and accommodation. It will discourage rather than encourage, I fear, more exchanges between Arabs and Jews.

I concluded my opening statement with the hope that "here in
the United States Arabs and Jews will choose tolerance and civility
as more appropriate weapons in the search for understanding and
accommodation" and that this debate might contribute to such
tolerance and civility. I expressed the hope that this debate would
not "deteriorate into an exchange of accusations about some specific
atrocities, real or alleged." The real atrocity is war itself. The basic
challenge is how to end the war between the Jews and the Arabs in
the Middle East—and thus to eliminate the basis for such atrocities.
But my hope was not realized. Mr. Abourezk leans almost exclusively
on the argument that in order to retain their hold on land they never
had a right to in the first place, the "racist" Jews of Israel have
continuously engaged in wanton terrorizing and murdering Arabs.

Such a state, presumably, has no right to exist—but, at the very least, does not deserve the support of the United States.

The temptation is almost uncontrollable to match his horror stories with an even longer list of Arab atrocities over the years directed not only against Jews in Israel but against Jews and non-Jews anywhere and everywhere around the globe. The urge is strong to describe each of these atrocities with the gruesome details that shocked the world at the time of each—and which, cumulatively, have produced the image he understandably wishes to erase—that image of "Arab terrorism." It is tempting, for example, to remind readers of those hours when they were glued to their television sets on September 5, 1972, hearing the details of the terrorist assault on eleven Israeli athletes at the Munich Olympics. I could take up page after page describing the mutilated bodies of the twenty-one children from Safed killed while spending the night at Maalot—or the twenty-four people killed and eighty wounded at Lod Airport in 1972—or any of the eight thousand (yes, *eight thousand!*) acts of terror in the period from February 1969, when Arafat became leader of the p.l.o., through 1984, as documented in *The Threat of PLO Terrorism* produced by the Israeli Ministry of Foreign Affairs in 1985. These are the acts that resulted directly in 650 deaths ("not very many," Abourezk says of this number) and many thousands wounded. And these are the acts that prompted Israel—as they should any self-respecting state concerned with the welfare of its citizens—to take retaliatory and preventive actions that, tragically, caused many more deaths, Arab and Jewish, including innocent civilians unfortunately caught in the cross-fire of violence.

I will have more to say about the many allegations of Israeli "terrorism" before I finish this rebuttal, but not too much more. I see no point in using precious pages for a case-by-case refutation of the many citations that have, over and over again, been either fully disproven or shown to have been grossly distorted and exaggerated. Some of the citations are accurate, or accurate enough, to prompt an observation I have made before and that I believe strongly. War *is* hell. People and nations at war *are* capable of cruelty. I do not exclude Israel or Jews from this obvious truth. That is why the search for peace and the need for accommodation are so crucial.

I find particularly offensive the repeated charge that Israelis (or *Zionists* or *Jews*) are totally uncaring about the lives of Arabs, that we grieve only over the death of our own. Now, Mr. Abourezk may choose to ignore or to reject the poignant comment of Golda Meir that I quoted, that she might some day forgive the Arabs for killing Israeli sons, but that she could never forgive them for making Israeli soldiers kill *their* sons. But I am proud to associate myself with that comment, and I am proud to assert here that every Jew I know also associates himself or herself with that view. That *is* the morality, the ethic, we have been taught all our lives. I do not contend that no Arab shares this reverence for life, but if any current or recent Arab leader has expressed such universal respect for human life, I have somehow failed to hear it.

In several separate sections of his presentation Mr. Abourezk refers to the tragic death of Alex Odeh in California—as an example of Jewish resort to terror, of lack of respect for Arab life, and of society's failure to react to such an outrageous act against an Arab. It is mind-boggling that my opponent could write so much and so often about the Odeh incident and not acknowledge my own personal role in the aftermath. Did he really think that I would fail to react to such a graceless omission? The event occurred long before this debate was planned. There can be no suspicion of planned self-serving behavior on my part. The murder of Alex Odeh was so disturbing to me that I did two things immediately. First, I consulted with the New York national headquarters and the California office of the American Jewish Committee. There was immediate agreement that we should all speak out firmly, both to express our condolences and to call upon all appropriate public bodies to take forthright action to apprehend those responsible for this outrageous act. I then placed calls to Mr. Abourezk in his capacity as head of the American Arab Anti-Discrimination Committee, to the professional head of ADC, and to Mr. Odeh's widow in California. I recall praising and thanking Mr. Abourezk for what I thought was a thoughtful and statesmanlike comment on the situation. He knows that Dr. David Gordis and I, sitting only a few feet away from him, reiterated our concerns at the hearing on July 16, 1986, before the House Judiciary Committee.

He knows that, at that hearing, I asked him to introduce me to Mrs. Odeh, and that we then had a very warm exchange. He knows that this meeting with Mrs. Odeh so impressed the nationally syndicated columnist Coleman McCarthy that he devoted a full column to the significance of this Jewish reaction to an anti-Arab atrocity. I received many calls and letters about this column from around the country, and also from around the world because the *International Herald-Tribune* had printed the column. "For Norma Odeh," Mr. McCarthy concludes his column, "the support of Hyman Bookbinder is an unexpected comfort. Both people, Arab and Jew, are the stronger for it."

But this is much more than a personal story. Lest Mr. Abourezk contend that I was a lonely exception, I hasten to add that there was widespread reaction throughout the American Jewish community— even though, it must be stressed, Jewish culpability has to this day been no more than conjecture, a hypothesis, rather than a proven fact. The American Jewish Committee's president, Howard Friedman, expressed "deep shock" and said, "The resort to violence here and abroad to settle political differences is creating a cycle of terror that civilized societies must unite to halt. We express our sincerest sympathies to the families of the dead and injured, and we urge law enforcement officials to spare no effort to apprehend the perpetrators of this latest horror."

The Anti-Defamation League of the B'nai B'rith condemned the bombing as "domestic terrorism which cannot be tolerated." The Orange County Jewish Federation's chairman, Rabbi Bernard King, declared, "We unequivocally abhor such violent acts no matter where they occur or who the perpetrators may be."

American Jews have not been spared from senseless violence and terrorism, of course. The Odeh incident brings to mind the bombing several years ago of the home of Morris Amitay, then the executive director of the American-Israel Public Affairs Committee (AIPAC), while he and his family were asleep. It was not far-fetched to speculate that the bombing may have been executed by pro-Arab forces, though no conclusive evidence has surfaced. But I recall no expressions of concern from any American-Arab sources.

The reaction to the Odeh murder is one response to the careless and calumnious charge by Mr. Abourezk that Jews are indifferent to the loss of Arab life. That case occurred in the United States. An even more important and much more publicized case occurred recently in Israel and involved Jewish soldiers and the state. When an Israeli journalist broke the story of Shin Bet agents having apparently beaten to death two Palestinian terrorists who had hijacked a bus in the Gaza area in 1984 and killed a woman soldier, the Israeli public was outraged. I have read scores of editorials, feature articles, texts of letters and petitions demanding full investigation and appropriate punishment for those responsible. The final outcome may not please Israeli or American critics, and the last of the case may not have been heard, but I cite the general reaction and revulsion over the revelations in Israel itself and among American Jews only to further rebut the Abourezk indictment of Israel and Jews as uncaring. As they demonstrated in that 400,000-strong demonstration in Tel Aviv at the time of the Sabra-Shatila massacre, Israeli citizens are sensitive to any indication of brutal, inhumane treatment of any people, Arabs included.

I feel compelled to ask: Is there a history of similar concern for Jewish life among those for whom Mr. Abourezk presumes to speak? Would it not be a more civilized world if we heard about people's protests in Jordan or Syria or Saudi Arabia or other Arab communities after reports of senseless terrorism directed against Jews—or if we could see the rulers and judges of those countries diligently pursuing known murderers and terrorists?

It appears, moreover, that the professed concern over loss of Arab lives seems often to be limited to losses attributable to Israeli or Jewish groups. Arab-Jewish or Palestinian-Jewish conflicts are always highlighted and fully reported, including reports of casualties. But surely he knows that *substantially* more Arabs have been killed by other Arabs or by Muslims (as in the Iran-Iraq war) than by Israelis. The history of internecine war within the Arab and Muslim worlds is characterized by seeming indifference to mass killings. According to Amnesty International, as many as twenty-five thousand Arabs were slaughtered in the 1982 Syrian purge of the Muslim Brotherhood in Hama. In seven years of Lebanese Civil War *prior* to the 1982 Israeli incursion, an estimated 100,000 Arabs had been killed. At least one million have been killed or wounded in the Iran-Iraq war. The IDF reported that between June 1967 and March 1986, the P.L.O. had murdered 429 residents of the territories, and injured 3,110, including a high proportion of women and children. News reports early this year revealed the murder of more than two hundred Suni Muslim fundamentalists in a Syrian-backed sweep in the slums of Tabbaneh, Lebanon.

Mr. Abourezk's failure to acknowledge Jewish caring is not difficult to understand. It would interfere with the dominant theme of his argument: Israel is racist, and Jews are, by inference if not explicit characterization, racists. Therefore, acknowledge nothing, cite no history that would dilute the case against these "racist," "aggressive," "terrorist," "brutal" Jews who—without any legitimate claims—decided to oust the "less-than-human" Arabs from their land. Just keep repeating these charges. Keep using words like *racist* and *exclusive* and *brutal* in tireless repetition. Throw in a statistic here and there, allege another incident—but never make the mistake of grappling with any degree of balance with the basic issues involved in the settling of a complex conflict resulting from competing claims.

Mr. Abourezk, oddly enough, rejects precisely the tactic he has himself used in this debate. "Attack the person, but avoid debating the issue. Make [them] into a pariah so their words and thoughts are discredited, but avoid discussing the substance. In this way," he correctly warns, "a debate on the correctness or incorrectness of u.s. policy in the Middle East can be avoided." I submit that by being an incessant scold, charging Israel with racism and brutality and aggression, Mr. Abourezk has tried to divert attention from the real issue.

But there are indeed basic issues that must be discussed. And they are implicit in the case Mr. Abourezk has made. In rereading my opening statement, I believe I have already essentially provided much of the rebuttal called for. Space does not permit a page-by-page response, and so a number of the specific contentions will remain unchallenged. In order to deal adequately with the principal issues requiring elaboration, I must take the risk that it might appear that unchallenged items are really unchallengeable.

The Basic Issue: Israel's Legitimacy

Nothing better states the central substantive issue of this debate than the failure of my opponent, in a presentation of more than thirty-five thousand words, to include even a single, unambiguous sentence in which he would put to rest the issue of Israel's very legitimacy. Before this book is completed, I continue to hope Mr. Abourezk will find it possible to state—if I may suggest words that he could conceivably accept—that "Whatever mistakes or unfairness surrounded the creation of Israel, its right to exist in peace, with

recognized, negotiated borders, should no longer be challenged."
Over and over again in his presentation he rejects this basic
right of Israel ever to have laid claim to any part of Palestine. Early
in his opening statement he refers to the Zionists' "forcible conquest of a new state." In his last section, he reveals his "ideal"
formula for undoing that historic mistake: "The Palestinians . . .
should be allowed the right to return and the right to vote on what
kind of government they want." His reluctant acknowledgment
that this "ideal" solution is not likely to occur does not lessen the
significance of his unyielding rejection of Israel's legitimacy. Instead of calling on the Arab states and Palestinian leadership at
long last to abandon their dream of eliminating the only Jewish
state in the area, he is willing only to consider the "pragmatic"
steps he deems appropriate under the circumstances, knowing full
well that for the rejectionist Arab states and for the various P.L.O.
factions, such "pragmatic" steps are viewed as tactics in their goal
of final, full "liberation."

In the Abourezk interpretation of history, there came a time at
the end of the nineteenth century, when a Zionist movement decided that the world's Jews, who allegedly had no current or recent
connection with Palestine, should leave the diaspora and make the
land of Palestine their new home, replacing the Arab Palestinian
state with a Jewish state, and driving out the Arab people, by force
if necessary. Repeatedly, he argues that Jews may be entitled to their
own state, but by what right, he asks, do they acquire one by taking
over a state occupied by some other people?

So it is necessary at this point to restate the basic case for Israel's
rights in Palestine, and to offer some additional documentation. The
Abourezk question is based on two major distortions of history that
must be corrected. First, the Jews were never "foreigners" in Palestine; they had maintained ties to their historic homeland, physical
and spiritual, for three thousand years, since the time of Abraham.
Second, there had *never* been an Arab political entity in Palestine.
For many, many years there had been two peoples in the area—the
Jewish people and the Arab people, both governed without their
effective participation. Their respective numbers fluctuated over the
years, each community experiencing both immigration and emigration of its respective people depending on circumstances both inside
and outside of Palestine.

While each of these communities yearned for recognition and political sovereignty, their respective goals did not clash in any threatening way until the twentieth century. Jewish "peoplehood" was an obvious and recognized concept. Arab Palestinian's "peoplehood" was less obvious—though, in time, appropriately identified and recognized—because they shared a religion, a culture, and a history with a large Arab community, with recognized states that surrounded them, and with which they had relatively easy access.

What is not really arguable is that during the early decades of the present century, there were *two* peoples living in Palestine and that there was need to effect some kind of political accommodation that could meet their respective needs with the least possible dislocation to the affected people.

It is one thing to argue that one or the other of the affected peoples got shortchanged in the solutions offered and the resulting arrangements, but it is simply turning history on its head to deny that both Jews *and* Arabs came to this historic conflict with legitimate bases for their respective claims. No matter how many times, no matter in how many ways, Mr. Abourezk repeats that the Zionists took over another people's country by "conquest," that charge cannot meet the test of documented history.

The Balfour Declaration of 1917 may still disturb enemies of Israel, but it is surely a reflection of the reality of significant Jewish presence and striving in Palestine. In order to minimize the significance of the Balfour Declaration, Mr. Abourezk quotes briefly from the Churchill Memorandum of 1922 to suggest a major "re-interpretation" of the declaration, the ruling out of what he calls "an exclusive Jewish state." While the memorandum did make it clear that the intent was not to contemplate a Jewish national home in *all* of Palestine as then constituted, it reasserted, by quoting favorably the 1921 Carlsbad resolution of the Zionist Congress, "the determination of the Jewish people to live with the Arab people on terms of unity and mutual respect, and together with them to make the common home into a flourishing community, the upbuilding of which *may assure to each of its peoples an undisturbed national development.*" There is no reference to any "exclusive" Jewish state.

Noting that apprehensions had been voiced by some Jews, the Churchill Memorandum declares that "fears of abandonment of the Balfour commitment are unfounded." After noting the many ways in which the Jews in Palestine had become a productive, creative community, the memorandum states:

> But in order that the community should have the best prospect of free development and provide a full opportunity for the Jewish people to display its capacities, it is essential that it should know that it is in Palestine as of right and not on sufferance. That is the reason why it is necessary that the existence of a Jewish National Home in Palestine should be internationally guaranteed, and that it should be formally recognized to rest upon ancient historic connection.

Neither the Balfour nor Churchill documents at the time spelled out exactly what form of political arrangements would be justified or required to assure the "national development" of the Jewish national home. As we have already noted, by 1942 the Zionist movement had determined that nothing less than statehood was appropriate.

Churchill never talked about an "exclusive" Jewish homeland. Neither did the Jews. His memorandum rejects only the notion that *all* of the Palestinian land of the time should become the Jewish homeland. Actually, as we soon saw, about 80 percent of that land was excluded even from consideration and became part of Transjordan. The remaining 20 percent was subsequently partitioned for the proposed Palestinian-Arab and Jewish states. Thus, only about 13 percent of the original territory available for the national Jewish home actually was granted for the new state of Israel.

Perhaps the most telling evidence of the reality of Jewish presence and entitlement to statehood at that historic stage is the role of Emir Faisal, son of the acknowledged leader of the Arabs, Sherif Hussein. During the 1919 Paris Peace Conference, Faisal met with Chaim Weizmann and other Zionist leaders. They signed an agreement that, "mindful of the racial kinship and racial bonds existing between the Arabs and the Jewish people," called for the "closest possible collaboration in the development of the Arab state and Palestine." The agreement looked to the fulfillment of the Balfour Declaration and called for "all necessary measures . . . to encourage and stimulate immigration of Jews into Palestine on a large scale . . ."

On March 3, Faisal wrote to Felix Frankfurter, a Supreme Court justice and Zionist leader:

> The Arabs, especially the educated among us, look with deepest sympathy on the Zionist movement. . . .We will wish the Jews a hearty welcome home. . . .We are working together for a reformed and revised Near East and our two movements complete one another. The Jewish movement is nationalist and not imperialist. Our movement is nationalist and not imperialist. And there is room in Syria for us both. [Under Turkish rule, Syria included part of Palestine.] Indeed, I think that neither can be a real success without the other.

This Faisal record remains an eloquent and decisive testimonial to the legitimacy of the Zionist cause and of Israeli statehood, despite Faisal's subsequent repudiation of his earlier action in the course of his turbulent reign first as king of (Greater) Syria and then as king of Iraq.

Rights of the Palestinians

My opponent starts his case with the charge that "the Palestinians have been betrayed, consistently and viciously, by the world powers, and terribly wronged by the Israelis." In the pages that follow, however, his angry barbs are aimed almost exclusively at the Israelis. What he fails to acknowledge is that the principal blame for any "betrayal" must be attached to the Arabs themselves.

If justice for the Palestinians is to be seen only in terms of an independent state—a subject to which we will return—then the record is abundantly clear that over and over again Arab rejectionism of Israel was matched by Arab indifference to or rejection of Palestinian independence. And the record is clear, too, that there was no principled Israeli objection to a Palestinian state until the "liberation" movement, as defined in the P.L.O. covenant and elsewhere, became a threat to Israel's own independence and security.

Solving the Palestinian question is obviously a critical political challenge, as well as a basic moral issue. But it has always been, and remains today, a *reflection* of the central issue rather than the central issue itself. This is not meant to denigrate the issue, but to put it in some perspective. The central issue, I am compelled to repeat once again, is the unwillingness or the inability of the Arab world to do what only Egypt has been willing thus far to do: accept without reservation the right of Israel to live in peace with recognized borders, and to repudiate the threat of force and the use of terrorism to achieve political results. Failure to have done this over the last forty years has created new realities, new "facts," new suspicions and resistance. The Palestinians have suffered from the Arab-Israeli impasse, and may have to live, at least for a while, with something less than full independence as a consequence.

This point cannot be overstressed: The struggle for a Jewish state and then its creation was *not* antithetical to the development of an Arab Palestinian entity. On the contrary, Arab-Palestinian independence, or at least greater self-governance, was clearly encouraged and made *more* achievable as a result of the struggle for Israeli independence and authority in the area. Over and over again, however, when the Arab world said "no" to Israel, they were thereby saying no to Palestinian aspirations too. But Israel persevered, fought wars forced upon it, and has never forsaken its "right to exist." Palestinians were the principal losers in the long list of "missed opportunities."

It may be instructive to highlight some of the principal "missed opportunities" that in the past might have resulted in a Palestinian homeland—or, at the very least, have provided substantially greater rights for Palestinian Arabs.

■ The Balfour Declaration, if implemented at the time, could have resulted in a Palestinian state too.

■ The Peel Commission recommendations in 1937, accepted reluctantly by the Zionists, would similarly have led to a Palestinian state.

■ The 1947 Partition Plan explicitly and generously provided for a Palestinian state.

■ Jordanian rule of the West Bank for nineteen years (1948–1967) provided opportunity for Palestinian self-determination, but Jordan and the other Arab states did not want this, preferring to use the "refugee" issue as a weapon against Israel.

■ Khartoum Summit in 1967, with its three "nos" ruled out post-Six-Day-War recognition and accommodation that could have, at that time, included Palestinian self-determination.

■ Camp David treaty in 1978 called for negotiations to provide for "autonomy," the most far-reaching self-governance ever offered the Palestinian Arabs, with the possibility of negotiating even more after a five-year period. The Arabs said no to Camp David.

A telling example of Arab hostility or indifference to Palestinian independence was revealed by Lord Caradon, the British delegate who drafted the final text of Resolution 242 after the Six Day War in 1967. When asked why that resolution makes no direct reference to the Palestinian people, only to "refugees," he explained that the omission was deliberate, for none of the Arab states at the time asked for a separate Palestinian state, but demanded instead that the territories under Israeli control be returned to Egypt, Syria, and Jordan.

In 1979, I recall a private session at which President Carter was briefing a group on the Middle East situation. When asked why the administration limited its Palestinian position to the autonomy called for in the Camp David accords, he reported that none of the several Arab governments with which he had been consulting favored an independent Palestinian state. Mr. Carter later included this account in his published memoirs.

Mr. Abourezk finds it convenient to ignore this long history when he deplores the plight of displaced Palestinians, holding Israel "solely responsible for the Palestinian diaspora, not the Arab countries." And he chooses to ignore, too, the many opportunities Arab Palestinians had either to remain in or return to their original homes. Thus, he refers to the "million and a half refugees" along the Suez Canal during the War of Attrition, but fails to note that all of these "refugees" returned to their homes when the fighting ended. One of the accomplishments of the Camp David accords between Egypt and Israel, Sadat said, was the resumption of normal life in the cities along the Suez Canal.

Similarly, in his reference to those who left the valley of the Jordan in that War of Attrition, he fails to note that this was the period when the P.L.O. controlled the East Bank of the Jordan and shelled Israeli farmers. Israeli retaliation did cause Jordanian and Palestinian farmers to flee, but after Jordan expelled the P.L.O. in 1970, the farmers returned. With improved irrigation, these Jordanian/Palestinian farmers live peacefully and productively right up to the Jordan River.

Going back to 1948 when the major displacement of Palestinians took place, there could have been much more extensive repatriation, or resettlement of refugees with compensation, under the terms of a U.N. resolution. But that resolution called also for Arab-Israeli talks leading to peace. If the Arabs had not refused to negotiate, who can tell how much of the refugee problem might have been solved at that critical moment?

Above all, it cannot be stressed too much that there never had to be as many Palestinian refugees as there were in 1948. Palestinian Arabs, over the years, had developed a tradition of temporary flight to avoid involvement in war, frequently inter-Arab wars. As soon as the establishment of a Jewish state was proposed, a significant portion of the Palestinian Arab middle and professional classes left Palestine with their possessions. The overwhelming majority, as already indicated, left because they were urged by their Arab leaders to do so. Only a small percentage left directly because of Israeli military operations that took place when residents resisted capture of their towns.

Writing in the Jordanian newspaper *Al Urdun* (April 9, 1953) a prominent Palestinian from Deir Yassin wrote, "The Arab exodus from other villages was not caused by the actual battle, but by the exaggerated description spread by Arab leaders to incite them to fight the Jews."

It is sad that, forty years later, Mr. Abourezk still engages in such "exaggerated description" in order to "fight the Jews"!

The issue of "self-determination" for Palestinian Arabs today cannot be considered in abstract, philosophical terms alone. Appealing and morally attractive as the concept is, it cannot be divorced from the realities of the times. What was feasible ten or twenty years ago *may* not be so any longer. It is naive, it is simplistic, to suggest that any group of people who can define a common trait—language, religion, race, geography, political preference—can unilaterally declare, at any time it chooses, that it has the right to "self-determination," without regard to the impact it has on its current government, administering authority, or neighbors. There could be no stability in society if the right of "self-determination" were so interpreted.

Any group, of course, has the "right" to *seek* any status it wishes. There are, basically, two ways of achieving such status. It can, through persuasion and negotiation, peacefully resolve the issue. Or, it can seek its desired status through revolution or war. The governing authority has a comparable "right"—the right to yield or the right to resist. There is nothing in history or in common sense that supports the idea that any nation has an obligation to make it easy for its enemies or any of its constituents to create threats to its own security and stability. Israel sees a P.L.O. state as such a threat. America agrees with this judgment and I believe that position is right.

But I do believe that a generous interpretation and implementation of the "legitimate rights" of the Palestinians has always been in order, and is very much in order today. If a period of peace and cooperation, under autonomy, perhaps in conjunction with Jordan, should lead to agreement among the parties involved that full "self-determination" is now feasible, I will be the first to cheer.

I acknowledged in my first presentation that a poorly-phrased statement attributed to Golda Meir in 1969 had given the impression that she and her government refused even to recognize the existence of Palestinians. But Mr. Abourezk himself quotes the full statement, and it proves indeed that she was denying the existence, to that point in history, of a Palestinian *entity,* rather than Palestinians as such. "When was there an *independent* Palestinian people with a Palestinian state?" she asked. "It was not as though there was a Palestinian people and we came and threw them out and took their *country* away from them. They *did* not exist."

Mr. Abourezk recklessly labels this reasonable account of history as "anti-Arab racism," and seeks to explain the whole sorry plight of the Palestinians on such "racism." Such name-calling cannot wipe out the simple truth that at Camp David the Israelis were prepared to start a new chapter in Palestinian self-governance and freedom. Instead of encouraging responsible Palestinian leaders to start a process that could have brought immediate improvements as well as the possibility of full independence, Arab leaders urged non-cooperation, the P.L.O. threatened and murdered those who would cooperate, and James Abourezk can think of nothing more constructive to do than to shout "racist!"

Is it too late for a reasonable solution to the Palestinian problem—the kind that might have been negotiated ten, twenty, thirty years ago? I don't know. I hope it is not. What I do know is that every day of delay makes it less likely. There are still many Israelis—

probably still a majority—who would support territorial compromise on the West Bank, in conjunction with Jordan. There is still substantial support for "genuine autonomy."

But with whom is there the opportunity for Israel to show flexibility and generosity, as it did so impressively and courageously with Egypt at Camp David? Jordan has been unable, unwilling, or afraid to sit down, without preconditions, with Israel and negotiate. And if Israel should go so far as to end its boycott of the P.L.O., *which* P.L.O. should it be? If Israel surprised the whole world and were willing even to deal with Arafat, would Syria permit such recognition of its arch-enemy?

Instead of full-time Israel-bashing, Mr. Abourezk should be using his influence to help get responsible Arabs and Palestinians together to offer good-faith negotiations with Israel. He should read and heed more than what he has quoted from Meron Benvenisti. The clock was running, this Israeli expert had warned, but the situation was not hopeless, he added. He expressed disappointment at the failure of the Jordanians and the Palestinians to present an acceptable negotiating team and take initiatives that would force the Israelis to make political choices. Until that happens, it is both futile and unfair to place the blame solely on the Israelis.

Israeli settlements in the West Bank have long been a controversial subject—in Israel itself, in the United Nations, and in the United States. The wisdom, timing, and nature of settlements have always been subjects for debate and negotiation among the parties involved. There were several occasions when my own organization, the American Jewish Committee, expressed some concern about aspects of Israel's settlements policy. But the issue is *not* the *legality* of such settlements, or the *right* of Jews to purchase land and live in the West Bank.

Backed by eminent authorities such as Eugene Rostow, Sterling Professor of Law and Public Affairs and former Undersecretary of State for political affairs, Israel takes the position that there is no international law that can be invoked to rule out settlements in the West Bank. As Rostow has persuasively argued, the 1949 Geneva Convention does not apply to the West Bank because of the unique status of the area. Jordan never had recognized authority over it; it was itself a military occupant between 1948 and 1967 after a war of aggression. When it tried to annex the West Bank in 1951, no other Arab state was willing to recognize Jordanian sovereignty over it. "Israel's claim to the area under the mandate is at least as good as that of Jordan," Rostow has commented. U.S. policy is in agreement.

As long as Benvenisti's admonitions to get on with negotiation are not heeded by the Palestinians and Jordan, they will have to face the reality that either for security reasons or for ideological ones Israelis will feel they have the right to settle on the West Bank. Those, like Mr. Abourezk, who are so concerned about settlements, should heed Mr. Benvenisti's admonitions.

Racism, Democracy, Pluralism

The reckless ease with which Mr. Abourezk makes the "racist" charge is demonstrated early in his opening statement when he attacks even those Israelis "on the left" who demand justice for Palestinians. They do so, he contends, not out of a sense of justice but because they wish to protect the "ethnic purity" of Israel!

Israel's purpose was and is, of course, to be a state with a Jewish character. History, religion, and peoplehood combine to make this a reasonable and appropriate national aspiration. Human history is crowded with many similar national aspirations. That such an entity is not the same as "racism" or "ethnic purity" can be recognized by any observer of Israeli conduct. Mr. Abourezk can use the word "exclusive" as often as he wishes, to distort the truth, but the facts do speak louder than his words. Hundreds of thousands of Arabs have always enjoyed full citizenship in Israel; there have always been Arab members of the Knesset. There are thousands of Catholics and Protestants similarly enjoying the full citizenship guaranteed by the state's Declaration of Independence and by many laws.

Israel's laws permit easier naturalization for citizenship—for people of all faiths—than those of most countries in the world, including the United States. There is, admittedly, one important preference for Jews—the "right to return." This is not the first country to build a preference system into its immigration laws. Israel operates on the humane principle that its exit doors must always remain open for anyone choosing to leave. (Would that this were so in the Soviet Union, in Syria, in Ethiopia, in Iran, and many other countries!) But no country can have unlimited *immigration* and it has the inherent right to determine priorities, as do most countries. Given the history of the Jewish people and of Israel's own national aspirations, is it unreasonable for Israel to afford this preference for Jews?

Mr. Abourezk can't have it both ways. He argues that "there is, in fact, no democracy in Israel for Arabs." And then, on the same page, he wonders what would happen if Arabs become the majority and *vote* (my emphasis) to change the nature of the state. Well, now, do the Arabs enjoy democratic rights in Israel, or don't they?

Israel, despite widespread misunderstanding on the subject, is *not* a theocracy. Religious freedom is guaranteed, and religious pluralism is a fact in Israel. Since many Arab nations are in fact theocracies, does Mr. Abourezk call *them* "racist"? Jordan is a de facto *Judenrein* country. Does he consider Jordan "racist"?

The word "racist"—at least in America—is seen primarily in terms of color. So it is appropriate to note the poignant story of Operation Moses several years ago, when thousands of dark-skinned Ethiopian Jews were smuggled out of that country and absorbed into Israeli society. Sephardim now constitute a majority of Israeli Jews. Major cultural differences between them and the Ashkenazim have produced some problems, but overall the blending and the cooperation of the two communities constitute one of the great success stories in human history. Israel's record of assistance to black nations has been noted previously.

The charge of anti-Arab "racism" is a cheap shot, obviously intended to destroy the credibility and integrity of Israelis and American Jews. There is, unfortunately, hostility; there is suspicion; there is fear between Arab and Jew in the Middle East—more than there once was and more than there should be. There are Arabs who hate Jews, and there are Jews who hate Arabs. The longer the conflict remains unresolved, the greater the danger of even more hatred and more ugliness.

But "racism" implies American or Israeli or Jewish policies and/or doctrines that are intended to demean, to humiliate, to reject, and to refuse to acknowledge the humanity of the Arab people. As an American, I reject such an indictment of my country. As a Jew, I reject this calumny against my people. And as a friend of Israel, I reject this distortion of a beleaguered country's singular record of adherence to democratic principles.

And I deeply resent the implication that American Jews are no longer committed to the civil rights struggle in the u.s. I write these particular words, it so happens, on the second celebration of the national holiday in honor of Martin Luther King, Jr. Last week, on the actual birthday of Dr. King, I was present at a memorable event. It was at the embassy of Israel here in the nation's capital. Almost a thousand people, almost equally divided between white and black, were tightly packed in the largest room at the embassy. Coretta Scott King, Washington Mayor Marion Barry, and Israel's Ambassador Meir Rosenne spoke. A film featuring Prime Minister Shamir and Foreign Minister Peres was shown. The Howard University Choir sang. All their messages were variations on the same theme: blacks and Jews have always struggled together—and continue to struggle today—for human rights for all people, against segregation and bigotry at home, against apartheid and fascism and colonialism abroad, for the rights of Jews to a homeland and the right of Jews to emigrate from the Soviet Union. In Israel, Dr. King's works and dreams are honored by memorial forests and parks and boulevards named for him—and his words are studied by Israeli children in their schools. What other foreign nation, what other community in America, has so fully and so consistently identified with the struggles of black people and every other oppressed people?

In 1983, as I had done on several previous occasions, I testified before the Congress in favor of a bill establishing a Martin Luther King national holiday. Here is a brief excerpt from that testimony:

A Martin Luther King holiday could be both the occasion for celebrating the freedom, the unity, the tolerance that characterizes pluralist America and the occasion for assessing our progress towards the ideals we have set for ourselves. That holiday could and should become the occasion for recognizing and hailing the cultural differences among our many religious and ethnic and racial groups, even as we hail the unity and brotherhood among all. . . . It would be, I hope, the day when, as Dr. King said, when all of God's children would join hands in celebration of freedom.

I believe, in all humility, that I spoke for the overwhelming majority of Jews that day. And I assert here that, close and warm as we feel about Israel, we do not suspend our commitment to human rights when we look at Israel. When, as it does on almost all occasions, it lives up to its own extraordinarily high standards, we are proud. When, on occasion, it does not, we grieve. And we have found ways, private and public, of expressing that grief.

Allegations of Misconduct

As the reader has seen, the case made against Israel by my opponent is essentially that Israel had no legitimate rights to statehood in the land of Palestine in the first place, and that it forced and reinforced its illegitimate existence through illegal and improper actions. A tiresome litany of allegations consumes much of my opponent's presentation. Space here permits only brief comments on some of the more glaring or spectacular allegations—to illustrate the quality of those allegations. The reader is referred to some of the volumes listed in the Notes on Sources for additional information.

Deir Yassin, 1948: As I have indicated earlier, this was a tragic exception to the general practice and was roundly condemned. Terrible as it was, however, it cannot explain the mass exodus of Arabs. To the extent that it did, it was due to the Arab exploitation of the tragedy. As cited by Mr. Abourezk himself, Menachem Begin notes in his memoirs, "Not what happened to Deir Yassin, *but what was invented about Deir Yassin,* helped to carve the way to our decisive victories on the battlefield." *What was invented* was, of course, the lie that Deir Yassin was the established, authorized tactic of the Israelis and therefore all Arabs should flee. This Arab tactic backfired on them.

King David Hotel, 1946: The Abourezk reference makes it seem as if the King David was a tourist hotel. It was, in fact, the site of the British Military Command at a time of great tension, specifically Jewish resentment over the British invasion of Jewish Agency headquarters and a roundup of some 2,500 Jewish leaders. The Irgun placed bombs in the hotel's basement and then made several calls warning the British to evacuate. British denials of such calls were conclusively refuted in 1979 when a British officer testified he had heard other officers joke about a Zionist threat to bomb the hotel.

Israeli-Arab Village Attack, October 1956: During the tensions preceding the Sinai operation, citizens of the village were under curfew. In a tragic mix-up, Arabs returning from work had not been informed of the curfew. Israeli soldiers, not aware of this failure of communication, followed orders to shoot violators. But they *were* tried, convicted, and sentenced. This was a painful exception to generally good relations that were prevailing between Israeli Arabs and Jews.

Straits of Tiran, 1967: Egypt's President Nasser did not have the "legal right," as alleged, to close the straits to Israeli shipping. Under the 1958 U.N. Law of the Sea Convention (known as the Eilat clause), it was stipulated that free passage through straits to reach the port of a third country could *not* be stopped by the riparian states even if the waters were narrow enough to be territorial waters. This "legal right" argument cannot be used to charge Israel with having been the aggressor in the Six Day War. Egypt's action was, in international law, an act of war.

Jordan and Six Day War of 1967: Israel did not, as alleged, strike Jordanian airfields without warning. The record is clear. Israel explicitly asked Jordan to stay out in a message relayed by an agent of the U.N. Only after Jordan shelled the Jewish section of Jerusalem did Israel strike back at Jordan.

Libyan Airliner Downed, 1973: Qadaffi had threatened to bomb Tel Aviv. The IDF sighted this Libyan plane, and thinking it was on a suicide mission, ordered it to land, which it failed to do. A tragic but understandable error.

Sabra-Shatila Massacre, 1982: The gruesome details of the massacre are related by the Israeli journalist Amnon Kapeliouk. But why is this listed among a litany of alleged *Israeli* atrocities? All of these horrible acts had been committed by *Arabs.* Israel conducted a full inquiry to determine possible *indirect* responsibility on the part of Israelis. Why was there no outcry over a lack of a Lebanese inquiry to determine who was *directly* responsible? Why was there no outcry about more recent Palestinian-Shiite actions in the same Sabra and Shatila district?

Looting of Lebanese Villages: The I.D.F. has strict policies against such looting. In rare circumstances of misbehavior, Israeli soldiers have been punished. The question must be asked: Has Mr. Abourezk spoken against the twelve years of P.L.O. terrorizing and looting of the villages they controlled in south Lebanon?

Attacks on Civilians: The sweeping allegation is made that Israel has regularly used U.S. arms to "devastate" Lebanese, Syrian, Egyptian, Jordanian, and Palestinian civilians. There has *never* been any credible evidence that Israel has ever *targeted* civilians. Tragically, some civilians have been among casualties in some of the retaliatory attacks Israel has been compelled to aim at P.L.O. sites, which are deliberately placed in close proximity to civilians. On the other hand, there is abundant evidence the P.L.O. and several Lebanese factions have regularly and indiscriminately attacked civilians.

Serving the American Interest

Perhaps the most serious problem I have with the Abourezk presentation is that he pays so little attention to the *American* record and *American* interest. His preoccupation is bashing Israel. He cannot deny the long record of American commitment to the establishment of the Jewish state in Palestine—and the overwhelming endorsement of that commitment by the American people. So he seeks to change that commitment by trying to make us feel ashamed about supporting such a "racist," "brutal," "Nazi-like" state. And he seeks to blame this great American mistake, as he sees it, on a press which has misled the American people—a subject I will deal with later.

In this debate we were asked to address whether America's Middle East policy is in our national interest. This is not, after all, a proceeding before a court of justice in which Israelis and Arabs are competing for a favorable verdict over alleged grievances. Each of us could not avoid, and we did not, expressing judgments about the behavior of Israel and the Arab states, but judging the American role must go beyond such an exercise.

"We are constantly reminded that both Israel's and America's policies are identical," Mr. Abourezk writes in his concluding section. That's sheer nonsense. I have never heard the most ardent American or Israeli supporter of the U.S.-Israel special relationship say this or anything close to it. The two nations do have many common values and goals and interests—but they are not identical. There is *no* nation on earth—Britain, France, Japan, Australia, Switzerland—whose policies or interests are identical with ours. It is sufficient, and important for the shaping of our foreign policy, to recognize that the interests of Israel and America are essentially congruent—and substantially more congruent and compatible than they are with the other nations in the area.

Even if I were to agree—*which I emphatically do not*— that every one of the Abourezk indictments and allegations charged against Israel was well-founded, it would still be appropriate to ask

whether America's judgment to have a special relationship with
Israel is in our best interest. I will not repeat here the arguments I
presented in my opening statement. But I never argued that Israel
is a perfect country that never made mistakes or acted contrary to
American interests or requests.

If Israel is less than perfect, which of our other allies *is* perfect?
When we decided to pour billions of dollars into the Marshall Plan
and then spend billions more each year on NATO, did we believe that
every Western European country was and would be forever a perfect, flawless, pure, trusting, obedient ally? Have they been? When
we decided to help our former foes—Germany, Italy, Japan—become economically viable and democratic, could we be sure that
everything they did would always please us? Ask Detroit auto workers or Tennessee textile workers that question. When we provide
foreign aid to dozens of nations around the world, do we thereby
endorse every aspect of their societies? No, we have provided our
resources and our diplomatic support because in each case we made
the judgment that the security and the health of those countries
benefited us, either directly or because it made for a better world,
a world less endangered by economic collapse or Soviet encroach-
ment or authoritarian rule.

Similarly, we have operated on the simple principle that the
health and security of a democratic Israel in one of the most critical
areas of the globe is a worthy goal fully compatible with and essential
for America's own interests in an unstable world. Our interests in
that area have not been limited to Israel's welfare, however. We
have sought to help other nations, too, find economic security and
peace. We are the only major nation in the world able to deal
trustingly with both Israel and much of the Arab world.

Does Mr. Abourezk really think this does not serve the American
interest?

Does Mr. Abourezk think that the United States is less interested in obtaining justice for the Palestinians than the Arab states
have been over the years?

Does Mr. Abourezk think that fifty million Egyptians are sorry
that the United States helped make peace possible for the last nine
years—or sorry that we provide about $2 billion a year to help their
economy?

That policies and interests of Israel and the United States are not always identical was perhaps most clearly seen, on several occasions, in the issue of arms sales to Arab states, primarily Saudi Arabia and Jordan. On some of those occasions, the White House—in both Republican and Democratic administrations—was able to muster enough congressional support to go through with proposed sales. On others, the resistance in Congress was too strong. Such differences between the White House and the Congress can and do exist without destroying the basic consensus on the value of that special relationship.

And differences, sometimes serious ones, between Israel and the United States can and do exist without threatening the basic relationship.

In the United Nations, such occasional differences have led to American votes or abstentions that have displeased Israel. In January of 1987, for example, the Security Council criticized Israel's handling of violent West Bank demonstrations. Mr. Abourezk bemoans the record of twenty vetoes cast over the years by the United States "protecting Israel." He fails to state that most of these were rejected by the United States only because they were obviously and crudely one-sided, condemning Israel for taking some action against Arab or Palestinian sites without noting the provocations that had prompted those actions.

Not only does Mr. Abourezk fail to acknowledge the American votes and abstentions on resolutions critical of Israel, he has no comment to make about the two most critical resolutions ever adopted by the Council on the Middle East, 242 and 338, both adopted *unanimously.* These reflected an international consensus supporting the principle of trading territory for peace and the end of belligerence. But, except for Egypt, the Arab nations have yet to give their unambiguous approval to these peace-seeking resolutions or to act in the spirit of these fundamental commitments of the U.N.

Mr. Abourezk may regret that the United States does not fall in line every time the Soviet and Third World blocs, joined at times with less-than-courageous, oil-hungry European nations, provide a voting majority in the United Nations to excoriate Israel. I haven't always approved of American votes, but it's good to know that most of the time those votes reflect loyalty to a long-time ally and a demonstrated application of balanced judgment rather than hostile prejudgment.

Moreover, it should be noted that no nation on earth has shown greater support of U.S. positions in the U.N. than Israel.

We are preparing these rebuttals early in 1987, when public interest in the Iran-arms-Contra controversy is at its height. Neither of us now knows the final outcome or meaning of that sad chapter, but it is clear that significant misjudgments were made. They deserve rejection and criticism even as we sympathize with the compelling need to take risks in order to get American hostages released.

I would hope that my opponent in this debate will not yield to the temptation to use demagoguery to score a point or two, by scapegoating the Israelis for their role in the affair. After some early suggestions that Israel had given us poor advice, the White House itself made it clear that no blame should attach to Israel. Evidently we did have some discussions with Israelis to tap their expertise in such matters. And evidently we sought and received their cooperation in implementing some of the arrangements. In doing so, Israel proved it was a good and loyal ally, even if the help it gave resulted in the service of an ill-considered course of action.

Blame It on the Media

Obviously unhappy about the strength and durability of pro-Israel sentiment in the United States, Mr. Abourezk looks for easy explanations. He has found two basic culprits for this unhappy reality—politicians and the media. As for the politicians, I feel no need to add to my earlier comments, except to stress that it is mischievous and irresponsible for a former member of the Senate to contend that over the years every president and the overwhelming majority of the members of Congress placed their immediate political interests ahead of their concern for the national interest.

Throughout his presentation, Mr. Abourezk keeps bashing the American press for withholding or slanting news that would be harmful to Israel. The freedom with which he makes such reckless charges is perhaps best illustrated in his discussion in "Terrorism and the Media" of the P.L.O. role during the evacuation of American residents in Lebanon. "I have no question that American journalists posted in Beirut reported these actions," he writes, "just as I have no question that news editors in the United States quashed the stories written." Why does he *not* have any question? Why does he *assume* such a major indictment against America's free press?

It is simply astonishing for anyone to *assume* that the press would ignore any documented, credible accounts of the P.L.O. protecting American evacuees or the American embassy. Such a man-bites-dog story would seem absolutely irresistable. If in fact he had asked the question, he would have learned that there had been reports of such action. I distinctly recall reading or hearing about it. Whatever the explanation might be for the story not rating major headlines, there is no excuse for baseless allegations of editors *quashing* filed stories.

In one single sentence, Mr. Abourezk's uncontrollable yen to defame hits at both the Israelis and at the American press. "The brutality of the Israelis easily matches that of the South Africans, but the difference in media treatment can only be explained in terms of racist attitudes toward Palestinian and Lebanese Arabs," he writes. Because American journalists cannot accept this blatantly false equating of Israeli and South African conduct, he pins the ugly label of *racist* on them.

Can anyone who reads American newspapers or watches television news even only occasionally take seriously the charge that "we were never shown Arabs mourning for their dead children." Or that "op-ed pieces seem to belong solely to those with a Zionist point of view." Or that there is reluctance to cover stories "such as Israeli spying in the United States or Israeli arms deals with Iran." Just repeating this nonsense is all the rebuttal I need to offer.

Anyone familiar with the American media treatment of the entire Lebanon war knows—as surely Mr. Abourezk must—that the American press gave that war so much coverage and so much editorial comment that embarrassed and hurt Israel's image that friends of Israel complained bitterly of the *anti*-Israel tone of the press. They were particularly incensed over what they charged was quick and unchallenged acceptance of pro-Arab propaganda—primarily about numbers of casualties and about innocent civilian victims.

A particularly disturbing reaction during the Lebanon war developed over the heavy use—by every newspaper and every TV program—of a pathetic UPI wire photo of a seven-month-old baby in an East Beirut hospital, swathed in bandages. The *Washington Post* (August 2, 1982) described the baby as having lost both arms as a result of an Israeli bombing. So shocking and so widely used was this photo that Secretary of State Shultz was quoted as having said, "The symbol of this war is a baby with its arms shot off." There were two things wrong with that story. Within a few weeks, Israel had presented evidence that it was a shelling from P.L.O. forces in West Beirut that had caused the injury. And, it turned out, the baby did *not* lose its arms, the injury not having been very severe. As is almost always the case, the subsequent "corrections" hardly wiped out the vivid memories of this awful "symbol" of the war.

That was the poignant story of a single baby. But similar careless-ness—and deliberate falsifying—led to reports of tremendously ex-aggerated numbers of killed and wounded and displaced in the first days of the fighting. It took weeks before corrections started to appear. Perhaps the most comprehensive and credible account of those early reports was written by *New York Times* correspondent David Shipler.

"It is clear to anyone who has travelled in Southern Lebanon," Shipler wrote, "that the original figures of 10,000 dead and 600,000 homeless, during the first week of the war, were extreme exaggera-tions." His credibility and objectivity were reflected in other reports in which he challenged Israeli figures too and criticized Israeli cen-sorship. But, again, corrections never catch up with initial misreport-ing, and even today Mr. Abourezk continues to use discredited statistics.

In the course of the Lebanese war there were innumerable in-stances when American broadcast journalists failed to draw the tradi-tional, professional line between reporting and editorializing—and almost always to Israel's disadvantage. Thus, John Chancellor on the "NBC Nightly News," which reaches millions of American homes, on August 2, 1982 reported: "What in the world is going on? What's an Israeli army doing here in Beirut?" His answer: "We are now dealing with an imperial Israel." (He had, in that short time, forgot-ten that on June 16 he had commented that "no one is questioning Israel's legitimate security problems in Lebanon.")

To cite just one more instance of Israel-bashing, ABC's Richard Threlkeld, on June 25, 1982 broadcast that "Israel . . . has suddenly started behaving like the neighborhood bully." Other major, popular television journalists—Roger Mudd, Peter Jennings, Barrie Dunsmore, among others—used their "news" reports to reflect their personal hostility to Israel's actions in Lebanon.

It was precisely because American coverage of the Lebanon war was so thorough and so critical that, as I noted in my opening statement, the relative approval of Israel over the Arab nations among Americans fell from ratios of about seven-to-one to three-to-one during the months of that unpopular war. It has since rebounded to the more traditional ratios.

I found it almost amusing, but not quite, to read the frequent allegations that the *Washington Post* was particularly partial to Israel. I can hear the editors of that paper chuckling when they read the Abourezk charges. For years now they have had to contend with an incensed Jewish community because of what it considers a very strong anti-Israel bias in the *Post,* especially in its news coverage and among some of their regular columnists. While I have personally not shared that harsh judgment of the *Post,* I have participated in several meetings with the paper's top editors in an effort to urge fair, balanced handling of the Middle East news.

No, the problem is with the message, not the messenger. If American citizens retained a three-to-one attitude toward Israel even at the height of a difficult, controversial, poorly-explained Lebanese war, it is because over the years they have gotten message after message that persuaded them that Israel is a nation we can identify with, that its welfare is a legitimate concern of ours, that it is ready and anxious for peace. And they have gotten message after message of Arab resistance to direct negotiation and accommodation, of Arab endorsement or tolerance of terrorism.

When, as in the case of Sadat and Camp David, Arabs start sending different messages, America's media will report it.

Some Random Notes

Space will permit only brief reactions to a few other items in the Abourezk opening statement that I simply cannot permit to stand unchallenged.

■ Mr. Abourezk: "The horrors of the Holocaust should not justify similar crimes against the Palestinians . . ." Similar crimes!

This is an inexcusable, reckless comparison of Hitler's state-enforced policy of genocide aimed at exterminating an entire people, and succeeding in the case of six million, with, at most, some cases of excessive violence by Israeli forces or individuals involved in combat with Palestinian or other Arab terrorists. It is an abomination to level such an obscene charge against a people still haunted by the memory of families consumed by the Holocaust.

In the Camp David accords, both Israel and the United States invited the Palestinians "to participate in the determination of their future," starting with autonomy. Like the opportunities Hitler offered the Jews?

■ "I am opposed to violence in any form," Mr. Abourezk declares in "Terrorism and the Media," and I found myself pleasantly surprised. But only a few pages later, in "Occupation," he refers to "violence as the only alternative for the Palestinians" in their resistance to Israeli settlements. If he indeed believes that "the most practical resistance to occupation is nonviolence," why does he not urge the Palestinians and the Arab leaders to follow the Sadat model, to sit down with the Israelis and negotiate the issue, rather than accept violence as the "only alternative"?

■ Mr. Abourezk challenges the integrity of a "class of American Jews who have learned that the route to political and financial power in America lies in using broad Jewish support for Israel as a club to enhance their own power." But Mr. Abourezk has himself been accused of consciously carving out a career of Israel-bashing. When he ran for the Senate, the record will show, he sought Jewish support and, for a while, seemed rather friendly to Israel's case for American support. Would it be fair to conclude that *he* found Israel-bashing a better "route to political and financial power in America" than his earlier stance?

■ To bolster his "racism" indictment, Mr. Abourezk distorts and exaggerates Israel's relationship with South Africa. Israel has never failed to support U.N. resolutions condemning apartheid or to be bound by U.N.-imposed sanctions on South Africa. Israel provides a very small percentage of South Africa's arms needs, the bulk coming from European nations. Only about *1 percent* of all international trade is with Israel, less than the level with several black nations. Most of South Africa's oil comes from Arab nations in violation of the embargo on oil shipments. Opposition to apartheid is so strong in Israel that even the present modest relationship is being reconsidered, at this writing.

In Conclusion

In my opening statement I acknowledged that u.s.-Israel relations, sound and valuable as they have been, have not been free of occasional "suspicions, irritations, and resentments" resulting from blunders or transgressions. "They cannot and should not be ignored," I wrote, "but they should not blind us to the bigger picture."

I regret very much that Mr. Abourezk seems indeed to be blind to the bigger picture. So intent has he been on destroying the integrity and character of the Zionists who built modern Israel, the leaders who have governed it for the last forty years, and those in America, Jews and others, who have identified with it, he has either ignored or carelessly distorted that bigger picture.

It remains for me now to express the hope that in the rebuttal he is preparing concurrently with mine, he has addressed himself to some of the questions I have raised explicitly or implicitly. Let me restate some of them:

■ Is it not true that through the seventy years since the Balfour Declaration, every president and every Congress has been committed to the idea of a Jewish state in the Middle East—and has seen it as consistent with the American interest?

■ Is it not true that the United States has always sought to balance its support for Israel with a search for friendly and supportive relationships with Arab nations?

■ Is it not true that there would be today an Arab Palestinian homeland if the Arab world had chosen to take advantage of the opportunities offered and had supported such a homeland—especially during the nineteen year occupation of the West Bank by Jordan?

■ Is it not true that Israel is a political democracy with basic civil liberties and freedoms substantially greater than any other state in the area?

■ Is it not true that America's strategic interests and needs in the Middle East are advanced by the presence of an economically healthy and militarily secure Israel?

■ Is it not true that Jews both in Israel and in the United States have always engaged in frank debate about how best to pursue the peace process and how best to assure the "legitimate rights the Palestinians"?

These may sound like rhetorical questions, but they go to some of the basic issues we must all try to understand better. I have said *true* to all these questions, but I am willing to continue debating them. That's why I have expressed disappointment at Mr. Abourezk's preoccupation with alleged blunders and transgressions—all of which, I now state for the last time, could have been avoided if seventy (Balfour) or forty (partition) or twenty (Six Day War) or ten (Camp David) years ago the Arab world had said *yes* to Jewish presence in the area. Because they said *no*, Jews *and* Arabs have suffered needlessly.

It is not too late for that *yes*. The present coalition government in Israel has eased its definition of acceptable Palestinian participants in negotiations. It has not ruled out some kind of international conference to start the negotiating process. Everything can be on the negotiating table. There is no need for the United States, for the United Nations, for—with all due respect—James Abourezk to spell out in advance what the results of such negotiations should be.

He can continue to repeat as often as he wishes that the Israeli-Egyptian treaty was a mistake. I will continue believing that it serves as a model and as a hope. Faced with the possibility of a broader peace, I am confident Israel will demonstrate again, as it did at Camp David, that it is prepared to be flexible and generous. But it must be given the opportunity to do so. It should not be expected to do so unilaterally.

I hope that the United States continues to use its resources and influence not only to "help" Israel as a faithful and helpful ally, but to encourage Arab-Israeli negotiations that can finally bring peace and justice to both Arabs and Jews.

JAMES G. ABOUREZK

hen I was in law school one of my professors gave what he called sterling advice to future lawyers: If you don't have the facts, pound the law. If you don't have the law, pound the facts. If you don't have either, pound the table.

Mr. Bookbinder has followed that advice in his presentation, but he has gone far beyond table-pounding. He has used a time-honored technique developed over the years by the Israeli lobby—that of pounding guilt. And he does so in a most disingenious way, first by renouncing any use of the Nazi Holocaust as a basis for American Middle East policy, then virtually making it the centerpiece of his presentation.

It is important at the outset to deal directly with use of the Holocaust as a political weapon.

Hitler's attempted extermination of Jews was one of history's greatest crimes, approached in viciousness by his slaughter of Gypsies, Russians, and Poles, and, in more recent times, Pol Pot's attempted extermination of his fellow Cambodians. The Holocaust was a crime committed against not just Jews, but against all of humanity. As others have said before me, its remembrance and warning belongs not just to Jews, but to the entire human race.

One of the great ironies—and outrages—of the Middle East is that even though Jews have claimed the Holocaust as an exclusive property, Israel is now conducting a brutal occupation and killing of Palestinians and Lebanese, and trying to justify its action in the name of preventing a repeat of the Holocaust of Jews. The outrage lies not only in the fact of these Israeli actions, but also in the way Israel's supporters attempt to rationalize them. There are many reasons for this moral double standard, some political and some racial, but whatever the reason, this behavior cannot be justified on the basis of the Nazi Holocaust.

The Holocaust is worthy of commemoration because of its preventive value. But to insert it into a political debate, whether in these pages or anywhere else, is to cheapen its meaning and dilute its message to future generations. If, because of its use as a political tool, its value as a warning wears thin, it will most certainly place future races and ethnic groups in great danger. The disservice to humanity of such a tactic far outweighs any temporary political benefit that might derive from it.

The Holocaust was a powerful argument in favor of creating a Jewish state after World War II (although not for displacing another people in the process), but it should not and cannot rationally be used as an argument to continue a brutal occupation policy by Israel, and support of it by the United States.

And neither, of course, can the other assertions made by Mr. Bookbinder.

Presidential Support of Israel and the Israeli Lobby

The series of presidential statements offered by Mr. Bookbinder in support of Israel sound impressive, but they hardly justify Israel's policy of occupation, paid for by the American taxpayer. Trying to rationalize American support for Israel's occupation and its accompanying violation of human rights by labeling it as "support for Israel" mixes two entirely different concepts. Support for a Jewish state is not the same as support for an illegal Israeli occupation, or for Israel's armed expansion at the expense of its Arab neighbors.

There is something else about the presidential statements Mr. Bookbinder is not telling his readers. Washington politicians will issue any statement, sign any letter, or make any speech written for them by members of the Israeli lobby on the grounds that doing so cannot hurt them, and will only help their electoral chances.

As former National Security staffer William Quandt has written in his book on the Camp David accords, "A gap often appears between what a president thinks and says in private and what he says for domestic political effect."

Seeking to explain how presidents make policy in the Middle

East, Quandt wrote that as a new president gains experience with the realities of domestic politics, it reinforces his tendency to emphasize one-sided support for Israel—particularly in election years and in public statements.

As evidence of "basic American support" for Israel, which was, as he says, "clear and firm even before the Holocaust," Mr. Bookbinder cites the statements made by a number of American presidents, beginning with President Woodrow Wilson's endorsement of the Balfour Declaration. It is useful to take a brief look behind such ringing endorsements.

In his book, *Israel in the Mind of America,* Peter Grose describes President Wilson's purely opportunistic reasons for his support of Zionism:

> There were good political reasons for doing so. The American Federation of Labor, under Samuel Gompers, was endorsing the principle of a Jewish homeland, as Jewish immigrants threatened to glut the American labor market. Theodore Roosevelt and his Republicans were leaning toward the Jewish national cause, and no Democrat would willingly abandon the potential Jewish support in the big eastern cities to the opposition. Zionist leaders were members of Wilson's political family—Brandeis, his protégé Frankfurter, the crusading New York rabbi Stephen Wise . . . to wish to satisfy their Zionist interests was only normal for a political leader, especially in the absence, before 1917, of arguments to the contrary.

The King-Crane Commission of 1919 was sent by the U.S. government to Palestine to see if the idea of a Zionist homeland was a good one. Again, according to Grose, its finding was decidedly negative. The commission concluded that a Jewish state could not come into being "without the gravest possible trespass upon the religious and civil rights" of the Arabs.

Whenever there was no political pressure from the Israeli lobby, there was, over the years, strong official objection to the establishment of an exclusive Jewish state in Palestine. At a meeting of the U.S. delegation to the United Nations on September 15, 1947, six weeks before the fateful partition vote, American diplomat Loy Henderson warned that partition would "result in much bloodshed and suffering, and that many people throughout the world would

lose their trust in the United States," writes Evan M. Wilson in
Decision on Palestine.

"He [Henderson] predicted that the existence of a Jewish state
in Palestine would cause injury and damage to the United States for
many years to come."

In a long and thoughtful memorandum submitted to Secretary
of State George C. Marshall, on September 22, 1947, Henderson
detailed his strongly held opinion against partition. His views, he
said, were shared by "nearly every member of the Foreign Service
or of the department who has worked to any appreciable extent on
Near Eastern problems."

Other points Henderson made in his memo:

> The UNSCOP [United Nations Special Committee on Palestine]
> Majority Plan is not only unworkable; if adopted, it would guaran-
> tee that the Palestine problem would be permanent and still more
> complicated in the future. . . .
> We are under no obligations to the Jews to set up a Jewish state.
> The Balfour Declaration and the Mandate provided not for a
> Jewish state, but for a Jewish national home. Neither the United
> States nor the British Government has ever interpreted the term
> "Jewish national home" to be a Jewish national state. . . .

In his study of Truman's 1948 decision to recognize Israel, John
Snetsinger recorded that Truman refused to do so until Clark Clifford presented him with the options—either recognize Israel, or
lose the critical Jewish vote in the November elections.

And in his memoirs, Truman admitted to the tremendous political pressures exerted on him personally and on his administration
when he was being pressed to recognize Israel. "I do not think I ever
had as much pressure and propaganda aimed at the White House
as I had in this instance," he wrote.

Evan Wilson writes that Postmaster General Robert E. Hanne-
gan, who was also chairman of the Democratic National Committee,
brought up at cabinet meetings the Palestine question in the context
of the "very great influence" the administration's support of Zionism had on fund raising for the party.

During the winter and spring of 1948, as the various government
departments put together their assessments, George F. Kennan,

head of the State Department's newly created Policy Planning Staff, also weighed in with an assessment questioning the wisdom of Truman's course.

Kennan's views made the rounds and other officials added their arguments and observations. When the department's final position paper emerged from this ponderous, but thorough process, the view it offered was grim and negative. So were similar assessments by the Defense Department and the c.i.a.

President Eisenhower, of course, understood the difference between Israel and its territorial objectives, and expressed it in strong terms after the 1956 Israeli/French/British invasion of Egypt. He was the last president to stand up to the Israeli lobby, but not the last one to feel its heavy-handed pressure.

Henry A. Byroade, director of the State Department's Office of Near Eastern, South Asian, and African Affairs under Eisenhower, warned Israel on March 28, 1954, to "drop the attitude of conqueror and the conviction that force and a policy of retaliatory killings is the only policy that your neighbors will understand. You should make your deeds correspond to your frequent utterances of the desire for peace."

Byroade returned to the attack on May 1 with a warning to Israel that it should not contemplate waging a war of expansion. The Arabs, Byroade said, "should have the right to know the magnitude of this new state. Their fears are enhanced by the knowledge that the only limitation imposed by statute on immigration into Israel is, in fact, the total number of those of the Jewish faith in the entire world. They see only one result—future attempt at territorial expansion—and hence warfare of serious proportion."

President Richard Nixon, for all that he said in public favorable to Israel, had no illusions privately. In his memoirs, he complained of "the unyielding and shortsighted pro-Israeli attitude in large and influential segments of the American Jewish community, Congress, the media and in intellectual and cultural circles."

Other presidents since Nixon have had the same complaint, perhaps none more so than Jimmy Carter. Carter wrote in his diary on November 8, 1978, that Begin only wanted peace with Egypt so he could keep Gaza and the West Bank.

How does one reconcile the private disagreement and outright animosity with the public statements of support cited by Mr. Bookbinder? How does one explain the fact that all three living former presidents have, since they left office, changed their public positions on the Middle East? The answer lies in the entity whose influence Mr. Bookbinder tries hard to downplay—the Israeli lobby, perhaps the best organized and most well-financed pressure group in Washington.

We are constantly told, by Mr. Bookbinder, and by others who defend the practices of the lobby, that its members are only practicing democracy, that what they do is no different than what is done by other lobbies.

The Israeli lobby may very well be doing just what other lobbies do. No one can deny that they have figured out the system and have learned how to beat it. But they have gone over the line of proper conduct for any lobby in this particular democracy.

The Israeli lobby takes its orders from Israel, a foreign power whose interests are not only different from ours, but at times in total opposition. It is a lobby that has used every conceivable tactic, including political and economic intimidation, to bring members of Congress and the administration into line with its thinking. It has used the threat of loss of advertising against segments of the media to prevent negative coverage of Israel and positive coverage of Arabs. It has learned to concentrate its money on congressional races either against candidates who refuse to spout its line or for those who agree to do so. We need to be clear that we are not discussing here the lobby for the tobacco farmers, the American Medical Association, or the construction industry. Domestic, and even other foreign lobbies, are expected to push for favorable consideration of their goals and objectives, but not even the toughest of them threatens political extinction or personal embarrassment if the candidate disagrees with them.

No amount of foot-shuffling and aw-shucks denials can alter the reality of the heavy hand of the lobby on Capitol Hill. Many have written about this deplorable phenomenon, including Stephen Isaacs, in *Jews and American Politics*, and Paul Findley, in *They Dare to Speak Out*. But one need only find a member of Congress willing to speak in private and off the record to hear it firsthand and in greater detail.

One can find scores, no, hundreds of statements written by AIPAC, or other components of the Israeli lobby, but inserted by senators and representatives under their own names in the *Congressional Record*—statements on every issue affecting the Middle East—in favor of Soviet Jewish emigration, against OPEC, against the P.L.O., generally in support of Israel and in opposition to Arab "perfidy." In return for such "cooperation," politicians receive from the Israeli lobby what has been called the mother's milk of politics— money for their campaigns.

My own experience in the U.S. House and the U.S. Senate confirms what William Quandt and others say, and what Mr. Bookbinder denies—that the Israeli lobby in Washington exerts undue influence on U.S. Middle East policymaking, the result of which is to skew American policy against American interests. The Israeli lobby is exclusively a one-issue lobby, caring little about how candidates stand on other issues of importance to the United States interest—whether domestic or foreign. Only Israel's interests and Israel's objectives are used as a gauge either for supporting or opposing a candidate.

Simply put, American politicians generally view the Israeli lobby as a plentiful source of money for their reelection, seeing little harm in taking the money in return for meeting its legislative demands. Cooperation with the lobby also keeps money from going to the opposition.

Beyond money, the lobby has applied a variety of pressure tactics on various groups around the United States when Israel feels it needs a public relations push. Newspaper ads in support of Israel signed by show business people, retired military officers, church groups, academics, labor leaders, all come about in much the same way as statements and votes by politicians.

The influence of the lobby is such that American politicians who will freely, and properly so, criticize a president of the United States, are afraid to voice even the mildest criticism of a prime minister of Israel. Similarly, although the attitude of the American media is now changing somewhat, there is a great deal more criticism of Israeli government policies in the Israeli press than there is in the American press. There is more debate among Israelis about the future of the West Bank than there is among American Jews, a phenomenon that can be attributed solely to the Israeli lobby's heavy-handed pressure on the American Jewish community.

It's natural that Mr. Bookbinder would seek to downplay the

Israeli lobby's influence. It would not fit too well with his thesis that the huge amounts of American aid and political support in the U.N. for Israel's transgressions result from a ground swell of public support.

But people who have served in Congress have a different—and more accurate—perspective. The network of pro-Israel campaign fund raising—and spending—extends to virtually every state in the union, which answers Mr. Bookbinder's question of how to explain support of Israel by politicians from states "like Montana or Oregon or Tennessee or North Dakota?" When I ran for the U.S. Senate in 1972, I was asked by my campaign chairman—a man whom I later learned was a Zionist—for a written statement of my position on the Middle East. I could, he told me, raise money from American Jews in New York if the statement was adequate. After I furnished the statement—a bland, non-committal position paper—I was put on an approved list, which enabled me to raise a considerable amount of money from American Jews in New York.

Not much has changed since then. As the 1986 congressional campaign was getting underway, I was called by the campaign manager of a member of the U.S. House of Representatives who intended to run for the U.S. Senate.

"How much money can Arab Americans raise for my candidate's senate race?" he asked me.

"Not as much as American Jews can raise," I replied.

A few weeks later, the congressman in question inserted a speech in the *Congressional Record* calling for increased emigration of Jews from the Soviet Union, a clear signal that fund raising for his Senate race had begun. The congressman, until that speech, had never discussed the issue of Soviet Jewish emigration, and had, in fact, been in favor of a Palestinian state.

Zionist Michael Goland, a wealthy Californian, openly boasts of having spent $1.5 million to defeat Illinois Senator Charles Percy in 1984. Goland is frequently trotted out by Minnesota Senator Rudy Boschwitz as a reminder to other senators of what can happen to them if they step out of line.

In the winter of 1973–74 I traveled through the Middle East, visiting most of the Arab world as well as Israel. I spoke with the leaders of Syria, Saudi Arabia, Jordan, Egypt, and Lebanon, all of whom told me they were prepared to recognize Israel provided it would withdraw to its pre-1967 borders, allowing the Palestinians an independent state. Upon my return I made a speech advocating just that as a way to bring an end to the Arab-Israeli conflict. Wolf Blitzer, then a correspondent for the *Near East Report*, AIPAC's newsletter, was in the audience and asked a few extremely hostile questions before he left. The next issue of the *Near East Report* carried an article implying that I had sold out to the Arabs, totally misrepresenting what I had said in my speech.

Not long after that, a friend from New York—an American Jew—who had contributed to my campaign sent me a letter she had received from I. L. Kenen, then the editor of the *Near East Report*, enclosing a copy of the article in question. His letter asked her to read the article, then suggested that Abourezk was not worthy of further political contributions because of what the article contained. It was obvious that Kenen had sent this article and a similar letter to others listed as contributors on my campaign report who had Jewish-sounding names.

One of the more outrageous results of the influence of the Israeli lobby is the ongoing rape of the American taxpayer. Aside from the billions sent to Israel each year, one example is the congressional funding of an Israeli warplane, the Lavi. The *Washington Post* reported on January 8, 1987, that after Congress had given most of the money for the plane's development, the Pentagon sent one of its officials, Dov Zakheim, to Israel to try to convince the Israelis to scrap the Lavi and buy cheaper, American-made aircraft.

Production of the Lavi, in competition with the U.S. aircraft industry, would cost the United States taxpayer a great deal more than the nearly $2 billion already sunk into its development, with projections of many billions more needed for completion. But Zakheim's job was not made easier by the fact the project represents billions in contracts to the Israeli military-industrial complex. The outcome of his visit might have been foretold in a suggestion made by *Yedioth Aharonoth*, Israel's largest daily newspaper. In an editorial commenting on the U.S. request, the newspaper said that "if Israel could not overcome Pentagon opposition, it should, 'make another appeal to those parties that overcame this opposition in the past'—a reference to Congress, which has readily earmarked $400 million annually for the project."

In an attempt to buy Israeli support for abandoning the Lavi project, Zakheim, a rabbi, offered to give Israel up to three hundred F16 fighters, with licenses for Israel Aircraft Industries to provide 50 percent of the engine parts and make the final assembly. The Pentagon will be forced to wait for its answer until Israel calculates which offer will benefit it the most.

Because of the tactics of the Israeli lobby, it becomes much easier to understand why ordinarily strong budget-cutters in the Congress become high-rolling, profligate spenders when Israel's budget is up for consideration. It also explains why congressional human rights advocates suffer from instant amnesia and laryngitis when it comes to Israel's brutal occupation of Arabs, and to military aggression such as Israel's invasion of Lebanon.

Israel: Strategic Asset or Costly Liability?

George Washington was remarkably prescient when, in his Farewell Address to the nation on September 17, 1796, he said:

A passionate attachment of one nation for another produces a variety of evils. Sympathy for the favorite nation, facilitating the illusion of an imaginary common interest, in cases where no real interest exists, and infusing into one the enmities of the other, betrays the former into a participation in the quarrels and wars of the latter, without adequate inducements or justifications. It leads also to concessions to the favorite nation, of privileges denied to others, which is apt doubly to injure the nation making the concessions, by unnecessarily parting with what ought to have been retained, and by exciting jealousy, ill will, and a disposition to retaliate in the parties from whom equal privileges are withheld; and it gives to ambitious, corrupted or deluded citizens who devote themselves to the favorite nation, facility to betray or sacrifice the interests of their own country, without odium, sometimes even with popularity; gilding with the appearances of a virtuous sense of obligation, a commendable deference for public opinion, or a laudable zeal for public good, the base of foolish compliances of ambition, corruption, or infatuation.

As avenues to foreign influence in innumerable ways, such attachments are particularly alarming to the truly enlightened and independent patriot. How many opportunities do they afford to tamper with domestic factions, to practise the arts of seduction, to mislead public opinion, to influence or awe the public councils!— Such an attachment of a small or weak, towards a great and powerful nation, dooms the former to be the satellite of the latter.

I once watched New York's Senator Jacob Javits question a State Department official during a Senate Foreign Relations Committee hearing. Javits was pressing the official for an answer he wanted. "Tell the committee why you believe Israel is a strategic asset to the United States," Javits asked over and over again. The hapless bureaucrat was unable to think up an answer on the spot. But that did not stop Javits from continuing to press him until he got what he thought was a satisfactory response.

The point of it all was that Israel's supporters have desperately tried over the years to create a "strategic asset" concept in the public mind—a selling point that includes making believe that Israel will allow itself to be used by the United States whenever it is convenient. Javits's efforts were just one more contribution to the cause.

Even if common sense tells us that no country would offer itself for such use, Israel's behavior has provided us with stark and overwhelming evidence that it will pursue its own interest whenever it chooses, whether or not it is against America's interest.

This was proven true by Israel's vicious attack on the uss *Liberty*, in which 34 American sailors were killed and 171 were wounded. It was true when America wanted Israel to free the Lebanese hostages it held in Israel in exchange for the Americans held on twa Flight 847. It was true when the Israeli government wanted to keep the Iran-Iraq war going and convinced President Reagan to approve an arms sales scheme to Iran. It was true when Israel paid Jonathan Pollard and his wife to steal American military secrets. It was true when Israel was found to have sent military aid to the Contras in Central America in defiance of a congressional ban on such aid.

The chain of events leading from Israel's refusal to return Arab territories after the 1967 war culminated in the 1973–1974 Arab oil embargo against the United States because of our continued blind support of Israel.

Israel's actions, like those of all nations, are self-serving. We would be foolish in the extreme to buy the line put out by Israel's propagandists that whatever they do, they do for us.

Seeking to cite the benefits for America of a "partnership" with Israel, Mr. Bookbinder describes as a vital component what he calls the "principal foreign policy challenge—how to deal with and triumph over our number one adversary, the Soviet Union. . . ." His attempt to build up the straw man of a nonexistent Soviet military threat to the Arab world, then offering Israel's protection is overreaching to the point of near tragedy. What does he mean by "triumph" over the Soviet Union? Is he contemplating nuclear war to achieve this triumph? Does he mean it in terms of conventional warfare? Certainly he does not expect us to believe either that Israel will challenge the Soviets militarily or that the Arab world would stand for Israeli "protection." Certainly the Israelis know that the Arab world fears Israel more than it does Russia, even if Mr. Bookbinder appears not to know.

His astounding claim that Israel would be able to wipe out the Soviet's Mediterranean fleet is no less illusory, and does as much justice to reality as offering Israeli protection to the Arabs.

Former c.i.a. Director Admiral Stansfield Turner's assessment of Israeli intelligence capabilities (long on public relations, short on capabilities) was augmented by testimony given by Robert McFarlane, former director of the National Security Council staff. Testifying to the Senate Foreign Relations Committee on January 16, 1987, McFarlane said because the c.i.a. had no independent intelligence to support the value of selling arms to Iran, the Reagan White House relied on Israeli intelligence for an analysis of the situation. It was later disclosed that the Israeli intelligence service, the Mossad, relied for the most part on an Iranian arms dealer for its information about Iran—an arms dealer who had more than a passing interest in encouraging the sale of arms to Iran. He was so unreliable that, since 1980, the c.i.a. had refused to deal with him. As the Senate Intelligence Committee draft report on the Iran arms sales scheme informs us, he failed a c.i.a.-administered lie detector test, yet Israeli officials continued to insist that the u.s. rely on him for intelligence.

Israel's "strategic value" to the United States lay helplessly inert when the Khomeini revolution toppled the shah of Iran in 1979. Israel stood by and watched its friend the shah go under, choosing only to sell American weapons to the new government once the Iran-Iraq war was underway. It's clear that neither Israel nor the United States could have changed the course of the Iranian revolution, but that is the real point. If it could do nothing to assist a regime with which it was friendly, how can anyone believe its claim that it stands ready to help the various Arab regimes?

Even as strong a friend of Israel as Henry Kissinger could, on occasion, resort to an honest assessment about Israel. He told a group of Jewish leaders in 1975, that, "the best defense against the spread of communism in the Middle East is to strengthen moderate Arab governments. The strength of Israel is needed for its own survival, but not to prevent the spread of communism in the Arab world. So it doesn't necessarily help United States' global interest as far as the Middle East is concerned."

Mr. Bookbinder spends a great deal of time trying to set up a confrontation between the Soviet Union and America, hoping to sell Israel's value to the United States within that context.

Trying to justify Israel's current policy of brutal occupation of the Arabs with geopolitical ramblings about Israel's strategic location and value is pure nonsense. There is already enough paranoia in official u.s. circles without this additional appeal to the darker side of our politics. Add all of this to the shameless boasting of how American weapons were more efficient at killing Arabs than Soviet weapons were at killing Jews and you have what could be called a zero sum game.

It is an argument whose intention is to avoid making peace, either with the Soviet Union, or with the Arab world. It is an appeal by the most reactionary elements in Israel to the most reactionary elements in the United States.

The use of the Soviet Union as a foil by Israel and its supporters is perhaps the ultimate in *chutzpah*. "Israel is the only bulwark against Soviet expansion in the Middle East," goes the cry by Israel's propagandists. "Israel will carry the struggle against the Soviets and their surrogates who seek to move against the oil resources there," is another.

Yet the reality is the opposite. Because of Islamic antipathy toward Soviet atheism, it is abundantly clear that the Soviets could have never entered the Middle East had it not been for Israeli expansionism and the u.s. policy of unquestioning support for Israel. Soviet military influence began in earnest in 1955 and is clearly traced to an action undertaken by Israel on February 28 of that year. In a major nighttime raid, Ariel Sharon's terrorist unit struck a small Egyptian army post on the outskirts of Gaza in the Sinai peninsula. The Israelis killed thirty-seven Egyptians and wounded thirty more, causing even the United States to join in sponsorship of a u.n. Security Council resolution condemning Israel.

The raid stunned Egypt's new leader, Gamel Abdel Nasser. Under the terms of the Tripartite Declaration of 1950, Egypt, Israel, and other Mideast countries were to be denied major Western arms. But France was secretly supplying Israel through the 1950s, and even through the 1960s.

According to Kennett Love's *Suez: The Twice Fought War,* the humiliation of the raid caused Nasser to begin a search for weapons to defend Egypt. The Soviets had long sought influence in the Middle East, but the Western powers had successfully kept them out, until 1955 that is. Nasser had repeatedly pleaded with the United States to sell him weapons. He also asked the British, but both countries turned him down flat on the basis of the Tripartite Declaration. Finally, in desperation, he asked Moscow, which was only too happy to oblige. A major weapons deal between Egypt and Czechoslovakia was officially announced on September 27, 1955, propelling the Soviets squarely into the center of the Middle East conflict. The West's long-time monopoly in the Middle East was broken and Nasser overnight became the hero of the Arab world.

The Soviets greatly increased their presence, and their influence, as a result of their criticism of the Israeli/French/British invasion of Egypt in 1956, establishing a permanent naval presence in the Mediterranean.

The 1967 war once again brought Russia and the United States into confrontation, this time with greatly increased Soviet naval power in the Mediterranean. After Israel violated the cease-fire to invade Syria's Golan Heights on June 9, 1967, the Soviet Union dramatically broke diplomatic relations with Israel—they remain broken today—and activated the "hot line" to the White House to deliver a harsh threat. As in 1956, the two superpowers nearly came to combat because of Israel's aggression. They came close to nuclear confrontation again in 1973 when Kissinger placed u.s. forces on nuclear alert in response to Soviet threats stemming from Israel's repeated violations of the cease-fire agreement.

In 1971, the Soviet Union signed a treaty of friendship with Egypt, in 1972 with Iraq, and in 1980, with Syria. It currently sells military supplies to Libya, Syria, and Iraq. Its hold on South Yemen, the only Arab state to embrace communism, has remained firm, and its relations with Egypt, which were severed in 1981, were resumed in 1984.

Rather than acting as an obstacle to Soviet influence in the Arab world, Israel has been a catalyst. For Israel to make such a claim is tantamount to an arsonist seeking to make himself a hero by offering to put out a fire he started.

Hyping Camp David,
or
Who Are the Real Rejectionists?

*I*t's not clear whether, in its television advertising, the Hewlett Packard Company has copied Mr. Bookbinder, or vice versa, but one of the major themes running through his presentation is, "What if . . .?" What if the Arabs had decided in 1947 to acquiesce to the partition plan for Palestine? What if, in 1967, the Arabs had agreed to the legitimacy of Israel and had negotiated secure, recognized borders?

I have a couple of "what ifs" of my own.

What if the Zionist movement had chosen Illinois instead of Palestine as a site for an exclusive Jewish state? Or New York? Or Washington State? Would Americans be as tolerant if they were being driven out of their homes as the Palestinians have been?

What if the United States and Britain had permitted entry by helpless Jewish refugees trying to escape from Hitler's oppression? What if Zionists then had not resisted such entry because they wanted to try to push as many Jews as possible into Palestine?

What if the Palestinian Arabs had been allowed to decide their own future instead of superpowers and minipowers deciding for them? What if the Israeli lobby were prohibited from intimidating members of Congress? How much richer would the American taxpayer be? How many lives would have been saved, and how much suffering would have been avoided?

What if President Carter had used his energy and his leverage over Israel to bring about a comprehensive peace settlement that included a Palestinian state? Would the United States interest have fared better than it has from promoting Israel's interest by buying a separate peace with Egypt?

We are treated as well by Mr. Bookbinder to constant references to "Arab rejectionism," in the context of Israeli "risks" to make peace. But lest we forget, in the wave of Israeli propaganda, it is Israel that is sitting on Arab lands. No Arab state or entity has ever taken Israeli territory by force in violation of the u.n. Charter. The only war ever started by the Arabs—in 1973—was started in large part to recover the Golan Heights and the Sinai, Arab territories occupied by Israel.

The anger the Arabs vented over the forcible taking of Arab lands in 1948 was cooled by reality after the 1967 war when they finally learned that Israel was too much of a military power. As Cheryl Rubenberg notes in her book, *Israel and the American National Interest,* since the 1967 war, the Arab states have moved one by one to seek accommodation with Israel. Rubenberg confirms that, by 1982, all of the Arab governments had accepted Israel on the condition that it be limited to its pre-1967 boundaries. Except for Egypt, all have conditioned their acceptance of Israel on the creation of a Palestinian state.

Even u.n. Resolution 242 has been stood on its head by propagandists for Israel. As though history can be changed with his typewriter, Mr. Bookbinder makes an effort to lay the failure of Resolution 242 to Arab "rejectionism" again.

An excellent exposition of the background of 242's passage is found in Donald Neff's history of the 1967 war, *Warriors for Jerusalem.* It is based on interviews with the participants as well as a State Department study of the resolution's background undertaken in the late 1970s. Our u.n. ambassador at the time of the resolution's passage, Arthur Goldberg, a self-declared Zionist, played a key role in misleading Jordan's King Hussein with respect to Israel's intentions after the 1967 war.

King Hussein, who negotiated on behalf of the Arabs, received continuing assurances from President Lyndon Johnson and from Ambassador Goldberg that Israel had accepted the concept of only minor border adjustments before withdrawal from the territories they had occupied, assurances which gave Hussein the confidence to agree to Resolution 242. Neff disclosed that a written memorandum confirming Israel's agreement to this concept has disappeared from government files, but he was able to verify its existence from the memorandum's author, the u.s. official who acted as the go-between with King Hussein and Ambassador Golberg.

In contrast to Mr. Bookbinder's assertion that the resolution was rejected by the Arabs, not only was it accepted, but Israel has ignored it along with numerous Arab offers of peace which have been rejected by Israel. Some examples of such offers detailed by Ms. Rubenberg follow:

■ In 1970, Egypt's President Nasser offered a peace agreement with Israel provided it evacuated the occupied territories and accepted a settlement of the Palestinian refugee problem. Israel rejected the offer.

■ In 1971, President Anwar Sadat of Egypt offered a full peace treaty to Israel, with secure guarantees if Israel would return to the pre-1967 borders. Israel did not respond.

■ In 1972, King Hussein of Jordan offered to confederate Jordan and the West Bank. Israel rejected the proposal.

■ In the aftermath of the 1973 war, Jordan offered extensive concessions and a full peace to Israel, which was rejected by Israel.

■ In 1976, Egypt, Syria, Jordan, and the p.l.o. supported a resolution introduced in the u.n. Security Council by the Soviet Union calling for a Middle East settlement based on the 1967 borders with "appropriate arrangements . . . to guarantee . . . the sovereignty, territorial integrity, and political independence of all states in the area [including Israel and a new Palestinian state] and their right to live in peace within secure and recognized boundaries."

Israel asked the United States to use its veto to kill the resolution.

■ In 1977, Egypt, Syria, and Jordan informed the United States that they would sign peace treaties with Israel as part of an overall Middle East peace settlement. Nothing happened.

■ The P.L.O. endorsed the Soviet-American joint statement in 1977 on a comprehensive peace in the Middle East.

■ Israel flatly rejected the Fahd plan in 1981, and the Fez plan in 1982, in which the Arab countries formally accepted Israel.

■ In 1982, Israel rejected the Reagan peace proposal out of hand, which was also later rejected by the Arab states as well.

Israel has illegally annexed Jerusalem and the Golan Heights, and is making preparations to annex the West Bank and the Gaza Strip. It has adamantly said no to a Palestinian state, or to Palestinian self-determination. Yet it consistently denounces what it calls Arab "rejectionists." It has been able to sell its argument that only Israel seeks peace and the Arabs seek war because of the propaganda assistance it has received over the years by the American media, which downplays peace efforts by the Arabs and focuses instead on Israeli statements, whether or not they are true.

To repeat the obvious but often forgotten truth: it is Israel that occupies Arab lands and not the other way around. It is Israeli settler colonialism that is the obstacle to a peace agreement, and no amount of propaganda and finger pointing can alter that truth.

It's not surprising that propagandists for Israel happily ballyhoo the Camp David agreements. Israel had for years been trying to neutralize Egypt. In fact, as Donald Neff wrote in his history of the 1967 Middle East war, *Warriors for Jerusalem,* Israel offered exactly the same deal to Egypt immediately after the 1967 war. Nasser turned down the offer on the ground that it would abandon the Palestinians to the mercy of Israeli occupation.

As the most important and powerful Arab nation, Egypt's presence on the Western front restricted Israel's freedom of military movement, keeping pressure on Israel to negotiate with the Palestinians. Making a separate peace with Egypt had been a dream of Israeli leaders from the beginning. Until Anwar Sadat came along, however, Egypt, like the rest of the Arab world, had demanded that Israel withdraw from the territories it had occupied in the 1967 war and that the Palestinians be given self-determination, meaning a state of their own.

It was Sadat's willingness to ignore the Palestinians that has brought about the recent physical suffering of Lebanese and Palestinians and the political stalemate in the Arab-Israeli dispute. It was President Carter's rush to win a "political victory" by pushing Sadat into the waiting arms of Menachem Begin that brought on the ensuing difficulties. Carter lent his own influence along with the prestige and bankroll of the United States government to the effort to obtain a separate peace treaty between Israel and Egypt. He ignored the principal cause of the Middle East conflict—Palestinian statelessness. As Cheryl Rubenberg commented, ". . . it might have been expected that the President of the United States would have understood that American interests in the Middle East are greater than the sum of individual Israeli and Egyptian interests."

When the Camp David agreements were finally signed, it became clear what had happened. Sadat had caved in under pressure from Carter and Begin and allowed the concept of Palestinian rights to die out. Begin was allowed to cut any linkage between the Palestinian autonomy agreement and a peace treaty with Egypt. This gave Israel its long sought separate peace without requiring any movement on Palestinian self-determination, virtually guaranteeing Israel's permanent occupation over the Palestinians. Finally, Sadat acquiesced to Israel's claim to sovereignty over all of Jerusalem.

For his part, Carter gave Israel additional billions from the U.S. Treasury to build new air bases in the Negev, to pay for withdrawal from the Sinai, as well as giving in to a long list of Israel's other demands. Carter was in such a hurry to make an agreement—any agreement—in the Middle East he even fell for the Begin line that Israel would give up settlement activity in the occupied territories for five years. Begin not only began allowing illegal Jewish settlements immediately after signing the agreement, but directed Israeli lobby pressure on Carter to push the final peace treaty with Egypt. Carter responded to Begin's pressure each time he applied, putting pressure in turn on Sadat, pushing him to complete the treaty and to include a clause giving it priority over existing treaties Egypt had with the Arab world.

Thus, the great peace agreement that has received so much hype from members of the Israeli lobby has turned out to be nothing more than a license for Israel to work its will on the rest of the Arab world. And so it has, in Lebanon, on the Golan Heights, and in the occupied territories. The American taxpayer is paying for Israeli arms with cash, and the Palestinians and Lebanese are paying in blood.

Mr. Bookbinder decries Arab stereotyping, but immediately asks if Arab Americans are doing enough to eliminate the invitation to such hostility toward Arabs as a result of the racist anti-Arab campaign. He says that if "Arab Americans do not wish to be thought of as Qadaffis or Arafats or Abu Nidals—they cannot remain as silent as they have been when terrible crimes are committed in the name of Arab aspirations."

I know Mr. Bookbinder's intent is not to blame the victims of racism for racist attacks against them. But he would quickly understand the meaning of his assertions if someone were to suggest that, to avoid being associated with Ivan Boesky, American Jews should rise up as one in denunciation when he is convicted of bilking the public out of billions of dollars. One could extend this antilogism to Meyer Lansky, Bugsy Siegel, and the dozens of other American Jews who actually have been convicted of crimes. Surely in America, those who commit no crimes are not expected to apologize, even if they are Arab Americans. And finally, the reason that some people wrongly wrap Arab Americans in a terrorist blanket is because of the Israeli lobby's successful campaign to taint all people of Arab blood.

Israel's Right to Exist, Revisions of History, and Other Ways to Change the Subject

*T*here's an old story about two men who were about to enter into negotiations. One of them brought a goat into the room and the other strenuously objected to its presence. But the goat's owner refused to remove it until his adversary first conceded a point dealing with their original negotiation.

Israel leaders have brought, in a sense, a goat into the Middle East negotiating arena when they insist that the P.L.O. must first recognize Israel's right to exist before it will even talk to them.

Of course Israel exists, and if and when it agrees to sit down with P.L.O. negotiators, the fact of their meeting face to face is itself recognition of Israel's right to exist. The Israelis are playing upon a fiction in order both to humiliate and to avoid talking to the P.L.O., principally because talking to them would mean ultimately returning the occupied territories to create a Palestinian state. Refusal to talk to the P.L.O. has a simple logic behind it—the longer Israel can delay a peace negotiation with them as the Palestinians' representatives, the longer it can keep the West Bank and Gaza.

Israel exists, but no one, including Israel, knows what its boundaries are. It is the only nation in the world that refuses to define its own boundaries, presumably because, in its own mind, it is not yet finished expanding. As Israeli Michael Bar-Zohar, David Ben-Gurion's biographer wrote:

> Ben Gurion certainly did not want to issue a specific declaration [of independence] that would curtail his aspirations to extend the boundaries of the state. He proceeded to reveal some of his ideas to his colleagues: "If the U.N. does not come into account in this matter and they [the Arab states] make war against us and we defeat them . . . why should we bind ourselves?" By a single vote, five to four, his view was adopted: the state's boundaries would not be mentioned in the Proclamation of Independence.

Mr. Bookbinder asserts that even if there were no Israel, we would be concerned about the rise of militant fundamentalism; the Iran-Iraq war; the explosion of terrorism; and the ominous threat posed by Soviet intrusion into the area. Although he implies that these concerns center in the Arab world, he is glossing over Israel's role in each one. As Israel's scheming to sell arms to Iran comes more into focus, it is eminently clear that Israel became involved for one reason only—to prolong the Iran-Iraq war, since it sees both countries as enemies.

Militant fundamentalism is indeed a concern, not only with respect to Islam, but also with respect to Jewish fundamentalists in Israel who are trying to hold Israelis to their concept of a theocratic state. Israel's alliance with militant Christian fundamentalists in the United States cannot be brushed aside, since its outcome wishes no one well.

After the Israeli invasion of Lebanon in 1982, a flood of world criticism descended on Israel, some of it even coming from the United States. Tragically, all of the great human rights advocates in the u.s. Congress headed for cover during that summer of Israeli slaughter. But the atrocities were too much even for a complacent press corps, which soon began filming and writing about the damage done by the Israeli blitzkrieg. This prompted some components of the Israeli lobby to regroup their forces, again taking the propaganda offensive in an effort to erase the memory of Jews killing Arab civilians on a mass basis, and to try to rewrite the history of the invasion.

Robert Friedman has detailed the lobby's public relations drive in an article in the February/March 1987 issue of *Mother Jones* magazine titled, "Selling Israel to America: The Hasbara Project Targets the u.s. Media." Friedman's is a story of American Jewish pressure on American newspapers and television to limit the flow of information about the Israeli occupation, of economic threats by advertisers to prevent advertising for Congressman Findley's book on the Israeli lobby, and of news editor and advertising agency cooperation with the Israeli government to restore Israel's image following the Lebanon invasion.

There were several thrusts to this propaganda campaign, some of which are repeated by Mr. Bookbinder in his presentation.

Bookbinder: "There was general understanding and even public statements of approval of Israel's determination to wipe out the base of p.l.o. terrorism which had made life unbearable for those living in the northern part of Israel."

Documented History: An eleven-month-long cease-fire arranged by u.s. diplomat Philip Habib had been scrupulously observed by the p.l.o. despite innumerable Israeli attempts to provoke the p.l.o. into responding.

Bookbinder: "Israel, it was widely believed, was invoking its right, under international law, to pursue those who threaten the security of its citizens. 'Peace for Galilee' as the operation was called, was a legitimate goal."

Documented History: It was widely believed that Israel was in total violation of international law, the u.n. Charter, and general rules of morality which dictate against bullying the weak. As one

Israeli writer said, in order for there to be Peace in the Galilee, Sharon and Begin had to start a war there.

Bookbinder: Yasir Arafat's brother, head of Palestinian Red Crescent, had gotten the world's media to broadcast the fabricated figures of "10,000 civilian deaths and 600,000 homeless" in southern Lebanon during the first few weeks of the incursion." (In propagandists' terminology, it is "incursion" rather than "invasion.") "Even Evans and Novak . . . accepted the Israeli estimate that the right numbers were 460 dead and 20,000 displaced."

Documented History: The Lebanese government reported a total of more than 18,000 killed, more than 30,000 wounded, and more than 600,000 made homeless, many of them permanently, during the Israeli invasion. Israel's supporters are extremely defensive on this issue, but how they expect to salve their conscience by altering the number of civilian dead for which Israel was responsible is beyond me.

Bookbinder: "[Israeli] spokesmen insisted that the action around Beirut had been necessary to complete the rout of the P.L.O., to rid Lebanon of all foreign forces, and to help create a central, stable, pro-democratic Lebanese government." (He adds that Syria was too solidly entrenched to achieve most of these goals, and that the Syrians assassinated Bashir Gemayel.)

Documented History: Israel's government wanted to destroy the P.L.O. and Yasir Arafat because the P.L.O. gave too much political backbone to the resistance in the West Bank and Gaza, according to Israeli author Ze'ev Schiff in his book on the Lebanon invasion. So far as the creation of a "central, stable, prodemocratic government," that bit of fiction describes with less than total accuracy the election of Israel's ally, Bashir Gemayel as Lebanon's president, which was "democratically" accomplished when Israeli tanks and guns surrounded the Lebanese Parliament during its voting on the president.

To get the flavor of official Israeli thinking when it comes to domination of those who get in their way, one must hear the words of Uri Lubraini. Lubraini is currently Israel's expert on Shiite affairs, and was interviewed concerning Iran on February 1, 1982, on the BBC documentary program, "Panorama." Ever the calm professional, he told the interviewer, "I believe, I very strongly believe that Tehran can be taken over by a very relatively small force, determined, ruthless, cruel—I mean the men who would lead that force will have to be emotionally geared to the possibility that they'd have to kill ten thousand people."

Other efforts by Mr. Bookbinder to rewrite history follow:

Bookbinder: The original partition plan in 1947 allotted Israel only 13 percent of Palestine.

Documented History: Although Palestinian Arabs vastly outnumbered Jews in Palestine, the partition plan allotted 56 percent of Palestine to the Jewish settlement and 44 percent to the Palestinians.

Bookbinder: "Israel's cooperation with White House officials in [the Iranian arms sales] gambit was embarassing to Israel, but it nevertheless did illustrate its willingness to help a trusted ally when such help was deemed important."

Documented History: Israel, which had been selling arms to Iran since 1981, wanted to increase its sales of American weapons and devised a scheme to bring Ronald Reagan and his administration along with it to make its own efforts legitimate.

Bookbinder: There is general recognition of Israel's extraordinary intelligence capability, which has been of benefit to the u.s. as well as European and Arab nations.

Documented History: It was the Mossad, the Israeli intelligence service, which was responsible for the killing of an innocent Moroccan waiter in Norway, mistaking him for one of its targets. It was the Mossad that provided the extremely faulty intelligence on Iran for the Reagan administration's arms sales scheme in 1986. It was the Mossad which allowed a complete surprise attack on Israel by the Egyptians in 1973.

Bookbinder: "The media has been very fair to the pro-Arab side of the debate. TV coverage of hostage situations and other terrorist events almost always has provided opportunities for angry denunciations of Israel and their presumed unfair treatment of Palestinians."

Documented History: During the 1982 invasion of Lebanon by Israel, I asked ABC news anchorman Ted Koppel how many times an Israeli spokesman had appeared on his "Nightline" show as opposed to the number of times an Arab spokesman had appeared. His response was that Israeli spokesmen had appeared twelve times and

Arab spokesmen appeared four times. Gordon Peterson of Channel Nine news in Washington, D.C., became convinced that the media was treating Israel unfairly by its coverage of the slaughter of civilians in Beirut during the summer of 1982. He then produced and aired on Channel Nine a ten-part series about Israel that was, at its best, a travelogue, and should have been labeled as advertising for the government of Israel. I offered Mr. Peterson a documentary I had produced for ADC on the impact of the Israeli invasion on civilians in Beirut, but he refused to air it. In addition, the Public Broadcasting System refused to air the documentary on the ground that it was produced by an advocacy organization and therefore against their policy. However, PBS has consistently violated this so-called rule, airing at about that same time a series of interviews conducted by lawyer Stanley Rosenblatt with various Israeli leaders, such as Peres, Sharon, and Shamir. When Alan Conwell, the spokesmen for the hostages on TWA Flight 847, expressed himself on the need for changing American Middle East policy, he was savaged by Israel's propagandists, among them *Washington Post* columnist, ABC commentator, and Ronald Reagan debate coach George Will. Will once wrote a column describing a videotape he had been shown by an Israeli that purportedly showed young Syrian children eating live snakes, among other distasteful activities. The clear intent of the column was to brand the Syrians as total barbarians, but when I wrote to Will asking him if I could see the videotape in order to judge for myself, he never bothered to respond. Few readable descriptions of Will exceed the one delivered by his friend, William F. Buckley, who said in his January 27, 1987, column:

> The problem with devising peaceful solutions in the Mideast, where George Will is concerned, is that there he sees only a single position: Israel's—at all times, in all places. George sometimes sounds a lot like Rabbi Kahane, who is properly scorned by the majority of Israelis for his anti-Palestinian fundamentalism. If progress of any kind is going to be made in the Mideast, you don't begin by siding with Israel on every single point.

Buckley's observations apply, of course, to all of the propagandists for Israel who make it impossible to discuss a peaceful solution to the conflict.

The issue we are discussing is whether American policy should be continued, or whether it should be changed. Mr. Bookbinder has made a strong effort to shore up his arguments by changing the subject in a number of places in his presentation. Nowhere is this effort more glaring than when he says,

> Historic realities simply have to be accepted as the basis for resolu-
> tion of current problems. It surely would not be argued by Mr.
> Abourezk—or would it?—that American Indian claims and griev-
> ances against the original settlers for their conduct in the New
> World can today serve as appropriate grounds for undoing what has
> come to be the American nation?

Over the years I have believed that American Indians are entitled to self-determination, just as I have believed that Palestinians are entitled to self-determination. I have tried—against heavy odds—to preserve what land is left for American Indians, and to make their condition less like an occupation by the Bureau of Indian Affairs. I believe the Palestinians deserve the same.

There is one difference, however, between the occupation of American Indians in the last century and the occupation of Palestinians today. In 1945, those nations that organized the United Nations did so because of the consensus that territory should no longer be acquired by force of arms. Sickened by the kind of aggression initiated by Germany and Japan in this century, and by the forcible grabbing of land from the Indians in the 1800s, the United States—and later, Israel—ascribed to the u.n. charter, forswearing any such future acquisition of territory. There is a sound reason for recognition of this principle. Stated bluntly—those who live by the gun will die by the gun. Stated a bit more elaborately—the world community can no longer afford the kind of empire-building which may very well result in the introduction of nuclear weapons, an ending that no rational person can want. The principles of the United Nations charter are directed toward doing away with any kind of colonialism, whether it is of the settler variety or not. Should Israel, and Mr. Bookbinder, be allowed to justify commission of a crime because someone else committed one? This is a principle which we should all hope does not become accepted practice.

In the last half of the twentieth century no one should

attempt to justify taking land by force by pointing to more primitive times.

Among other attempts at revising history, Mr. Bookbinder asserts that Israeli resistance to Arab "invasions" resulted in large areas of Israeli dominance as the fighting ended. "Surely not unknown in the history of wars among nations," Mr. Bookbinder continues, "the victor lay claim to some of these lands it had been *compelled* to occupy in its self-defense." (Emphasis added.)

This is a propagandist's technique. "Invasions" of what? Could the Arabs invade themselves? The history of wars among nations should be just that—history, not propaganda. In fact, Israel has never been invaded. It started the 1956 and the 1967 wars and fought them on Arab land. The 1973 war was fought totally on Arab land as well, in the Sinai desert and the Golan Heights. The invasion of Lebanon, of course, was also fought completely on Arab land.

As do most supporters of Israel, Mr. Bookbinder becomes highly defensive when talking about Palestinian refugees and how they came to leave Palestine in 1948. Putting aside all the other arguments, neither Mr. Bookbinder nor anyone else has ever answered the question of why, if Israel wanted so desperately to have the Palestinians stay, did they not allow them to return to their homes after the fighting was over? The answer is obvious, of course. They were driven out, and allowing them to return would have vitiated the entire Zionist strategy of creating a Jewish majority.

When one sweeps aside all of the fluff, and all of the propaganda about how great Israel is, and how bad the Arabs are, the real issue still remains. Is it in the real interests of the United States to use its taxpayers' money for Israel's occupation of the Palestinians and the Lebanese? Is it in the real interests of the United States to add the Middle East as one more arena of potential nuclear confrontation, not only with the Soviet Union, but now with Israel and its nuclear arsenal added to the threat? Is it in the real interest of the United States to turn its head away from the gross violations of human rights committed on a daily basis by Israel? Is it in the interests of the United States to continually antagonize the large and potentially friendly Arab world? Forgetting about its oil resources, which are of tremendous economic value, can we say it's in our interests to write off the friendship of 150 million Arab people just to further the objectives of Israel?

It is important to keep in mind that changing American policy in the Middle East does not mean abandoning Israel. But it does mean we would once again live up to our revered ideals of self-determination and opposition to the taking of territory by force. It means we would once again stand tall in the United Nations and use our once rare veto for just causes, not for support of a cruel and inhuman occupation. It means America will no longer allow the use of its money for the barbed wire fences and iron bars that wrongly imprison Arabs resisting their occupiers. Changing our policy will mean that we stop buying bombs and airplanes that kill innocent civilians.

The most insidious feature of the Israeli lobby's campaign has been to prevent Americans from knowing how their money is being used. I do not doubt that Americans would instantly turn away from blind support of Israel once they became aware of its crimes. As is the case in other areas of policy, once the public is aware of wrongdoing, it will apply strong pressure on the politicians to put a stop to it.

Changing American Middle East policy would surely bring it more into line with the principles Americans hold sacred.

FACE-TO-FACE

DEBATE

Moderated by David K. Shipler

FACE-TO-FACE DEBATE

MR. SHIPLER: Anyone who has read this far has to be dismayed. Two Americans, both very well versed in the problems of the Middle East, look at the same shade of gray—one sees black, the other sees white. It raises questions about the purpose, the utility, of dialogue. So at this stage it's probably useful to conduct a search for common ground, to see whether these two men, having had their say at some length about the history and the politics and the violence of that region, can together find some reasonable course for progress.

To begin, we might try a mind-bending exercise, and ask each of you to criticize your own position; to answer the question, what wrongs have Arabs done to Israelis and what wrongs have Israelis done to Arabs? What criticisms do you have of your own argument and your own side of this question?

Let's begin with Mr. Abourezk.

MR. ABOUREZK: When you say Arabs, I assume you mean the Arab nations. Are there a number of sins committed by Syria and by Jordan and Saudi Arabia, and so on?

I don't speak for those governments. I think they are perfectly capable of speaking for themselves and defending their own position. I suspect each of them has committed a great many wrongs and sins. And you can justify some of them, perhaps, by saying, well, these are Third World countries coming out of colonialism, and that's what they're trained to do. That's a totally separate argument; it has nothing to do with this issue.

If I were to talk about wrongs committed by the Palestinian people themselves, they're guilty of being vulnerable and politically weak in a world where, in spite of the United Nations, might makes a great deal of right. And I think that's unfortunate.

So far as the Palestine revolution, the P.L.O. and its various

247

factions, I would rather see the P.L.O. undertake a struggle of non-violent resistance than the armed struggle that they have undertaken. But I'm not going to sit in the comfort of my Washington home and my Washington office and tell people who've grown up in refugee camps, "You can't go pick up a gun and go try to reclaim your land." That would be very difficult for me to do, even though I disagree with what they're doing. I'm not going to preach to them.

MR. SHIPLER: Well, take the role of analyst, then. You're trying to untangle this problem. You say that violence is not preferable, in your view.

MR. ABOUREZK: I happen to be a pacifist, and I absolutely believe violence is wrong, no matter what.

I think I could bring myself to defend my family and myself in a violent way, but I don't think that I can condone anybody undertaking acts of violence, because, as Joe Valachi used to say, "Them that lives by da gun dies by da gun."

I can't justify violence. But I have to hark back to what Oliver Tambo, the head of the African National Congress, said when he was in Washington in early 1987. In a speech at the Press Club he said, "Those who make political revolution impossible make violent revolution inevitable."

So you see, while you can ask me to lay blame and point the finger of blame on Palestinians and on Lebanese in southern Lebanon who are resisting the Israeli occupation, I have to lay it back on Israel. There really is no sensible alternative but to stop the occupation; let these people have their own country, let them have self-determination. Let's not just talk about self-determination in an abstract form; let's do it in reality.

MR. SHIPLER: Well, let's explore the political dimension before we turn to Mr. Bookbinder.

There is a spectrum of opinion in the Arab world, even among Palestinians, even within the P.L.O., about the appropriate political stand to take with respect to dealing with Israel, negotiating with Israel. How do you come out on that? Do you criticize one particular viewpoint or another? Where do you put yourself in that spectrum? For example, would you subscribe to the idea of a Palestinian-Jordanian delegation negotiating with Israel over the future of the West Bank?

MR. ABOUREZK: I think there ought to be an international conference with every state in the region involved, including the P.L.O., the Soviet Union, and the United States.

I think there should be a P.L.O. delegation by itself. I don't believe we ought to continue to mask the refusal on the part of Israel to negotiate by allowing them to say that they won't accept certain Palestinians. It just doesn't make sense for Israel to choose the Palestinian negotiators, which is what they're trying to do. If they were successful in choosing a Palestinian negotiator, how valid and how solid and how long-lasting would the ensuing agreement be? Obviously, the Palestinians have their own representatives in the form of the P.L.O..

MR. SHIPLER: Well, Mr. Bookbinder, let's give you the same question. What Israeli positions do you criticize?

MR. BOOKBINDER: Well, first, if I may, Mr. Shipler, with all due respect, I do not accept your first comment about our presentations, that one sees it all black and one sees it all white. I ask the reader to go back and read the first part of this book. I've presented a gray picture, because I believe it is a gray picture. Over and over again I have said that both peoples have suffered as a result of the conflict, and both have made mistakes. Both have been wrong at times.

In your book, *Arab and Jew,* you said, quite properly, "Both peoples are victims; each has suffered at the hands of outsiders, and each has been wounded by the other."

I concur. That's why there is this great need to seek accommodation, to seek a way out of this terrible, horrible dilemma that two peoples with legitimate claims to the land and to peace and recognition find themselves in. This conflict must be solved somehow.

You also said, in dealing with the question of terrorism and violence, "The Arabs and the Jews have been quite asymmetrical on this point of terrorism, with the Arabs generally hailing their terrorists and the Jews punishing theirs."

That's the difference. That's a very, very important difference. While people in both groups have indeed engaged at times in violence, in horrible crimes, I believe it is fair to say that overall the Jews have themselves been repelled, repulsed, indignant at acts taken by their own people, while overall the Arabs have said they are compelled to engage in this kind of terrorism and violence.

Now, Mr. Abourezk may say that he's a pacifist, but it's a weird kind of pacifism that leads him to say, as he did in the very first part of this book—on more than one occasion—that he justifies the violence. He says they had no alternative but to do these terrible things. No pacifist should ever talk that way. No pacifist should ever justify violence of that type.

And there's a difference, of course, between violence that is a tragic part of war and violence that is initiated by a group specifically for the purpose of compelling political decisions, with innocent victims.

So, have Jews been guilty of incidents that one must reject? Yes, indeed, and I have said so in the earlier part of the book. No need to recite the specifics.

Have the Arabs been guilty? Yes, they have.

All of this—all of this—argues for a really serious effort to understand what can bring the parties together.

Finally, let me say this. I entered this exercise, this debate, with the hope that as a result each of us would indicate a readiness to understand and accept at least part of the other's viewpoint. I'm compelled to say that I feel less hopeful now that Mr. Abourezk is trying to understand our agony and our aspirations. I say "our" meaning Jewish.

I suggest that Mr. Abourezk can tell me right now that I'm wrong. Let him do it, and I'll be glad to acknowledge I'm wrong. I believe that Mr. Abourezk personally shares the hope of too many Arabs that, indeed, the state of Israel should cease to exist. I think he'd like to wake up tomorrow morning and find out that in one way or another Jews are no longer the majority in Israel, or that one way or another all of the Arabs who he says were forced out have returned, and either through electoral process or some other process have now undone the Jewish state. That's what he would like to see happen.

MR. SHIPLER: Mr. Abourezk, can you respond to his question about your desires on behalf of Israel, whether you would really like to wake up one morning and see the disappearance of the Jewish state?

MR. ABOUREZK: I would like to see true democracy come to Israel. And if the people allowed to vote want to continue the state, that's wonderful. I believe in self-determination. And if they vote not to have an exclusively Jewish state, that's fine with me as well.

But I think the people ought to be entitled to decide that, particularly because the people who support Israel and who speak for it consistently say it's the only democracy in the Middle East. Well, let's let the democracy work.

We know that most of the Arab countries are not democracies. They're monarchies and they're dictatorships and so on, but . . .

MR. SHIPLER: I assume you're talking about Israel within the pre-1967 boundaries, not including the West Bank and the Gaza Strip and . . .

MR. ABOUREZK: Well, I think the people in the West Bank ought to be entitled to vote, and, as I said in my initial presentation, the ideal situation would have been to allow all the Palestinians to vote who were in what is now Israel proper, or, what we think is Israel proper. But that ideal situation is past. You can't go back to that now.

MR. SHIPLER: I think I'd like to follow up on your remark just to focus it a little more closely if we can. One could debate the health of any country's democracy. Frankly, having lived in Israel for five years, I have no doubt that it's basically a democracy. There are flaws in it, of course. If you're talking about Arabs within the state of Israel, they do vote, and they vote in very high percentages.

MR. ABOUREZK: They're not allowed to form their own political parties, though.

MR. SHIPLER: That's correct, they're not allowed to form their own political parties, but the . . .

MR. ABOUREZK: It's not what you'd call a pure democracy.

MR. SHIPLER: . . . but the question of whether Israel would remain in existence, depending on majority vote, seems a moot point since the vast majority of Israeli voters are Jews, and therefore . . .

MR. ABOUREZK: But you're repeating what I said.

MR. SHIPLER: The question remains unanswered. What would you like to see happen?

MR. ABOUREZK: Since we've passed the ideal in what is now considered Israel proper, even though the country has never defined its own boundaries, let's put that aside.

Now, in the West Bank I would like to see some sort of opportunity for the residents to decide their own future and their own government. We keep hearing about a Jordanian federation and five years of autonomy. Nobody knows what that means, really. It means, let's put it off for another five years.

We do everything except follow our principles. Our principles say that people are entitled to decide who their government shall be. We're not following those principles so far as the occupied territories are concerned.

MR. BOOKBINDER: I want to go back to what started this particular part of the dialogue. I believe you have failed to respond to my challenge. I'd like to hear you say that history, compassion, justice, and plain humanity now justifies the existence of a Jewish state in that part of the world.

MR. ABOUREZK: I've already said that.

MR. BOOKBINDER: No, all you've said so far in the book is that you accept as a fact that Israel exists. Would you amend that at least to say you believe it has a right to exist?

MR. ABOUREZK: Well . . . .

MR. BOOKBINDER: It has earned the right to be there as a Jewish state?

MR. ABOUREZK: Would you want me to say that?

MR. BOOKBINDER: Yes.

MR. ABOUREZK: I tell you what. I will say that if you'll say the Palestinians have a right to a state. How's that?

MR. BOOKBINDER: I want to remind our readers that in my presentation I drafted a single sentence, "Whatever mistakes or unfairness surround the creation of Israel, its right to exist in peace with recognized, negotiated borders should no longer be challenged."

Now, are you saying you're willing to say something like that . . .

MR. ABOUREZK: You add another condition, I won't answer that . . .

MR. BOOKBINDER:. . . You're willing to say something like that, if I'm willing to say something else. I'll tell you exactly what I feel. It's implicit in the first hundred pages of the book, but I'll say it now very, very directly.

I believe that the last several decades of Arab-Palestinian aspirations should now be recognized and that they should be entitled to the maximum possible amount of self-governance consistent with peace and recognition in that area.

MR. ABOUREZK: What does that mean?

MR. BOOKBINDER: I'll tell you exactly what it means. I am not ready to declare that the formula for that self-governance is what you call self-determination, what most people call a state. That is something to be negotiated between the parties involved.

Now, there is a process that has been agreed to by the major Arab state in the area, Egypt, by Israel, and with the cooperation of the United States. A formula exists for the beginning of this process of maximum self-governance for the Palestinians. That process would now be in its ninth year if Camp David had been followed. If that process, starting with maximum autonomy—genuine, generous autonomy—demonstrates to the Arabs, to the Palestinians, to the Israelis, that they can move even further into a full state, I will be the first to cheer.

Now, that's a long answer to your question, but that's exactly the way I feel about it.

MR. ABOUREZK: It sounds to me like you're against the Palestinian state, Mr. Bookbinder, because you've got every conceivable excuse that you can think of, and what everybody else can think of for not having one. Why don't you say, these people are entitled to run their own destiny. Let them have a state; let them have a democracy, a dictatorship, whatever it is that they want, and not what you want.

MR. BOOKBINDER: No, I want to start out with substantially more self-governance than any previous occupying power gave the Palestinian Arabs.

MR. SHIPLER: I want to follow up on something that Mr. Bookbinder said, and that's on the question of the West Bank occupation, which Mr. Abourezk raised.

How do you characterize the occupation? Do you concede that it's a pretty terrible situation? Do you think Israel should be trying to find a way to withdraw from the West Bank?

MR. BOOKBINDER: First, it's necessary to stipulate again what's been implicit in the book so far. Even the word "occupation" raises some questions. The fact of the matter is that those we now refer to as the Palestinian Arabs never had a state and never had a political entity to be taken over by another people. There never was an Arab Palestinian state that was taken over by the Israelis. Palestinian Arabs have lived for a long, long time in a twilight zone at best, and they're still in that situation.

Today, and for the last twenty years, it is true that the administering power or the occupying power in the West Bank is Israel. It's a very unhappy situation. We all know that in Israel itself there is a major difference of opinion about how to ultimately resolve the West Bank issue. There are indeed many Israelis who obviously intend to maintain political control of that area forever.

I personally disagree with that. I don't think that ought to be the Israeli view. There are many Israelis who want, down the road, to have some kind of territorial compromise, with Jordan preferably and hopefully, so that the Palestinian Arabs will finally be recognized.

Now, there's also a school of thought that argues that there is indeed a Palestinian Arab state now; its name is Jordan. I know that's an oversimplification, and I hear Mr. Abourezk chuckling, but it's not without merit. There exists already the foundation for some kind of entity that would give Palestinian Arabs a feeling that they are recognized.

I would like to see the beginning of genuine autonomy. It's mind-boggling to remind oneself that it's been nine years since a very important chapter of Palestinian history might have started, the ninth year of what could still be autonomy or what might be much more than autonomy. But Mr. Abourezk was one of those who shouted down what was involved in Camp David, said it wasn't good; it wasn't right.

MR. SHIPLER: Well, without rehashing Camp David, Mr. Abourezk, do you see in Mr. Bookbinder's desire for some kind of Israeli disengagement from the West Bank, any seed of hope there that you can pursue?

MR. ABOUREZK: No, I don't, not by the government of Israel. Why should Mr. Bookbinder sit here in Washington and decide what kind of government the Palestinians will have? He wants to give them autonomy, which neither he nor anybody else knows the meaning of; he wants to give them a state called Jordan, and he's never asked the Jordanians if they will agree to that, or if the Palestinians will themselves.

MR. BOOKBINDER: I have.

MR. ABOUREZK: What did they say?

MR. BOOKBINDER: They skate around the issue.

MR. ABOUREZK: Do you suppose that means yes or no, when they skate around it?

MR. BOOKBINDER: You know, because you've referred to it at times. You know that in the Camp David accords, a very historic step was taken, the Palestinians were invited to join the talks about their future. You can't call that an unimportant piece of history. It's inherently critical . . .

MR. ABOUREZK: The Camp David agreement was basically designed to keep the Palestinians from having a state. If it was designed to allow for a state, why would the Israelis be allowed to veto everything that was decided by the administrative council? And why would the Palestinians themselves object to it if they saw the possibility of a state? Do you think that they don't want a state, so that's why they're doing all this?

MR. SHIPLER: Both of you have already addressed this question, and there's no point in going over it.

MR. ABOUREZK: All right. I want to get back to the statement attributed to Mr. Shipler that "Arabs hail terrorists and Jews punish theirs." The first thing in my memory in this regard was when the Israelis landed a commando battalion in Beirut in 1973 and assassinated four Palestinian leaders. They weren't fighters, they were intellectuals and one poet, Kemal Nasser. These people were not soldiers or terrorists; they were assassinated simply because they were intellectuals and they were leaders.

And Golda Meir, in a public forum, said what "a splendid operation it was."

Now that was some punishment. You can go right on through history up until 1986, when the Shin Beth people beat to death two Palestinian prisoners accused of hijacking a bus. While handcuffed, they were beaten to death. And what happened? Everybody involved, all the way up to the head of Shin Beth, was pardoned, every single one of them.

In his rebuttal Mr. Bookbinder says that everyone was angry

about the outcome of this incident. Wonderful—they were angry. But you can't continue to say, Mr. Bookbinder, that the Jews are humane and the Arabs are not. It doesn't wash. There's inhumanity on both sides. So I really ask you to be fair and honest in this regard. Don't keep trying to paint Arabs all bad. You say that you agree with me that Arabs get critized and blamed too much and you want to put a stop to it.

MR. BOOKBINDER: I really don't enjoy being called unfair and dishonest. Let me remind you, and let our readers know, that literally twenty-four hours ago, I picked up the phone and I called you, I called the White House, I called the Justice Department, I called Tony Lewis of the *New York Times,* because I was distressed over the reports in yesterday's paper, which might be accurate, of harassment of P.L.O. supporters in California.

You know that this isn't a new exercise for me. You know that I did the same thing a year ago when Alex Odeh was assassinated. I'm not saying I'm a saint, but I want to tell you that what I did I feel is totally consistent with the basic ethic that guides Jews, both here and in Israel. We understand, we sympathize when there are lives lost. I'm not being a hypocrite when I talk about the crimes committed on both sides.

But the point is, where do we go from here? We cannot ignore the way we just heard Mr. Abourezk dismiss the possibility, the potential, in a Camp David formula over and over again.

As I prepared for this book, I was reminded and pained how again and again there were marvelous opportunities for possible progress, and people refused them. Sometimes the Jews were responsible for saying no. But much more often it was the Arab community that said no. No to the Balfour Declaration. No to partition. No to Camp David. No to this, no to that, no to 242.

And yes, I must say that, while it's not too often—but often enough—an Arab friend, an Arab colleague, somebody I meet at the American Enterprise Institute or somewhere else, will whisper lest someone else hear, that maybe we should have permitted Camp David to start operating. Maybe partition would have been better.

Again, in your book, Mr. Shipler, your own evaluation seemed to be that if the Arabs had said yes to partition back in 1947 or 1948, Israel today would be a much smaller country. The Palestinian Arabs would have benefited from saying yes. But saying no, no, no, no, constantly . . .

MR. ABOUREZK: When Mr. Bookbinder says somebody whispered in his ear that we should have permitted Camp David to start operating, I guess the question that immediately occurs is, who stopped Camp David from operating? Was it the Arabs themselves? Certainly they were against it, but they were not included in it.

The Syrians were against it, but they were not part of Camp David. It was Israel, the United States, Egypt, and Jordan, right? And they could have gone ahead without Jordan. It had nothing to do with Jordanian territory.

So what was set up in Camp David was this so-called autonomy plan, and an administrative council that would have administered the occupied territories. The administrative council was a unanimous decision-making body. Everything had to be unanimous.

In fact, as I say in my presentation, when I was briefed at the White House, I asked Jimmy Carter and Cyrus Vance right after the briefing, "Is this to be a unanimous body?" They replied that it was.

"That means," I said, "if somebody made a motion to create an independent Palestinian state, it would be vetoed by Israel?"

They said yes, and that they would agree with that. In fact, the U.S. would have vetoed it, if Israel hadn't.

But I'd bet money that Israel would have vetoed it.

So what we have is just another form of occupation, under a better name. You can put public relations names on everything you want to do, and that's exactly what the Camp David agreement was, nothing more, nothing less. And who stopped the Camp David agreement from operating? It was Menachem Begin. Instantly Menachem Begin got up and started making speeches, "We're never going to give up Jerusalem. We're never going to give up the occupied territories. We're going to start building settlements." They did, in fact, announce new settlements almost immediately after Camp David was signed. So don't give me all this jazz about the Camp David agreement being a historic opportunity. It was a historic failure. It brought on the invasion of Lebanon in 1982, and there's no way you can deny that if you want to be realistic. Now let's talk about the future, if you don't mind.

MR. SHIPLER: Okay. I'd like to start talking about the future by asking you to discuss the question of u.s. policy. We're now in 1987; the Camp David accords weren't implemented, and they didn't seem to have any chance of being for various reasons. There has been some effort to create a dialogue between Jordan and Israel which has not come to fruition.

Where do we go from here. If you were secretary of state, what would your approach be now?

MR. ABOUREZK: Well, the first thing I'd do as secretary of state is fire Elliott Abrams.

The second thing I would do is sit down with Prime Minister Shamir and say, "The United States position is that you should negotiate with all of the interested parties in an international conference, including the Soviet Union. Now, you don't have to, because you are a sovereign nation, but if you don't do it, the United States is going to withhold all future aid from Israel."

In my view, there is never going to be any sort of peaceful resolution of this matter unless the United States stops writing blank checks for Israel. That's why Israel does whatever it wants to. In contrast to the way things usually operate, it gets rewarded for its crimes and its sins, not punished for them.

MR. SHIPLER: Do you think that's politically realistic? Do you think a secretary of state would be able to do that?

MR. ABOUREZK: No, of course not. We're talking about the ideal situation. It's not politically realistic simply because the Israeli lobby has poured too much money into congressional campaigns and presidential primaries, to allow politicians to say, "Israel, you've got to make a deal."

MR. SHIPLER: And what would the outcome of an international conference ideally be, from your standpoint? What would the solution be?

MR. ABOUREZK: Ideally, I think, a peace treaty would be negotiated between Israel and all of its enemies in the Middle East, including the p.l.o. There would be a Palestinian state that Israel would finally have to recognize, and then define its own borders—I think that would be one of the major accomplishments of the conference—and the Palestinians would begin to administer their own state. There would be anti-hostility treaties among all of these nations, supervised by the Soviet Union and the United States.

The Soviet Union has indicated that it's interested in such an arrangement on more than one occasion. And I think the United States would be, provided there wasn't any influence from the Israeli lobby. I think that would be the u.s. position if it were not skewed by what we euphemistically call domestic politics.

MR. SHIPLER: And where would the Palestinian state be located?

MR. ABOUREZK: In the West Bank and the Gaza Strip, which is the only real territory left for such a state in the Middle East.

MR. SHIPLER: So you've answered Mr. Bookbinder's question here about recognizing Israel's right to exist, it seems to me.

MR. ABOUREZK: Well, of course, I've said of course Israel exists. Those are the very words I used in . . .

MR. BOOKBINDER: He still won't say "right to exist." You really do refuse to say that, don't you?

MR. ABOUREZK: Within whatever boundaries, and provided that you recognize the Palestinians' right to exist.

MR. SHIPLER: Now, let me ask you, Mr. Bookbinder—we may be making some headway here—let me ask you the same question.

MR. ABOUREZK: Let me just remind you I am not a nation, so it doesn't do much good for me to recognize Israel's right to exist.

MR. BOOKBINDER: But you want me to create a state for the Palestinians.

MR. ABOUREZK: No, I want you to let them decide for themselves.

MR. SHIPLER: Mr. Bookbinder, let me ask you the same question about u.s. policy if you were secretary of state. I would like to make the observation that there seems to be the potential here for some agreement between you about peace treaties between Israel and its Arab neighbors. How can you build on that?

MR. BOOKBINDER: Let me respond in the same multi-dimensional way. Because the reference has been made to the Israeli lobby, with all the implication that it is what keeps us from making the progress you're seeking, Mr. Shipler, I did a little research yesterday.

The reader knows my basic case about the Jewish lobby and its legitimacy. I reject the suggestion that the Jewish lobby simply buys the Congress of the United States. Let's examine the total campaign expenditures picture for the 1986 cycle, for the years 1984 to 1986. Total expenditures for all of the senate and house campaigns were between $400 and $500 million. Some of the reports have not yet come in. Note that: $400 to $500 million to elect the last Congress.

Total amount of pac—political action committee—contributions were $145 million. Total Jewish political action committee contributions were $3.5 million.

In other words, the total Jewish contributions to all campaigns were less than 1 percent of the total expenditures. We are 3 percent of the people, so we're spending even less than our proportion.

That's very important to keep in mind, because the suggestion is made over and over again that the only reason America and Americans are so supportive of Israel is not on merit, not on basic concerns about America's interests, but because the Jews have bought Congress.

Now to the heart of the question itself. We have heard from Prime Minister Shamir of his total opposition to any international conference. My personal judgment is that that's wrong. There ought to be more flexibility than that. But I'm also confident this is a matter for further discussion and deliberation. The Israelis have shown flexibility in the past in the negotiating process.

But we also ought to understand that such a conference should be no more than a formula to begin direct negotiations. I'm gratified by what the administration has said, that it's calling for an international conference as a preface to direct negotiations, because that's the only thing that will produce results.

The Soviet role in Middle East affairs has not been one that Americans should welcome. I don't want to recite that history now. It's not one we ought to be happy about. Moreover, whenever you bring all of the superpowers together they all vie for the position of most militant, friendliest to Arab aspirations, and you get nowhere.

Even though Mr. Abourezk is disappointed about Camp David, the only thing that should gratify us during these last forty years is that the major Arab state in the area, Egypt, saw the wisdom of direct negotiations and was willing to negotiate a treaty with Israel. Because of that, fifty million Arabs have been living in peace.

Now, if one Arab American named James Abourezk doesn't think that's very important, I would suggest, since he's the one always saying, let's ask the Arabs what they want, that we ask the Arabs in Egypt whether they would prefer war rather than the peace they now have.

If, in order to get a broader peace, it is necessary to deal one on one, or with only two countries or three countries or whatever the situation allows, we should be willing to do that and not insist that all the countries have to sit around the same table at the same time. But to go back to the first comment, I personally don't think it's necessary or wise to rule out totally the possibility of an international conference.

MR. SHIPLER: And what about a Palestinian state? What do you see as the final result of that conference?

MR. BOOKBINDER: I want that conference or that direct negotiation to bring us as close as possible to full self-governance for the Palestinians.

MR. SHIPLER: What does that mean?

MR. BOOKBINDER: It's easy enough for us to recite a pat formula that people are entitled to self-determination. How can anybody be against that version of motherhood? Of course, people should have the right to self-determination. What people? Under what circumstances? With what neighbors?

You cannot have an absolute doctrine that any group of people who say they want to be fully free and self-determinant, have the right to do it. You cannot say that the Indians of South Dakota have the right to self-determination, meaning their own state or their own country, with their own foreign policy.

Mr. Abourezk may say yes to that, but I think the absurdity of it is self-evident. I want that group of Palestinian Arabs who desire their own state either to negotiate it in peace and persuade their neighbors and persuade the world community that that's the proper next stage, or let them fight for it.

They have tried to fight for it in their own ways; they have not succeeded. But it's not for me to say in 1987 that the only answer to the Palestinian problem is their own independent state. At the same time, I don't want to rule it out.

MR. ABOUREZK: First of all, I have to reject your figures on what the Israeli lobby contributes to elections.

MR. BOOKBINDER: The Federal Election Commission has published these . . .

MR. ABOUREZK: Have they defined what Jewish PACS are in the Federal Election . . .

MR. BOOKBINDER: Yes. There are seventy identifiable organizations known as Jewish PACS.

MR. ABOUREZK: What about individual Jews who contribute; did you add that in? Contributions made independent of PACS? Let me tell you how I got money from individual Jews.

I was put on an approved list by my campaign chairman, who turned out to be a Zionist, and I started getting money from Jews all over the country. I went to fund raisers where Jews contributed money to my campaign.

MR. BOOKBINDER: Did you issue a statement that you didn't believe then; did you lie? Why did you get the support? You must have said something that you didn't believe in.

MR. ABOUREZK: No, I wrote a letter; I said I believed in peace in the Middle East. And my campaign chairman said that was fine.

MR. BOOKBINDER: What's your point?

MR. ABOUREZK: My point is this—for you to deny that the Israeli lobby influences Congress is absolutely ludicrous. If those people up on the Hill had any guts at all, I could take you by the hand and lead you into the Democratic cloakroom and hear what these senators and congressmen tell me privately: "I wish I had guts enough to say the things you do, Jim. I can't do it, I depend too much on Jewish contributions. I just absolutely cannot say that, but, by God, you're right." For the eight years I was in national politics, I heard that every day.

Now, with respect to the international conference, where Mr. Bookbinder says that only the most radical states will have influence, just try to make an international settlement without the radical states in the Arab world and see how far you get. Ask George Shultz about the May 17 agreement that he tried to organize between Lebanon and Israel, without Syria's participation. That went out the window.

MR. SHIPLER: Can you address the question about self-determination and Mr. Bookbinder's observation that not every ethnic group in the world has its own state?

MR. ABOUREZK: I agree not every ethnic group has its own state. But here we have a piece of vacant land. The Palestinians have been trying to create their state from the beginning of this whole thing. They were stopped in the first place by the partition plan, which never went through. They were stopped by Israel declaring itself a state. And now they say, "Okay, we'll settle for—we don't like it, but we'll settle for—the West Bank and the Gaza Strip."

Now, I see nothing wrong with them being able to vote within those areas for their own government. You say that, this goes along with the general concept that not every ethnic group can have its own state. Well, why can't they have their own state?

We're not talking about Poles living in Chicago who might want to start their own state here. We're talking about Palestinians who have a particular history that lends itself to having their own state. In fact, ideally, they would have had their own state years ago if Israel hadn't come in, declared itself, and hung on by force of arms.

The Palestinians weren't able to do that. They weren't strong enough militarily. So what happens now? They are entitled, I believe, and whether they get self-determination has nothing to do with any other ethnic group.

MR. BOOKBINDER: Between 1948 and 1967, Jordan occupied the West Bank. During that time did you make any public declarations about the fact that the Palestinians were being deprived of their own state?

MR. ABOUREZK: No.

MR. BOOKBINDER: You didn't? Could they have been granted statehood then without Israel preventing it from happening?

MR. ABOUREZK: Yes.

MR. BOOKBINDER: They could have.

MR. ABOUREZK: Yes.

MR. BOOKBINDER: But they didn't. So there was indeed a time, a significant time, when the Palestinians might have had their own state, but they were kept from having that state by the Arab world.

MR. ABOUREZK: We're talking about American policy, not Jordanian policy.

MR. BOOKBINDER: That's right.

MR. ABOUREZK: You're going back to what the Jordanians did in the past that might have been wrong to justify what Israel's doing in the present that's still wrong? Is that right? Is that logical?

MR. BOOKBINDER: You say that American policy ought to decree for the Jordanians, for the Palestinians, and for the Israelis, what the nature of statehood ought to be. Do you want American policy to be the one to decree that?

MR. ABOUREZK: American policy ought to follow the principles of self-determination which have been declared by every American government from the beginning. We ought to follow that principle and not make an exception for Israel.

MR. BOOKBINDER: You will have total chaos if you say that any group of people at any time—regardless of the recent history, regardless of the kind of allies that are involved—has a right to say they are a state.

MR. ABOUREZK: You cannot put words in my mouth. What I said was the Palestinians have a peculiar history that lends itself to self-determination. They're occupied by a foreign power and they ought to be entitled to have their own state. Let me hear you deny that. I want to hear it.

MR. BOOKBINDER: I deny the way in which you just formulated it. I have never closed the door to a group calling themselves Palestinians seeking maximum self-determination, even statehood, if the other parties in the area involved have been persuaded that that's the way to peace. I don't close the door to it, but neither do I want it open so wide that any group of people that you define, Jim, can simply declare they are a state. Existing states have a right to be concerned about their security, too. And there I identify with the pain . . .

MR. ABOUREZK: You're talking about Israel.

MR. BOOKBINDER: I identify with my people, my fellow Jews, who've gone through a history of pain, a history of discrimination, a history of persecution. If they want to have reasonable security, I don't want to deprive them of it.

There was a time when they did not, could not, stop the formation of another Palestinian state. But we have a history to contend with, a history of constant violation of understandings, a history of

Palestinian aspirations that have been pursued in the form of violence against the state of Israel, Palestinian aspirations that are expressed in the name of a P.L.O. that doesn't want Israel to exist, wants its death, and engages in terrorist activities day after day, year after year.

So a theoretical position about the existence of a Palestinian state on the West Bank or somewhere else cannot be considered in isolation from history.

MR. SHIPLER: Go ahead and respond, and then I have a couple of final questions I want to ask.

MR. ABOUREZK: You are absolutely right; you cannot divorce this from history. And that's precisely why I spent the first sections of my initial presentation talking about the history of this thing.

You see, it's not just Jews who've had violence perpetrated against them; it also has been perpetrated other people in this world.

MR. BOOKBINDER: Agreed.

MR. ABOUREZK: Including the Palestinians who didn't ask for it in the first place. Now, here's another one of your "what if" questions: what if Israel had not decided to come in and seize Palestinian land, which is what it was? You're not going to make me feel guilty, because it doesn't work. I have committed no sin and neither have the Palestinians.

MR. BOOKBINDER: Neither have I.

MR. ABOUREZK: I didn't say you did, and I'm not trying to make you feel guilty. What I'm saying is there's no way you can excuse Israel's activities toward the Palestinians by saying that your people had been the victims of violence. I happen to know that; I happen to be just as much against it as you are.

But you cannot justify the crimes of Israel today against the

Palestinians by saying that somebody else committed crimes against the Jews years ago.

MR. SHIPLER: Let me ask you one more question, and then I'd like to ask both of you a final question before we end.

Mr. Bookbinder talked about his own identity as a Jew shaping his views. How does your identity as an Arab American shape your views? How important is it, do you think?

MR. ABOUREZK: I don't feel like an Arab; I feel like an American. Because my parents were born in Lebanon, and because Arabs feel that they can come to me and talk to me, I've had a greater understanding of their aspirations, I think, than most ordinary Americans have. I think that's the real difference. Maybe it has an indirect impact, because I have talked to so many Arab people all over the Arab world, common people, government people, kings, presidents, dictators, whatever. It's just that I have a greater understanding of them, and I think that probably is the indirect result of being an Arab American.

But, very simply, I feel like an American, and I'm of liberal persuasion. I've always been an advocate of human rights for anybody.

MR. SHIPLER: I want to ask the last question. Having gone through this exercise now, do you still believe in dialogue? Is it fruitful?

MR. BOOKBINDER: I must say that I am saddened. I am saddened by the turn that this debate has taken.

Maybe it's inevitable that when two people feel this strongly about an issue, they tend to exaggerate the differences. The fact of the matter is that there has to be understanding between Jew and Arab, both in the Middle East and here, as friends of peace and progress. I'm sorry that I've heard and seen no concessions on Mr. Abourezk's part that Jews, because of their history, because of a lot of things, are basically entitled to a secure home in the Middle East.

I'd like to hear those words. I haven't heard them in this debate, in this book, or anywhere else. There can be peace in the Middle

East. There must be peace in the Middle East. The basic needs of all the peoples there can be satisfied.

I don't pretend to be an expert in this area, but Palestinian Arabs are Arabs, with a rich culture and a rich identity of interest among all of them. There would have been peace and harmony and progress for Palestinian Arabs these last forty years, these last seventy years. There could have been; there should have been.

I have contended all along that there is no Palestinian Arab state primarily because the Arabs of the world did not want an additional, separate Palestinian Arab state. The Jews, the Israelis, for many years could not have, would not have, did not want to stop that from happening. But because other significant things have now happened, the immediate creation of a hostile Palestinian state right next to Israel has caused great concern among the Israelis.

I hope that concern can be overcome, not by the kind of angry rhetoric we've seen in this book on the part of a man who believes strongly about it. I regret it very much. But I think we can overcome these differences, we must overcome these differences. There is room enough in the Middle East for the existence of a viable Jewish state that's not constantly threatened. There's room for Arab aspirations, and specifically Palestinian aspirations. I desire that. I want Palestinian Arabs to feel that they have a home and a homeland, whether it be with Jordan, whether it be ultimately their own new, independent state, if all the parties in the area agree that that's the right next stage.

I know many Israelis who share this dream and hope that there can be this kind of peace in the Middle East. If this book has not contributed to greater understanding, I will be very, very sorry. But I think perhaps the contribution we will have made in this volume is that in addition to expressing the hope that peace can break out, and that there can be civility in our discussion, the book may also contribute to having people understand that it won't be easy, and we have to continue working on it.

MR. SHIPLER: Mr. Abourezk, is dialogue fruitful?

MR. ABOUREZK: Yes, I think it's definitely fruitful. The big problem with dialogue as it has taken place in the United States is that it's been altogether too one-sided. Mr. Bookbinder talks about hoping that peace breaks out. The unfortunate part about his aspirations for peace is that he is somewhat like the Israeli government which would like to have peace only on their terms, not on anyone else's terms.

In other words, let's split off Egypt and make peace with them so they're not a threat to us anymore. Let's split off Jordan, let's try them next and see if we can get them out of the way. And then we'll work on Syria after that. Then we don't ever have to worry about the Palestinians once we remove these military powers from the equation. That was basically what was behind Camp David.

You just can't say, "Well, I'm hopeful for peace and I hope Mr. Abourezk would not be so angry and would not say all these things."

What has really happened is that the u.s. government and that segment of the American public that pays attention to Middle East affairs just has had no understanding of Palestinian aspirations. They just don't care about the Palestinians.

To have Mr. Bookbinder say that not all peoples are entitled to self-determination, to try to ring in the American Indians and the Sikhs in India and the Punjabis and on and on and on, is ridiculous. You're talking here about Palestinians living in occupied land under a military occupation, he's basically trying to say that they're not entitled to their own state.

He's saying that he doesn't like the occupation, but it's the best thing we have. He's saying that I won't talk about Israel's right to exist, but what he's really doing is dancing around this whole issue of the Palestinians' right to their own state. He won't come right out and say it, and I know why he won't—because Israel doesn't want a Palestinian state right next door. They just don't want it there, period, and they're going to use every conceivable excuse not to allow it.

You can talk from now until next year about our hopes for peace, but unless there is a real dialogue between the p.l.o. and the Israelis, it's not going to happen. And you won't get negotiations when one side is excessively strong and the other is excessively weak, and that's why Israel won't negotiate now.

It's incumbent upon the u.s. government, which gives Israel its strength, to come around and tell Israel that if they don't negotiate, if they don't want to sit down and talk peace with the P.L.O., then U.S. support of Israel will end.

It's got to be done that way or it just won't happen at all.

MR. SHIPLER: Thank you both very much.

CLOSING
STATEMENTS

HYMAN BOOKBINDER

*I*t is clear from a reading of the preceding pages that Mr. Abourezk and I do indeed see the Middle East "through different
eyes." Our face-to-face colloquy did not bring us much closer.
There are, obviously, clear contradictions in our presentations.

But the very fact this dialogue has occurred may be more important than the specific elements in it. If it encourages more study,
more thinking, more attention to the tragic hostility between Arab
and Jew, it will have served a useful purpose. Though our respective
eyes may see different truths today, the continuing search for truth
may some day bring us closer together.

I have participated in this debate as an American, as a Jew, and
as a citizen of the world committed to a just peace in the Middle
East. I remain satisfied that these aspects of my being have not been
in conflict with one another.

As an American, I am proud that my country has seen fit to lend
its standing and resources to the cause of peace and accommodation
in the Middle East, and that it has used its unique position to make
possible such breakthroughs as the Camp David agreement. With
the great majority of Americans, I am proud that, from the start, our
country has identified with the determination of the Jewish people
to build again a state of Israel on the land of their ancestors. There
have been some mistakes and vacillations over the years, but the
underlying American commitments have been right and the performance generally constructive. In the global struggle for human
rights and democracy, it is comforting to know that my country has
forged an alliance with the only fully democratic nation in the
Middle East. This relationship has served our own national interests
in a world threatened by totalitarianism, aggression, and terrorism.

As a Jew, I feel proud that my coreligionists, despite horrendous difficulties, have managed to build a state with doors always open to any Jews anywhere who need refuge from a world still hostile to Jewish presence. I am pleased that despite endless wars and threats to its very existence, Israel has remained essentially democratic and pluralist, and that it has shown generosity and flexibility whenever peace with Arabs seemed possible. As a Jewish American, it feels good to know that the great majority of Americans share this Jewish evaluation of Israel's history.

As a citizen of the world, I see America playing a constructive role in seeking to bring justice and peace to an area too long torn apart. I welcome America's interest not only in assuring Israel's security, but also in securing justice for the Arabs and recognition of the legitimate rights of the Palestinians.

American involvement in the Middle East has not been without difficulties or dangers or costs. Like other obligations undertaken by the world's foremost democracy, such involvement may at times be perceived as a burden rather than a boon. Its purposes can be honestly misunderstood by friends, and deliberately distorted by enemies. But the United States cannot be uninvolved in the currents and crosscurrents of Middle East developments. That it should be the one great power today which enjoys the confidence of Israel *and* much of the Arab world is the best possible evidence that its policies have been, overall, on target. By serving the cause of peace and reconciliation in that vital area, it has well served its own best interests.

By an unpredictable accident of timing, I find myself writing this concluding statement a few days after returning from what will probably be judged a historic "mission" to Israel. I was one of about fifty American Jewish officials and representatives who went to Israel in March 1987 to discuss several major issues that threatened to cause a serious rupture between the United States and Israel, and between the American Jewish community and Israel. Major public attention was focused on the Pollard spy case, the Pollards having been sentenced earlier that month. Particularly distressing were the inexplicable promotions of the two Israeli officials presumably involved in the Pollard operation.

Mr. Abourezk, I assume, will see and use the Pollard case as a refutation of my argument that it is in our national interest to maintain and strengthen the u.s.-Israel special relationship. I see it as a tragic exception to a very impressive record of trust and cooperation. I see it, moreover, as a test of the strength and durability of the u.s.-Israel relationship. Early in March, at the height of official and public indignation—including that of the American Jewish community—President Reagan placed the case in proper perspective: "Our relationship with Israel is long and strong, and is based on a large number of strategic and mutual interests, and that will not change."

Observing the way American Jews spoke out firmly on the Pollard case, both at home and in our frank talks with Israeli officials, could Mr. Abourezk bring himself to withdraw his reckless charge that the Jewish lobby "takes its orders from Israel"?

Upon arriving in Israel on March 16, I was widely reported in both the Israeli and American press as having declared that "Pollard is a criminal found guilty in our system of justice. It's as simple as that." I called upon Israel to give credible evidence that it understood the gravity of the offense and was prepared to take adequate corrective and preventive action.

But I also said then, and now conclude my contribution to this volume with these words:

"Serious as the Pollard case and its handling by Israel have been, it does not erase the impressive history of trusting relationships these past 40 years, nor does it refute the sound logic which prompted such relationships. The United States and Israel continue to be good for one another."

CLOSING STATEMENT
JAMES G. ABOUREZK

W hen all the history has been recited and the debating points have been made, the question of peacefully ending the Arab-Israeli conflict remains an inescapable issue.

Israel's hiring of an American citizen—Jonathan Pollard—to steal secrets from its main benefactor, the United States, and Israel's self-serving involvement in the Iran-Contra affair have revealed once again that Israel will always serve its own interests rather than those of the United States.

Those interests have always been expansionary and dangerous— both to the victims of its expansion and to world peace. Denials of such misconduct by Israel's supporters fly in the face of years of evidence.

American Jews should no longer allow themselves to be morally taxed to support Israel's empire building at the expense of its more vulnerable neighbors, the Arabs. By their policy of never questioning Israel's behavior, American Jews have effectively turned over to Israel's leaders their power to make political decisions on the merits of an issue. Israel's lobby has succeeded in mobilizing American Jews as a weapon capable of forcing Israel's wishes on the United States government. Israel's arrogance is a direct result of the power built up by the lobby, and no amount of denials and covering propaganda can change that reality.

The result has been the negation of the very principles for which American Jews have stood during much of their history. Blind support of Israel has obscured their long-held visions of social justice and self-determination, placing them in the position of denying these things to Palestinians only because Israel, out of a desire for empire, has decreed it to be so.

The Palestinians are entitled to their place in history, just as Jews were. It is unseemly to argue that somehow Palestinians do not qualify for the self-determination that Mr. Bookbinder demands for others. He and other Zionist spokesmen spend much of their time and energy denouncing apartheid in South Africa, the Soviet occupation of Afghanistan, and the violation of human rights in Russia, and at the same time will make petty excuses for Israel's occupying Arab land, violating human rights, and killing, imprisoning and torturing Arabs. His principles are quickly abandoned when it comes to Palestinians, because standing by them means he must criticize Israel.

It is revealing to know that Mr. Bookbinder will protest to the Israeli government the damage done by the Pollard affair to Israel's image and to Israel's relations with the United States, but that he will not protest the brutality of Israel's treatment of Arabs in Lebanon and the occupied territories of Palestine.

The Arab-Israeli conflict can be ended, in fact, it must be ended before more people—both Arab and Jew—are made to suffer. But it will not end until Israel is forced to give up its dreams of empire. That will not happen until American Jews begin to question seriously the premises of their blind support of Israel's aggressive acquisition policies. When Israel is made to realize that America will no longer support its violent adventures, then perhaps realism will replace arrogance, and Israel will begin to live within the confines of international law.

That is when this tragic conflict will end.

NOTES ON SOURCES
AND
SUGGESTED READING

NOTES ON SOURCES AND SUGGESTED READING

HYMAN BOOKBINDER

Despite sharp differences expressed in this book, the "facts" supporting our respective positions are not really as much in dispute as my opponent suggests. As the title of the book indicates, we have simply seen these facts "through different eyes." We have brought to these facts different personal and group histories, loyalties, and prejudices. I have not sought to hide mine in the preceding pages.

In the following paragraphs, I will note some of the principal sources which have contributed to my appreciation of the subtleties and complexities of the Arab-Israeli dispute and of the u.s.-Israel special relationship—sources which may help guide the reader interested in learning more about the subject. While these sources may be seen as largely pro-Israel, many of them reflect a balance and respect for the Arab point of view, which I have myself tried to reflect in this book—the kind of balance rarely seen in sources usually cited by pro-Arab authors.

I will not burden these pages with endless listings of sources to prove the obvious "fact" that, on hundreds of occasions, the p.l.o. and other anti-Zionist groups engaged in indiscriminate violence against civilian targets as a matter of deliberate policy. In the text, I have referred to several of these occasions to make the basic point. Nor do I see the need to list pages of sources to document the hundreds of explicit commitments to the destruction of the state of Israel voiced by major Arab and Palestinian leaders over the years.

While the resolution of current international disputes cannot rest primarily on centuries-old or even millennia-old events and aspirations—long before current generations of peoples can be judged responsible—it is helpful to understand the history and legacy of those peoples. Thus, an understanding of the history of the

Jewish people, with an unbroken commitment to the land of Israel over the ages, is critical to appreciating the Israeli attitude. Two works by Abba Eban are as readable as they are valuable: *My People: The Story of the Jews* (New York: Random House, 1968) and *Heritage: Civilization and the Jews* (New York: Summit Books, 1984). Abram Sachar's *A History of the Jews* (New York: Knopf, 1965) has long served as an authoritative research source.

Jewish history is an integral part of many books dealing with the history and nature of the modern Zionist story. Among those I found very helpful:

Herzl by Amos Elon (New York: Holt, Rinehart & Winston, Inc., 1975)

Chaim Weizman by Norman Rose (New York: Viking Press, 1986)

Ben Gurion: Prophet of Fire by Dan Kurzman (New York: Simon & Schuster, 1983)

The Making of Modern Zionism: The Intellectual Origins of the Jewish State by Shlomo Avineri (New York: Basic Books, 1981)

The Zionist Idea by Arthur Hertzberg (New York: Atheneum, 1981).

Among the books dealing generally with Zionism but focusing primarily on the specific struggles surrounding the creation of the state of Israel in 1948 and its defense in the years that followed are:

My Life by Golda Meir (New York: Putnam, 1975)

Story of My Life by Moshe Dyan (London: Weidenfeld and Nicholson, 1976)

The Israelis by Amos Elon (New York: Holt, Rinehart & Winston, Inc., 1971)

Founders & Sons by Amos Elon (London: Penguin, 1983)

Genesis 1948—the First Arab-Israeli War by Dan Kurzman (New York: World Publishing Company, 1970).

My opponent in this book may disapprove of reminders of the Holocaust to help explain Jewish *and* non-Jewish commitment to Israel, but the connection is as unavoidable as it is poignant. Lucy Dawidowicz's *The War Against the Jews—1933–1945* (New York: Holt, Rinehart & Winston, Inc., 1975) is already a classic. David Wyman, not himself a Jew, has written a brilliant account of the failures to do what was required in *The Abandonment of the Jews: America and the Holocaust 1941–1945* (New York: Pantheon Books, 1984).

Israel's current president and former ambassador to the United Nations, Chaim Herzog, has written a comprehensive account of the string of wars his embattled country has waged through its history in *The Arab-Israeli Wars* (New York: Random House, 1982).

Among the important works written by non-Jews in search of understanding the promise and the problems of the Jewish state are Peter Grose's *Israel in the Mind of America* (New York: Knopf, 1983), Joan Peters' *From Time Immemorial* (New York: Harper & Row, 1984) and David Shipler's *Arab and Jew: Wounded Spirits in a Promised Land* (New York: Times Books, 1986).

The willingness of Israelis to face realities and to promote policies not in vogue is reflected in many books, studies, and articles. One of the most respected and prolific authors is Meron Benvenisti. His *Conflicts and Contradictions* (New York: Villard Books, 1986) reflects his exhaustive studies and deep feelings about Israel, the Arabs, and the West Bank.

For the American reader who does not understand Hebrew, the best source for up-to-date accounts of developments in Israel is the weekly international edition of the *Jerusalem Post*. As in all Israeli publications, the freedom to engage in open, sharp debate is impressively reflected in the pages of the *Post*.

Despite assertions to the contrary, it is a fact that publications of American Jewish organizations, like those in Israel, reflect a wide range of opinion on how best to resolve the Arab-Israeli dispute. The American Jewish Committee, for example, publishes both *Commentary*, basically conservative and "hawkish", and *Present Tense*, basically liberal and "dovish." Reading both, and many others in between, helps one's understanding of the difficulties and ambivalences that surround the search for solutions to the dispute.

For current, specific information on what the "pro-Israel" lobby in Washington is advocating, the *Near-East Report*, a weekly newsletter, is indispensable.

Over the years, *Near-East Report* has published updated editions of its *Myths and Facts: A Concise Record of the Arab-Israeli Conflict*. Unabashedly and unapologetically pro-Israel and especially pro-special relationship, this publication is a very useful, convenient resource for direct refutation of the many myths and distortions that are regularly utilized in anti-Israel propaganda campaigns.

I am particularly pleased to recommend as a most reliable source of relatively current information on Israeli and Arab-Israeli developments the *American Jewish Year Book*, published annually by the American Jewish Committee and the Jewish Publication Society of America. Deservedly recognized as the authoritative "book of record" for the Jewish and general community, the volume each year contains chapters on every important Middle East development during the preceding year. Its objectivity and balance has been widely recognized and commended. This series of articles served as a primary source for me in writing this book.

A principal and frequent author of these *Year Book* segments, Dr. George Gruen, edited an important volume in 1982, *The Palestinians in Perspective* (New York: Institute of Human Relations Press, 1982). With contributions from several scholars, this volume does indeed provide perspective on a very critical issue.

While I do not agree with parts of them, two books by recent U.S. public officials merit serious consideration. William Quandt's *Camp David: Peacemaking and Politics* (Washington, D.C: The Brookings Institute, 1986) and Harold Saunders's *The Other Walls: The Politics of the Arab-Israeli Peace Process* (Washington, D.C.: American Enterprise Institute, 1985) reflect the doubts and misgivings some participants in the development of U.S. policy have had.

For the most complete and authoritative documentation of the U.S.-Israel special relationship, there are thousands of pages of hearings conducted over the years by various congressional committees, primarily the Senate Foreign Relations Committee, the House International Affairs Committee, and the respective Appropriations Subcommittees. With the possible exception of U.S.-Soviet relations, no other foreign affairs issue has received as much close scrutiny by the Congress as the Arab-Israeli conflict.

Wolf Blitzer's *Between Washington and Jerusalem* (Oxford: Oxford University Press, 1985) is a perceptive account of U.S.-Israel relations as recorded by an American reporter for the Jerusalem Post.

A number of "basic source" compendia volumes are available for the student. Two that have been especially helpful are:

The Israel-Arab Reader edited by Walter Laquer and Barry Rubin (4th Edition, 1984) (Facts on File Publications)

Israel, the Middle East and the Great Powers edited by Israel Stockman-Shamron (London: Shikman Publishing Co. Ltd., 1984)

With all the respect and attention all of the above works deserve, they do not serve as a substitute for the most relevant and current source of information and understanding: the news reported every day. In one bold stroke, Anwar Sadat in 1977 changed the course of history and made much of it irrelevant. Remaining informed and alert to other possible changes in course is of the utmost importance—if new "missed opportunities" are to be avoided.

Despite problems of omission and commission that do occur, I have no general "gripe" against the American media. The two papers, among others, that I read regularly and thoroughly—the *New York Times* and the *Washington Post*—have provided me with most of the knowledge I have needed to help me frame judgments. I do not share some of the shrill criticism directed at them from time to time by both pro-Arab and pro-Israel extremists.

It is my hope that *Through Different Eyes* may be considered worthy of a listing in future books on the Middle East.

JAMES G. ABOUREZK

As I wrote my part of this book I noted the available sources of information about each event that contributes to the background for my argument that Israel, not the Arabs, has been the aggressor in the Middle East. But because this book is essentially a debate, its reading should not be interrupted with periodic footnotes. Instead, this section discusses the major sources of information I have used. I have maintained a record of sources for all the statements made in my presentation, and I will make the appropriate source notes available to anyone who requests it. Please write to me in care of Adler & Adler, Publishers, Inc., 4550 Montgomery Avenue, Bethesda, Maryland 20814.

The actual story of how Israel was created and its behavior today is important because Israeli claims have gone unanswered for so long that many accept them as documented history. Yet if one reads what really happened at the beginning and in the years following, quite thoroughly documented in a great many books, one comes away shocked, and sometimes angry, at the dramatic differences between fact and propaganda.

1. Introduction

A number of histories of the creation of Israel exist, among which the best are: *Israel and the Arabs*, by Maxime Rodinson (New York: Penguin Books, 2nd Edition, 1982); *Israel and the American National Interest*, by Cheryl Rubenberg (Urbana, Illinois: University of Illinois Press, 1986); *The Fateful Triangle*, by Noam Chomsky (Boston: South End Press, 1983); *Whose Land Is Palestine?*, by Frank Epp (Grand Rapids, Michigan: William B. Eerdsman Publishing Co., 2nd printing, 1974); *Arab and Jew: Wounded Spirits in a Promised Land*, by David Shipler (New York: Times Books, 1986); *The Evasive Peace*, by John Davis (New York: New World Press, 1968); John Snetsinger's *Truman, the Jewish Vote and Israel* (Stanford, California: Hoover Institution Press, 1974). David Wyman's *The Abandonment of the Jews: America and the Holocaust 1941–1945* (New York: Pantheon Books, 1984) provides a thorough treatment of the policies of the United States which prevented Jews from escaping Hitler's persecution to seek refuge here.

2. Israel Consolidates Itself

For Israel's behavior following the truce agreements in 1948 and 1949, the best sources are Michael Brecher, *Decisions in Israel's Foreign Policy* (London: Oxford University Press, 1974); Stephen Green, *Taking Sides* (New York: William Morrow & Co. Inc., 1984); Livia Rokach, *Israel's Sacred Terrorism: A Study Based on Moshe Sharett's Personal Diary and other Documents* (Belmont, Massachusetts: Association of Arab American University Graduates, 1980), which is a translation of selected portions of former Prime Minister Moshe Sharett's diary, regarding a great many of the crimes committed by the Israeli government after the 1948 war.

The top people in the Johnson administration who spent a great deal of their time worrying about Israel's welfare included: Clark Clifford, Abe Fortas, Arthur Goldberg, Harry McPherson, John Roche, Walter and Eugene Rostow, and Ben Wattenberg. The internal documents regarding assistance to Israel created by Johnson's White House advisers include: State Department, NEA/

IAI:2/8/67; confidential, declassified April 16, 1981. W.W. Rostow, Memorandum for the President, May 21, 1966; secret, declassified, March 13, 1979. Unsigned, White House papers, May 19, 1966; secret, declassified, March 13, 1979.

For a detailed exposition of the American policy machinations which led to Sadat's decision to attack Israel in 1973, see the chapter on Standstill Diplomacy: 1971–73, in William Quandt's *Decade of Decisions* (Berkeley: University of California Press, 1977), pp. 128–64.

By far the best histories of the 1956 attack on Egypt by Israel, France, and England and the 1973 Middle East war are those written by Middle East historian Donald Neff, *Warriors for Suez: Eisenhower Takes America into the Middle East* (New York: Linden Press/Simon & Schuster, 1981); and *Warriors for Jerusalem* (New York: Linden Press/Simon and Schuster, 1981).

3. The Camp David Agreements: Egypt Opts Out

The primer on the Camp David accords was written by William Quandt, who, as a member of the National Security Council staff, was heavily involved in all the negotiations leading up to the agreements. William Quandt, *Camp David: Peacemaking and Politics* (Washington, D.C.: Brookings Institution, 1986).

Seth Tillman, who teaches at Georgetown University, has written an excellent text on United States' interests in the Middle East, entitled, *The United States in the Middle East: Interests and Obstacles,* (Bloomington: Indiana University Press, 1982).

4. Racism as an Aid to Conquest

Golda Meir's statement appears in Seth Tillman's book, cited in Part 3, above, p. 146. Menachem Begin's comments on Christians at the Baghdad nuclear reactor site were quoted in the *The New York Times,* June 9, 1981, p. A8, col. 1. Eytan's "cockroaches" comments were quoted by Reuters' Wire Service, April 12, 1983, Tuesday A.M. cycle. Christopher Mayhew's letter appeared in the *London Sunday Times,* October 19, 1986. Albert Speer's *Playboy* interview appeared in June 1971, p. 203. I was unable to find the date of Begin's quote after he ordered the bombing of the Fakhani district, but I have a distinct memory of his statement at the time. Amos Oz's *In the Land of Israel* is a Vintage Book, published in 1983.

5. Terrorism and the Media

The many incidents of Israeli and Jewish terrorism are recorded in dispatches from *The London Times, Facts on File,* and *Le Nouvel Observateur,* either on, or shortly after, the date of the act of terror. Terrorist acts committed by the Mossad are recorded in Richard Deacon, *The Israeli Secret Service* (New York: Taplinger Publishing Co., 1977). Surprisingly, books on Israel's Mossad abound, most of them boasting of the terrorist exploits of Israel's covert action organization. One of the most complete books on Jewish terrorism is J. Bowyer Bell's, *Terror out of Zion* (New York: St. Martin's Press, 1977). Bell writes as an admirer, but in the process he details virtually all of the gruesome acts of terror committed by the Irgun and the Stern Gang.

Lord Christopher Mayhew personally related to me the story of his secretary who was injured when opening a letter bomb addressed by Jewish terrorists to Mayhew, then a member of the House of Commons. Nathan Yalin-Mor, one of the triad heading the Stern Gang between 1944 and 1948, visited my Senate office in 1973, at a time when he had become a self-described "dove." He had spent the last years of his life searching for a peaceful solution to the Arab-Israeli conflict, visiting anyone who might listen to his plea for an end to the violence. I asked him during the first of our many visits if it was true that the Stern Gang sent letter bombs to British politicians, trying to verify what Mayhew had earlier told me. His answer was, "Oh, yes, we sent lots of letter bombs."

Mordechai Gur was quoted in the Israeli newspaper, *Al Hamishmar,* May 10, 1978. Writer Tony Clifton, of *Newsweek,* and photojournalist Catherine Leroy collaborated on a dramatic book entitled, *God Cried* (London: Quartet Books, 1983), which describes how the editors of the *New York Times* changed Thomas Friedman's dispatch about the bombing of Beirut. Jonathan Randal of the *Washington Post* published an excellent book on the right wing Phalangists of Lebanon and their alliance with Israel, entitled *Going All the Way: Christian Warlords, Israeli Adventurers, and the War in Lebanon* (New York: Viking Press, 1983); and Joseph Schechla reported on the little-covered aspects of Israel's occupation of Lebanon following its invasion and siege of Beirut in *The Iron Fist: Israel's Occupation of South Lebanon, 1982–85* (Washington, D.C.: ADC Research Institute, Issue Paper No. 17, 1985).

David Hirst, in *The Gun and the Olive Branch,* pp. 155–59, reported the bombings directed toward Iraqi Jews as the work of an underground Jewish group. In a new book written by Abbas Shiblak entitled *The Lure of Zion* (London: Al Saqi Books, 1986) we learn that those responsible for the attacks were members of the Israeli Secret Service, the Mossad.

Barney Rosset's interview appeared in *Small Press* (Westport, Connecticut: Meckler Publishing Corp., July/August, 1986) p.52.

6. Occupation

Lea Tsemel's example appeared in *OCCUPATION: Israel Over Palestine,* edited by Naseer Aruri (London: Zed Books, 1984), p. 58. Meron Benvenisti's West Bank Data Base Project provides a great deal of information on settlement activities in the Occupied Territories. Most of the information in this section is derived from his *1986 Report: Demographic, Economic, Legal, Social and Political Developments in the West Bank* (Jerusalem: West Bank Data Base Project, 1986, in conjunction with the American Enterprise Institute, Washington, D.C., and distributed by the Jerusalem Post). Benvenisti provided further information on the West Bank during a lecture at the American Enterprise Institute in Washington on November 10, 1986.

The *London Sunday Times* initial report was published June 19, 1977, the Israeli response on July 3, 1977, and a reply by the *Sunday Times* on July 10, 1977.

Information about Israeli activities in southern Lebanon in the early years was provided to me when I interviewed Ramon Edde, a member of the Lebanese parliament in August 1973. Edde escorted me to the Lebanese-Israeli frontier at that time specifically to show me Israeli tanks sitting on Lebanese territory at Chebaa.

7. Unquestioning Support for Israel: The Impact on America

A great deal of information on Israeli arms sales is available in Aaron Klieman's book, *Israel's Global Reach: Arms Sales as Diplomacy*

(McLean, Virginia: Pergamon-Brassey's International Defense Publishers, 1985).

Wolf Blitzer's *Jerusalem Post* article was reprinted in the *Los Angeles Times*, November 15, 1986.

Jane Hunter's newsletter, *Israeli Foreign Affairs*, published monthly in Oakland, California, tracks Israel's arms dealings and other relationships with South Africa and other right wing dictatorships.

For a full treatment of the Zionist-Fundamentalist connection, see Grace Halsell, *Prophecy and Politics: Militant Evangelists on the Road to Nuclear War* (Westport, Connecticut: Lawrence Hill & Co., 1986).

For a detailed account of how the Israeli lobby works, see Paul Findley, *They Dare to Speak Out* (Westport, Connecticut: Lawrence Hill Co. 1984), and Stephen Isaacs, *Jews and American Politics* (New York: Doubleday & Co., 1974). Edward Tivnan, *The Lobby: Jewish Political Power and American Foreign Policy* (New York: Simon & Schuster, 1987).

8. Searching for America's Interest

The information on U.S. aid to Israel is derived from the Library of Congress' Congressional Research Service, whose specialist, Clyde Mark, has compiled all the aid programs he has been able to find.

A P P E N D I C E S

A.
Israel's Declaration of Independence
(May 14, 1948)

Eretz-Israel* was the birthplace of the Jewish people. Here their spiritual, religious and political identity was shaped. Here they first attained to statehood, created cultural values of national and universal significance and gave to the world the eternal Book of Books.

After being forcibly exiled from their land, the people kept faith with it throughout their Dispersion and never ceased to pray and hope for their return to it and for the restoration in it of their political freedom.

Impelled by this historic and traditional attachment, Jews strove in every successive generation to re-establish themselves in their ancient homeland. In recent decades they returned in their masses. Pioneers, ma'pilim† and defenders, they made deserts bloom, revived the Hebrew language, built villages and towns, and created a thriving community, controlling its own economy and culture, loving peace but knowing how to defend itself, bringing the blessings of progress to all the country's inhabitants, and aspiring towards independent nationhood.

In the year 5657 (1897), at the summons of the spiritual father of the Jewish State, Theodore Herzl, the First Zionist Congress convened and proclaimed the right of the Jewish people to national rebirth in its own country.

This right was recognised in the Balfour Declaration of the 2nd November, 1917, and re-affirmed in the Mandate of the

*Eretz-Israel (Hebrew)—the Land of Israel, Palestine.
†Ma'pilim (Hebrew)—immigrants coming to Eretz-Israel in defiance of restrictive legislation.

League of Nations which, in particular, gave international sanction to the historic connection between the Jewish people and Eretz-Israel and to the right of the Jewish people to rebuild its National Home.

The catastrophe which recently befell the Jewish people—the massacre of millions of Jews in Europe—was another clear demonstration of the urgency of solving the problem of its homelessness by re-establishing in Eretz-Israel the Jewish State, which would open the gates of the homeland wide to every Jew and confer upon the Jewish people the status of a fully-privileged member of the comity of nations.

Survivors of the Nazi holocaust in Europe, as well as Jews from other parts of the world, continued to migrate to Eretz-Israel, undaunted by difficulties, restrictions and dangers, and never ceased to assert their right to a life of dignity, freedom and honest toil in their national homeland.

In the Second World War, the Jewish community of this country contributed its full share to the struggle of the freedom and peace-loving nations against the forces of Nazi wickedness and, by the blood of its soldiers and its war effort, gained the right to be reckoned among the peoples who founded the United Nations.

On the 29th November, 1947, the United Nations General Assembly passed a resolution calling for the establishment of a Jewish State in Eretz-Israel; the General Assembly required the inhabitants of Eretz-Israel to take such steps as were necessary on their part for the implementation of that resolution. This recognition by the United Nations of the right of the Jewish people to establish their State is irrevocable.

This right is the natural right of the Jewish people to be masters of their own fate, like all other nations, in their own sovereign State.

ACCORDINGLY WE, MEMBERS OF THE PEOPLE'S COUNCIL, REPRESENTATIVE OF THE JEWISH COMMUNITY OF ERETZ-ISRAEL AND OF THE ZIONIST MOVEMENT, ARE HERE ASSEMBLED ON THE DAY OF THE TERMINATION OF THE BRITISH MANDATE OVER ERETZ-ISRAEL AND, BY VIRTUE OF OUR NATURAL AND HISTORIC RIGHT AND ON THE STRENGTH OF THE RESOLUTION OF THE UNITED NATIONS GENERAL ASSEMBLY, HEREBY DECLARE THE ESTABLISHMENT OF A JEWISH STATE IN ERETZ-ISRAEL, TO BE KNOWN AS THE STATE OF ISRAEL.

WE DECLARE that, with effect from the moment of the termination of the Mandate, being tonight, the eve of Sabbath, the 6th Iyar, 5708 (15th May, 1948), until the establishment of the elected, regular authorities of the State in accordance with the Constitution which shall be adopted by the Elected Constituent Assembly not later than the 1st October 1948, the People's Council shall act as a Provisional Council of State, and its executive organ, the People's Administration, shall be the Provisional Government of the Jewish State, to be called "Israel."

THE STATE OF ISRAEL will be open for Jewish immigration and for the Ingathering of the Exiles; it will foster the development of the country for the benefit of all its inhabitants; it will be based on freedom, justice and peace as envisaged by the prophets of Israel; it will ensure complete equality of social and political rights to all its inhabitants irrespective of religion, race or sex; it will guarantee freedom of religion, conscience, language, education and culture; it will safeguard the Holy Places of all religions; and it will be faithful to the principles of the Charter of the United Nations.

THE STATE OF ISRAEL is prepared to cooperate with the agencies and representatives of the United Nations in implementing the resolution of the General Assembly of the 29th November, 1947, and will take steps to bring about the economic union of the whole of Eretz-Israel.

WE APPEAL to the United Nations to assist the Jewish people in the building-up of its State and to receive the State of Israel into the comity of nations.

WE APPEAL—in the very midst of the onslaught launched against us now for months—to the Arab inhabitants of the State of Israel to preserve peace and participate in the upbuilding of the State on the basis of full and equal citizenship and due representation in all its provisional and permanent institutions.

WE EXTEND our hand to all neighbouring states and their peoples in an offer of peace and good neighbourliness, and appeal to them to establish bonds of cooperation and mutual help with the sovereign Jewish people settled in its own land. The State of Israel is prepared to do its share in a common effort for the advancement of the entire Middle East.

WE APPEAL to the Jewish people throughout the Diaspora to rally round the Jews of Eretz-Israel in the tasks of immigration and

upbuilding and to stand by them in the great struggle for the realization of the age-old dream—the redemption of Israel.

PLACING OUR TRUST IN THE ALMIGHTY, WE AFFIX OUR SIGNATURES
TO THIS PROCLAMATION AT THIS SESSION OF THE PROVISIONAL COUN-
CIL OF STATE, ON THE SOIL OF THE HOMELAND, IN THE CITY OF
TEL-AVIV, ON THIS SABBATH EVE, THE 5TH DAY OF IYAR, 5708 (14TH
MAY, 1948).

David Ben-Gurion

Daniel Auster	Rachel Cohen	David Zvi Pinkas
Mordekhai Bentov	Rabbi Kalman	Aharon Zisling
Yitzchak Ben Zvi	Kahana	Moshe Kolodny
Eliyahu Berligne	Saadia Kobashi	Eliezer Kaplan
Fritz Bernstein	Rabbi Yitzchak	Abraham Katznelson
Rabbi Wolf Gold	Meir Levin	Felix Rosenblueth
Meir Grabovsky	Meir David	David Remez
Yitzchak Gruenbaum	Loewenstein	Berl Repetur
Dr. Abraham	Zvi Luria	Mordekhai Shattner
Granovsky	Golda Myerson	Ben Zion Sternberg
Eliyahu Dobkin	Nachum Nir	Bekhor Shitreet
Meir Wilner-Kovner	Zvi Segal	Moshe Shapira
Zerach Wahrhaftig	Rabbi Yehuda Leib	Moshe Shertok
Herzl Vardi	Hacohen Fishman	

B.
The Palestine National Charter

This Charter shall be known as "the Palestine National Charter."
Articles of the Charter:

Article 1. Palestine, the homeland of the Palestinian Arab people, is an inseparable part of the greater Arab homeland, and the
Palestinian people are a part of the Arab Nation.

Article 2. Palestine, within the frontiers that existed under the
British Mandate, is an indivisible territorial unit.

Article 3. The Palestinian Arab people alone have legitimate
rights to their homeland, and shall exercise the right of self-determi-

nation after the liberation of their homeland, in keeping with their wishes and entirely of their own accord.

Article 4. The Palestinian identity is an authentic, intrinsic and indissoluble quality that is transmitted from father to son. Neither the Zionist occupation nor the dispersal of the Palestinian Arab people as a result of the afflictions they have suffered can efface this Palestinian identity.

Article 5. Palestinians are Arab citizens who were normally resident in Palestine until 1947. This includes both those who were forced to leave or who stayed in Palestine. Anyone born to a Palestinian father after that date, whether inside or outside Palestine, is a Palestinian.

Article 6. Jews who were normally resident in Palestine up to the beginning of the Zionist invasion are Palestinians.

Article 7. Palestinian identity, and material, spiritual and historical links with Palestine are immutable realities. It is a national obligation to provide every Palestinian with a revolutionary Arab upbringing, and to instil in him a profound spiritual and material familiarity with his homeland and a readiness both for armed struggle and for the sacrifice of his material possessions and his life, for the recovery of his homeland. All available educational means and means of guidance must be enlisted to that end, until liberation is achieved.

Article 8. The Palestinian people is at the stage of national struggle for the liberation of its homeland. For that reason, differences between Palestinian national forces must give way to the fundamental difference that exists between Zionism and imperialism on the one hand and the Palestinian Arab people on the other. On that basis, the Palestinian masses, both as organisations and as individuals, whether in the homeland or in such places as they now live as refugees, constitute a single national front working for the recovery and liberation of Palestine through armed struggle.

Article 9. Armed struggle is the only way of liberating Palestine, and is thus strategic, not tactical. The Palestinian Arab people hereby affirm their unwavering determination to carry on the armed struggle and to press on towards popular revolution for the liberation of and return to their homeland. They also affirm their right to a normal life in their homeland, to the exercise of their right of self-determination therein and to sovereignty over it.

Article 10. Commando action constitutes the nucleus of the Palestinian popular war of liberation. This requires that commando action should be escalated, expanded and protected and that all the resources of the Palestinian masses and all scientific potentials available to them should be mobilised and organised to play their part in the armed Palestinian revolution. It also requires solidarity in national struggle among the different groups within the Palestinian people and between that people and the Arab masses, to ensure the continuity of the escalation and victory of the revolution.

Article 11. Palestinians shall have three slogans: national unity, national mobilisation and liberation.

Article 12. The Palestinian Arab people believe in Arab unity. To fulfil their role in the achievement of that objective, they must, at the present stage in their national struggle, retain their Palestinian identity and all that it involves, work for increased awareness of it and oppose all measures liable to weaken or dissolve it.

Article 13. Arab unity and the liberation of Palestine are complementary objectives; each leads to the achievement of the other. Arab unity will lead to the liberation of Palestine, and the liberation of Palestine will lead to Arab unity. To work for one is to work for both.

Article 14. The destiny of the Arab nation, indeed the continued existence of the Arabs, depends on the fate of the Palestinian cause. This interrelationship is the point of departure of the Arab endeavour to liberate Palestine. The Palestinian people are the vanguard of the movement to achieve this sacred national objective.

Article 15. The liberation of Palestine is a national obligation for the Arabs. It is their duty to repel the Zionist and imperialist invasion of the greater Arab homeland and to liquidate the Zionist presence in Palestine. The full responsibility for this belongs to the peoples and governments of the Arab nation and to the Palestinian people first and foremost.

For this reason, the task of the Arab nation is to enlist all the military, human, moral and material resources at its command to play an effective part, along with the Palestinian people, in the liberation of Palestine. Moreover, it is the task of the Arab nation, particularly at the present stage of the Palestinian armed revolution, to offer the Palestinian people all possible aid, material and manpower support, and to place at their disposal all the means and opportunities that will enable them to continue to perform their role as the vanguard of their armed revolution until the liberation of their homeland is achieved.

Article 16. On the spiritual plane, the liberation of Palestine will establish in the Holy Land an atmosphere of peace and tranquility in which all religious institutions will be safeguarded and freedom of worship and the right of visit guaranteed to all without discrimination or distinction of race, colour, language or creed. For this reason, the people of Palestine look to all spiritual forces in the world for support.

Article 17. On the human plane, the liberation of Palestine will restore to the Palestinians their dignity, integrity and freedom. For this reason, the Palestinian Arab people look to all those who believe in the dignity and freedom of man for support.

Article 18. On the international plane, the liberation of Palestine is a defensive measure dictated by the requirements of self-defence. This is why the Palestinian people, who seek to win the friendship of all peoples, look for the support of all freedom, justice and peace-loving countries in restoring the legitimate state of affairs in Palestine, establishing security and peace in it and enabling its people to exercise national sovereignty and freedom.

Article 19. The partition of Palestine, which took place in 1947, and the establishment of Israel, are fundamentally invalid, however long they last, for they contravene the will of the people of Palestine and their natural right to their homeland and contradict the principles of the United Nations Charter, foremost among which is the right of self-determination.

Article 20. The Balfour Declaration, the Mandate Instrument, and all their consequences, are hereby declared null and void. The claim of historical or spiritual links between the Jews and Palestine is neither in conformity with historical fact nor does it satisfy the requirements for statehood. Judaism is a revealed religion; it is not a separate nationality, nor are the Jews a single people with a separate identity; they are citizens of their respective countries.

Article 21. The Palestinian Arab people, expressing themselves through the Palestinian armed revolution, reject all alternatives to the total liberation of Palestine. They also reject all proposals for the liquidation or internationalisation of the Palestine problem.

Article 22. Zionism is a political movement that is organically linked with world imperialism and is opposed to all liberation movements or movements for progress in the world. The Zionist movement is essentially fanatical and racialist; its objectives involve aggression, expansion and the establishment of colonial settlements, and its methods are those of the Fascists and the Nazis. Israel acts as cat's paw for the Zionist movement, a geographic and manpower base for world imperialism and a springboard for its thrust into the Arab homeland to frustrate the aspirations of the Arab nation to liberation, unity and progress. Israel is a constant threat to peace in the Middle East and the whole world. Inasmuch as the liberation of Palestine will eliminate the Zionist and imperialist presence in that country and bring peace to the Middle East, the Palestinian people look for support to all liberals and to all forces of good, peace and progress in the world, and call on them, whatever their political convictions, for all possible aid and support in their just and legitimate struggle to liberate their homeland.

Article 23. The demands of peace and security and the exigencies of right and justice require that all nations should regard Zionism as an illegal movement and outlaw it and its activities, out of consideration for the ties of friendship between peoples and for the loyalty of citizens to their homelands.

Article 24. The Palestinian Arab people believe in justice, freedom, sovereignty, self-determination, human dignity and the right of peoples to enjoy them.

Article 25. In pursuance of the objectives set out in this charter, the Palestine Liberation Organisation shall perform its proper role in the liberation of Palestine to the full.

Article 26. The Palestine Liberation Organisation, as the representative of the forces of the Palestinian revolution, is responsible for the struggle of the Palestinian Arab people to regain, liberate and return to their homeland and to exercise the right of self-determination in that homeland, in the military, political and financial fields, and for all else that the Palestinian cause may demand, both at Arab and international levels.

Article 27. The Palestine Liberation Organisation shall cooperate with all Arab countries, each according to its means, maintaining a neutral attitude vis-à-vis these countries in accordance with the requirements of the battle of liberation, and on the basis of that factor. The Organisation shall not interfere in the internal affairs of any Arab country.

Article 28. The Palestinian Arab people hereby affirm the authenticity and independence of their national revolution and reject all forms of interference, tutelage or dependency.

Article 29. The Palestinian Arab people have the legitimate and prior right to liberate and recover their homeland, and shall define their attitude to all countries and forces in accordance with the attitude adopted by such countries and forces to the cause of the Palestinian people and with the extent of their support for that people in their revolution to achieve their objectives.

Article 30. Those who fight or bear arms in the battle of liberation form the nucleus of the popular army which will shield the achievements of the Palestinian Arab people.

Article 31. The Organisation shall have a flag, an oath of allegiance and an anthem, to be decided in accordance with appropriate regulations.

Article 32. Regulations, to be known as Basic Regulations for the Palestine Liberation Organisation, shall be appended to this Charter. These regulations shall define the structure of the Organisation, its bodies and institutions, and the powers, duties and obligations of each of them, in accordance with this Charter.

Article 33. This Charter may only be amended with a majority of two thirds of the total number of members of the National Assembly of the Palestine Liberation Organisation at a special meeting called for that purpose.

C.
U.N. Security Council Resolution 242
November 22, 1967

The Security Council,

Expressing its continuing concern with the grave situation in the Middle East,

Emphasizing the inadmissibility of the acquisition of territory by war and the need to work for a just and lasting peace in which every State in the area can live in security,

Emphasizing further that all Member States in their acceptance of the Charter of the United Nations have undertaken a commitment to act in accordance with Article 2 of the Charter,

1. *Affirms* that the fulfillment of Charter principles requires the establishment of a just and lasting peace in the Middle East which should include the application of both the following principles:

(i) Withdrawal of Israel armed forces from territories occupied in the recent conflict;

(ii) Termination of all claims or states of belligerency and respect for and acknowledgement of the sovereignty, territorial integrity and political independence of every State in the area and their right to live in peace within secure and recognized boundaries free from threats or acts of force;

2. *Affirms further* the necessity

(a) For guaranteeing freedom of navigation through international waterways in the area;

(b) For achieving a just settlement of the refugee problem;

(c) For guaranteeing the territorial inviolability and political independence of every State in the area, through measures including the establishment of demilitarized zones;

3. *Requests* the Secretary-General to designate a Special Representative to proceed to the Middle East to establish and maintain contacts with the States concerned in order to promote agreement and assist efforts to achieve a peaceful and accepted settlement in accordance with the provisions and principles in this resolution;

4. *Requests* the Secretary-General to report to the Security Council on the progress of the efforts of the Special Representative as soon as possible.

D.
U.N. Security Council Resolution 338
October 22, 1973

The Security Council

1. *Calls upon* all parties to the present fighting to cease all firing

and terminate all military activity immediately, no later than 12 hours after the moment of the adoption of this decision, in the positions they now occupy;

2. *Calls upon* the parties concerned to start immediately after the cease-fire the implementation of Security Council resolution 242 (1967) in all of its parts;

3. *Decides* that, immediately and concurrently with the cease-fire, negotiations start between the parties concerned under appropriate auspices aimed at establishing a just and durable peace in the Middle East.

E.
A Framework for Peace in the Middle East
Agreed at Camp David
Signed September 17, 1978

Muhammad Anwar al-Sadat, President of the Arab Republic of Egypt, and Menachem Begin, Prime Minister of Israel, met with Jimmy Carter, President of the United States of America, at Camp David from September 5 to September 17, 1978, and have agreed on the following framework for peace in the Middle East. They invite other parties to the Arab-Israeli conflict to adhere to it.

Preamble

The search for peace in the Middle East must be guided by the following:

—The agreed basis for a peaceful settlement of the conflict between Israel and its neighbors is United Nations Security Council Resolution 242, in all its parts.

—After four wars during thirty years, despite intensive human efforts, the Middle East, which is the cradle of civilization and the birthplace of three great religions, does not yet enjoy the blessings of peace. The people of the Middle East yearn for peace so that the vast human and natural resources of the region can be turned to the pursuits of peace and so that this area can become a model for coexistence and cooperation among nations.

—The historic initiative of President Sadat in visiting Jerusalem and the reception accorded to him by the Parliament, government and people of Israel, and the reciprocal visit of Prime Minister Begin to Ismailia, the peace proposals made by both leaders, as well as the warm reception of these missions by the peoples of both countries, have created an unprecedented opportunity for peace which must not be lost if this generation and future generations are to be spared the tragedies of war.

—The provisions of the Charter of the United Nations and the other accepted norms of international law and legitimacy now provide accepted standards for the conduct of relations among all states.

—To achieve a relationship of peace, in the spirit of Article 2 of the United Nations Charter, future negotiations between Israel and any neighbor prepared to negotiate peace and security with it, are necessary for the purpose of carrying out all the provisions and principles of Resolutions 242 and 338.

—Peace requires respect for the sovereignty, territorial integrity and political independence of every state in the area and their right to live in peace within secure and recognized boundaries free from threats or acts of force. Progress toward that goal can accelerate movement toward a new era of reconciliation in the Middle East marked by cooperation in promoting economic development, in maintaining stability, and in assuring security.

—Security is enhanced by a relationship of peace and by cooperation between nations which enjoy normal relations. In addition, under the terms of peace treaties, the parties can, on the basis of reciprocity, agree to special security arrangements such as demilitarized zones, limited armaments areas, early warning stations, the presence of international forces, liaison, agreed measures for monitoring, and other arrangements that they agree are useful.

Framework

Taking these factors into account, the parties are determined to reach a just, comprehensive, and durable settlement of the Middle East conflict through the conclusion of peace treaties based on Security Council Resolutions 242 and 338 in all their parts. Their purpose is to achieve peace and good neighborly relations. They recognize that, for peace to endure, it must involve all those who have been most deeply affected by the conflict. They therefore agree that this framework as appropriate is intended by them to constitute a basis for peace not only between Egypt and Israel, but also between Israel and each of its other neighbors which is prepared to negotiate peace with Israel on this basis. With that objective in mind, they have agreed to proceed as follows:

A. West Bank and Gaza

1. Egypt, Israel, Jordan and the representatives of the Palestinian people should participate in negotiations on the resolution of the Palestinian problem in all its aspects. To achieve that objective, negotiations relating to the West Bank and Gaza should proceed in three stages:

(a) Egypt and Israel agree that, in order to ensure a peaceful and orderly transfer of authority, and taking into account the security concerns of all the parties, there should be transitional arrangements for the West Bank and Gaza for a period not exceeding five years. In order to provide full autonomy to the inhabitants, under these arrangements the Israeli military government and its civilian administration will be withdrawn as soon as a self-governing authority has been freely elected by the inhabitants of these areas to replace the existing military government. To negotiate the details of a transitional arrangement, the Government of Jordan will be invited to join the negotiations on the basis of this framework. These new arrangements should give due consideration both to the principle of self-government by the inhabitants of these territories and to the legitimate security concerns of the parties involved.

(b) Egypt, Israel, and Jordan will agree on the modalities for establishing the elected self-governing authority in the West Bank and Gaza. The delegations of Egypt and Jordan may include Palestinians from the West Bank and Gaza or other Palestinians as mutually agreed. The parties will negotiate an agreement which will define the powers and responsibilities of the self-governing authority to be exercised in the West Bank and Gaza. A withdrawal of Israeli armed forces will take place and there will be a redeployment of the remaining Israeli forces into specified security locations. The agreement will also include arrangements for assuring internal and external security and public order. A strong local police force will be established, which may include Jordanian citizens. In addition, Israeli and Jordanian forces will participate in joint patrols and in the manning of control posts to assure the security of the borders.

(c) When the self-governing authority (administrative council) in the West Bank and Gaza is established and inaugurated, the transitional period of five years will begin. As soon as possible, but not later than the third year after the beginning of the transitional period, negotiations will take place to determine the final status of the West Bank and Gaza and its relationship with its neighbors, and to conclude a peace treaty between Israel and Jordan by the end of the transitional period. These negotiations will be conducted among Egypt, Israel, Jordan, and the elected representatives of the inhabitants of the West Bank and Gaza. Two separate but related committees will be convened, one committee, consisting of representatives of the four parties which will negotiate and agree on the final status of the West Bank and Gaza, and its relationship with its neighbors, and the second committee, consisting of representatives of Israel and representatives of Jordan to be joined by the elected representatives of the inhabitants of the West Bank and Gaza, to negotiate the peace treaty between Israel and Jordan, taking into account the agreement reached on the final status of the West Bank and Gaza. The negotiations shall be based on all the provisions and principles of UN Security Council Resolution 242. The negotiations will resolve, among other matters, the location of the boundaries and the nature of the security arrangements. The solution from the negotiations must also recognize the legitimate rights of the Palestinian people and their just requirements. In this way, the Palestinians will participate in the determination of their own future through:

1) The negotiations among Egypt, Israel, Jordan and the representatives of the inhabitants of the West Bank and Gaza to agree on the final status of the West Bank and Gaza and other outstanding issues by the end of the transitional period.

2) Submitting their agreement to a vote by the elected representatives of the inhabitants of the West Bank and Gaza.

3) Providing for the elected representatives of the inhabitants of the West Bank and Gaza to decide how they shall govern themselves consistent with the provisions of their agreement.

4) Participating as stated above in the work of the committee negotiating the peace treaty between Israel and Jordan.

2. All necessary measures will be taken and provisions made to assure the security of Israel and its neighbors during the transitional period and beyond. To assist in providing such security, a strong local police force will be constituted by the self-governing authority. It will be composed of inhabitants of the West Bank and Gaza. The police will maintain continuing liaison on internal security matters with the designated Israeli, Jordanian, and Egyptian officers.

3. During the transitional period, representatives of Egypt, Israel, Jordan, and the self-governing authority will constitute a continuing committee to decide by agreement on the modalities of admission of persons displaced from the West Bank and Gaza in 1967, together with necessary measures to prevent disruption and disorder. Other matters of common concern may also be dealt with by this committee.

4. Egypt and Israel will work with each other and with other interested parties to establish agreed procedures for a prompt, just and permanent implementation of the resolution of the refugee problem.

B. Egypt-Israel

1. Egypt and Israel undertake not to resort to the threat or the use of force to settle disputes. Any disputes shall be settled by peaceful means in accordance with the provisions of Article 33 of the Charter of the United Nations.

2. In order to achieve peace between them, the parties agree to

negotiate in good faith with a goal of concluding within three months from the signing of this Framework a peace treaty between them, while inviting the other parties to the conflict to proceed simultaneously to negotiate and conclude similar peace treaties with a view to achieving a comprehensive peace in the area. The Framework for the Conclusion of a Peace Treaty between Egypt and Israel will govern the peace negotiations between them. The parties will agree on the modalities and the timetable for the implementation of their obligations under the treaty.

C. Associated Principles

1. Egypt and Israel state that the principles and provisions described below should apply to peace treaties between Israel and each of its neighbors—Egypt, Jordan, Syria and Lebanon.

2. Signatories shall establish among themselves relationships normal to states at peace with one another. To this end, they should undertake to abide by all the provisions of the Charter of the United Nations. Steps to be taken in this respect include:

(a) full recognition;

(b) abolishing economic boycotts;

(c) guaranteeing that under their jurisdiction the citizens of the other parties shall enjoy the protection of the due process of law.

3. Signatories should explore possibilities for economic development in the context of final peace treaties, with the objective of contributing to the atmosphere of peace, cooperation and friendship which is their common goal.

4. Claims Commissions may be established for the mutual settlement of all financial claims.

5. The United States shall be invited to participate in the talks on matters related to the modalities of the implementation of the agreements and working out the timetable for the carrying out of the obligations of the parties.

6. The United Nations Security Council shall be requested to endorse the peace treaties and ensure that their provisions shall not be violated. The permanent members of the Security Council shall

be requested to underwrite the peace treaties and ensure respect for their provisions. They shall also be requested to conform their policies and actions with the undertakings contained in this Framework.

For the Government   For the Government
of the Arab   of Israel:
Republic of Egypt:

A. SADAT   M. BEGIN

Witnessed by:

JIMMY CARTER

Jimmy Carter, President
of the United States of America

ACKNOWLEDGMENTS

HYMAN BOOKBINDER

For whatever understanding and feelings I have about the Middle East I owe a debt to countless numbers of scholars, writers, government officials and colleagues, but I absolve them all of any mistakes or weaknesses in my contribution to this volume. Even within my own circle of friends and colleagues, we have occasionally seen things "through different eyes."

I am deeply grateful to several friends and colleagues whose counsel I sought in order to reduce to a minimum any errors in fact or misinterpretation of the available facts. The first draft of the opening statement was read by Michael Berenbaum, Andrew Baker, M.J. Rosenberg, Mort Yarmon, and Lolly Bram. Their suggestions were most helpful, although I did not accept all of them.

A long-time colleague of mine, Dr. George Gruen, to whom I have looked for almost twenty years for knowledge and insight, was my principal consultant and guide throughout this project. Invaluable research assistance was provided by Lee Berinstein. For conceiving the idea and developing it into appropriate book form, I thank Ron Goldfarb and Jim Adler. Dorothy Woodland patiently converted my sloppy handwriting and mistyping into a readable manuscript.

Above all, Ida Leivick provided encouragement and confidence, sounding board and sound common sense, throughout this effort, as she has over the years in every aspect of our partnership.

If I do not, in the years left for me, get to see all Jews and all Arabs finally at peace with one another, may this occur at least in the lifetime of my daughters, Ellen and Amy, and surely in the lifetime of my grandchildren, Michael and Rebecca and Rose. To them I dedicate this book and this dream.

JAMES G. ABOUREZK

Thanks go first of all to my dedicated research assistant, Beth Wait-kus, who worked not only weekends and nights, but also long days gathering source materials for my part of the manuscript. Also to Middle East historian Donald Neff, both for his research assistance and comments on the manuscript; to my oldest son, writer Charles Abourezk, for his comments on the manuscript; to Clyde R. Mark, specialist in Middle East Affairs at the Library of Congress' Congressional Research Service, who compiled and provided the only comprehensive and complete source of American foreign aid to Israel I have seen; to Philip Mattar and Samira Badawi at the Institute for Palestine Studies for source information on the P.L.O. charter and other documents relating to the Palestinians; to my agent, Ron Goldfarb, for providing the idea of a debate such as this one; and to our publisher, Jim Adler, for his compassionate interest in the subject, as well as his commitment to airing, in print, both sides of the Arab-Israeli story.

What I have written is dedicated not only to the Arab people of Lebanon and Palestine, whose suffering and resilience under the boot of a modern occupation sets an example for the rest of us, but to all those everywhere in the world who ask only for their freedom.

Special dedication goes to the memory of a friend, Alex Odeh, who was murdered by Jewish extremists in his ADC office in California on October 11, 1985, and to his widow, Norma, and his surviving children. Norma Odeh's courage and determination have given new strength to continue the struggle.

ABOUT THE MAKING OF THIS BOOK

The text of *Through Different Eyes* was set in Avanta by ComCom, a division of The Haddon Craftsmen, of Allentown, Pennsylvania. The book was printed and bound by Maple Vail. The typography and binding were designed by Tom Suzuki of Falls Church, Virginia.